3.50

Mother
from
Jack

1931

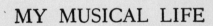

MY MUSICAL LIFE

WALTER DAMROSCH

MY MUSICAL LIFE

BY
WALTER DAMROSCH

NEW YORK
CHARLES SCRIBNER'S SONS
1930

To dearest M

This book I dedicate to you because you have walked hand in hand with me through most of the experiences related therein.

Because of you my disappointments have been cut in half and my happinesses made double, and if I have made known to you the wondrous muse of music, you in turn have brought into our home and given a permanent abiding place therein, the three gentle sisters—Faith, Hope and Charity.

CONTENTS

CHAPTER   PAGE

I. CHILDHOOD—1866–1875 1

II. BAYREUTH IN 1876—MY DOLL'S THEATRE . . . 13

III. FOUNDING OF THE SYMPHONY AND ORATORIO SOCIE-
TIES OF NEW YORK 23

IV. AUGUST WILHELMJ—TERESA CARRENO 28

V. LISZT AND WAGNER 36

VI. THE FOUNDING OF GERMAN OPERA AT THE METRO-
POLITAN—DEATH OF MY FATHER 51

VII. LILLI LEHMANN 63

VIII. HANS VON BÜLOW 74

IX. ANDREW CARNEGIE AND THE BLAINE FAMILY . . 90

X. THE DAMROSCH OPERA COMPANY, 1895–1899 . . 104

XI. ARTISTS 134

XII. ROMANCE 164

XIII. THE ORATORIO SOCIETY OF NEW YORK 169

XIV. THE NEW YORK SYMPHONY ORCHESTRA 186

XV. THE GREAT WAR 221

XVI. THE EUROPEAN TOUR 272

vii

CHAPTER		PAGE
XVII.	WOMEN IN MUSICAL AFFAIRS	323
XVIII.	BOSTON	333
XIX.	MARGARET ANGLIN AND THE GREEK PLAYS . . .	344
XX.	DEAD COMPOSERS	351
XXI.	MUSIC AND MODERN MAGIC	367
XXII.	POSTLUDE	380
	INDEX	383

MY MUSICAL LIFE

I

CHILDHOOD—1866-1875

I am an American musician and have lived in this country since my ninth year. I was born in Breslau, Silesia, on January 30, 1862, and my first memories are connected with war, the Austro-Prussian War of 1866. I was four years old and remember being with my mother in a room in our apartment in Breslau, which was filled with flowers and growing plants (mother always had a marvellous gift for maintaining and nursing plants) and various friends coming in to condole with her over the death of my baby brother, Hans, who had died of cholera, which was then raging in Breslau. The second child of my parents, born in 1860, had been christened Richard, after Richard Wagner, who had officiated as godfather at the ceremony. This child lived but a short time, and Wagner had vowed that he would never again stand as godfather for the children of any of his friends, as the ill luck which had pursued him all his life was thus carried even into their families.

In order to safeguard the rest of her children from the danger of the dread disease to which little Hans had succumbed, my mother took my older brother, Frank, myself, and a baby sister into the country near the Bohemian frontier, where the war was being fought. I can remember my brother and myself standing at a country road, each armed with a huge bouquet of flowers we had gathered, and watching for General Steinmetz and his army to pass on their way to the front. As they marched by, my brother bravely ran to one of the officers and gave him his flowers, but my courage gave out and I threw my bouquet so that it fell on the ground, from which one of the soldiers smilingly picked it up and stuck it on his bayonet. That same afternoon Frank and I lay on the ground with our ears closely pressed to it and we could plainly hear the booming of the cannon.

When peace was declared, King William of Prussia (afterward Emperor William the First) together with Crown Prince Frederick, Bismarck, Moltke, and a brilliant retinue of officers, made their triumphant entry into Breslau on horseback. My brother and I watched this gorgeous sight with delighted eyes from the balcony of our apartment. My mother threw a wreath, which fell on the neck of the horse carrying King William and he, looking up, saluted her.

Musical conditions when my father first came to Breslau in 1858, immediately after his marriage, were miserable enough, and it was not until he founded, together with some musical enthusiasts, the "Breslau Orchester Verein" that a regular symphonic orchestra was established with a series of subscription concerts. All the great artists of the day came to Breslau to take part in these concerts, and generally they stayed at our house, although our quarters were very simple—Liszt, Wagner, von Bülow, Clara Schumann, Tausig, Joachim, Auer, Haenselt, Rubinstein. Some of them I can remember vaguely, but of course many stories and anecdotes were current in the family regarding their visits.

When Tausig, Liszt's greatest piano pupil, spent a

night in our house, the bed in the guest-room broke down in the middle of the night and he calmly arranged his mattress on the floor and continued his slumbers. But his visit was connected in my brother's and my mind particularly with a certain apple pudding which he adored and which my mother always baked especially for him, so that it became known in our family as the "Tausigsche Apfel-Speise." It was a luscious mixture of apples, raisins, and almonds incased in a delicate, light pie-crust.

My father and Tausig would sometimes engage in the most violent discussions on musical or philosophical topics, and the latter would often become so enraged that he would rush out of the house, vowing he would never return. Then he would run around the block and come back in five minutes, smiling and saying, "Come, Damrosch, let us play a Beethoven Sonata together," and all would be well.

When Joachim arrived he found a large

"Willkommen Herr Joachim"

in green leaves over the door of our music-room, carefully arranged by my brother and myself. We adored him because he loved children and would cut all manner of wonderful figures out of paper for us.

Liszt came on especially to officiate as godfather at the christening of my older brother, Frank (Franz), who was named after him, but, as I was not born at the time, my memory of it is not very vivid.

Once when Hans von Bülow arrived for dinner, my mother herself had roasted a hare in his honor. To her despair she discovered at table that she had seasoned it with sugar instead of salt, but Bülow, perfect gentleman that he was, asked for a second helping, insisting that sugar always improved roast hare immensely.

My favorite reading at the age of eight was a wonderful edition of Homer's "Iliad" and "Odyssey" in a fine high-sounding metrical translation by Voss and with many beautiful illustrations by Friedrich Preller, of Weimar, at whose house my mother (Helene von Heimburg) became engaged to my father. As a result of reading these very exciting Greek chronicles I constantly enacted scenes therefrom. My mother's clever fingers fashioned for me from silver paper and pasteboard helmet, armor, and shield; and as Achilles I would drag Hector (my little sister, Marie) on my chariot (two overturned chairs) around the walls of Troy (the dining-room table).

In the winter there was always skating on the Oder, and I remember, aged seven or eight, being given money to buy a ticket of admission and to skate to my heart's content. Part of this ticket had to be retained and given up on leaving the ice. Of course I lost this ticket and being refused egress by the uniformed attendant, I dismally skated about for hours, becoming more and more frightened as the sun went down and the river became more and more deserted. I thought I would have to remain there for the rest of my young life, and it was a very tear-stained and miserable little boy who ran toward the dear Tante Marie who, having become anxious at my absence, had come to see where I was and who released me, by payment for another ticket, from my dreadful imprisonment.

Tante Marie is a younger sister of my mother's who came to live with us at the age of sixteen and who became my mother's closest helper during many years of storm and stress, whose gentle and patient self-sacrifice have never failed her and who, thank God, is still living and as wonderful as ever, the last link with that dim past of long ago.

I think I was somewhat afraid of my father in those days. He was rather stern and taciturn. Life was hard and the struggle for existence difficult. He was somewhat severe about my studies and as those were the days when whipping children for naughtiness was considered an essential of their education, I received my share of such punishment. In fact, sometimes I was whipped in school and then had to take my school report home to my father and he would perhaps repeat the dose. But with all that I was very proud of him and used to enjoy trotting by his side along the promenade on the banks of the Oder, because so many people would take off their hats to him deferentially as he passed.

He also gave us children a good deal of his time in reading to us books that would stimulate our imaginations and cultivate our instincts for the beautiful—Grimm's and Andersen's "Fairy Tales," the "Arabian Nights," and some of the parables from the New Testament.

But whenever I was sent supperless to bed or confined to my room for some misdeed, it was always mother who would comfort me and perhaps bring me a plate of soup or dessert secretly and talk to me gently until my obstinacy would melt and I would be ready to knock at my father's study and ask his forgiveness. Once I did not dare, but instead drew a picture of myself standing penitently at his door and underneath the words: "Seven times seventy times shalt thou forgive." This I shoved under the door into his study and it produced the desired effect, as it brought my father out and in a very forgiving mood.

One of my sins was that I simply could not bear to eat spinach, and as in those days it was considered the absolute duty of a child to eat anything that was put before him because "God had grown the spinach and other vegetables in order to feed hungry children," and "there were thousands of poor little children who would be only too glad to eat spinach," I was forced to eat it although it often choked me and made me ill. Even to this day I cannot bear spinach, and with all the reverence and deep affection that I have for my father, I do not think he was right in this particular case as regards his pedagogic theories.

The following excerpts from letters of von Bülow throw an interesting light on the conditions under which my father worked in Breslau at that time.

To the Princess Carolyn Sayn-Wittgenstein (Liszt's closest friend)

Berlin, Feb. 10, 1859.

. . . Anticipating Liszt's·promise I have sent the score of his "Ideale" to Damrosch who will have the parts copied and get the work to his public already during this month. If we could only have a half dozen soldiers like Damrosch at our disposal! . . .

To Felix Draescke (composer and disciple of Liszt for whom Bülow had tried to obtain a position)

Berlin, Oct. 16, 1860.

. . . I am assured of my complete lack of power to help. To achieve the like for Damrosch has also failed. D., with wife and child, and another one in the nearest future, is *quasi* near to starvation. It has taken me much time to find out finally that I cannot help. . . .

To Hans von Bronsart (mutual friend and musician. Intendant of the Royal Opera in Hanover. In relation to a joint concert with Bülow)

. . . A propos! Please fix Damrosch's honorarium as high as possible. He needs it. In order to recompense him the better, I do not desire any violoncellist. I had arranged with him in your name for eight Louis d'or. You had authorized me to give as high as ten for Laub. Damrosch is Laub + ½. . . .

Laub was a distinguished violinist living in Berlin.

To Richard Pohl (distinguished writer on music and propagandist for Wagner, Berlioz, and Liszt)

Berlin, Sept., 1861.

. . . Damrosch had been engaged by Tausig for joint soirées in Vienna and a long Russian concert tour, but the matter suddenly came to naught, and although one cannot accuse T. of irresponsibility, Damrosch is in such miserable fashion again bound to that sterile Breslau. Poor, greatly talented, honest chap—must fight his way through greatest *misère*. Is there still no chance for him in Weimar? . . .

To Joachim Raff (German composer of distinction)

Berlin, Nov. 10, 1860.

. . . Your piano and violin sonata I am to play in Leipsig. Laub and Singer are afraid of the Gewandhaus and are not keen about it, so I don't yet know whom I am to serve as accompanist. Damrosch, with whom I played the composition six weeks ago, conceives it according to my views quite exceptionally. The adagio, for instance, he plays far more beautifully than Laub. Very likely we shall turn to him. . . .

In 1870 the papers were filled with accounts of "the outrageous insult of King William by the French ambassador, Benedetti," and the hostile attitude of Emperor

Napoleon the Third. War was declared and of course
we boys immediately began to indulge in imitations of
the military drill of the soldiers of our city. The most
exciting and welcome news to me at the time was that my
piano teacher had been drafted and I had high hopes of
not having to continue to undergo the dreary necessity
of daily finger exercises, but alas, my hopes were rudely
dashed to the ground when a bald-headed substitute
appeared to continue the lessons.

Soon the trains were coming in, bringing the wounded,
and the French prisoners, among whom the dark-skinned
Zouaves and Turks especially excited our interest. We
looked with envy at the older boys of our school who,
having studied French, used to go up to the French officers
and ask them whether there was anything they could do
for them.

The war ended and my young piano teacher returned,
resplendent in his uniform with shining brass buttons,
in which he paid his first ceremonial visit to my father
and mother. My mother, wishing to put him at his ease,
asked him to tell something of his experiences in the war,
but he was not very articulate. Yes, he had been at the
beleaguering and capitulation of Metz.

"How wonderful," said my mother, "and what happened to you there?"

"Oh, well, they—they—shot at us."

And that was all we could get out of him.

In the meanwhile my father had become more and
more discontented with musical, social, and political
conditions in Breslau. He was really a Republican at
heart and the Prussian bureaucracy, which had become
more and more accentuated by the war, irked and angered
him. With greatest difficulty he could make a bare

living for his family, and he found the population of Breslau, except a small band of devoted followers, steeped in materialism and not particularly sympathetic toward art, especially the modern German composers.

In 1871 my father received an invitation through Edward Schubert, the music publisher of New York, to come to America as conductor of the Arion Society, and while this opening was small enough, it seemed to offer him an opportunity through which better and bigger things might develop and under conditions more free than were possible in Germany at that time. He therefore determined, at forty years of age, to take the plunge and to precede his family to America in order to find out whether a living and a new career might be made possible in the New World. The Arion Society occupied an honorable position in the social and musical life of the Germans living in New York.

I can remember his farewell concert, in Breslau, at which he performed Beethoven's Ninth Symphony. There were laurel wreaths, and chorus ladies in white, and there was a general atmosphere of enthusiasm and of many tears, but my memories are connected particularly with my astonishment at seeing my teacher of arithmetic whom I hated, suddenly stand up in the middle of the parquet during the intermission and ogle the ladies with a pair of opera-glasses. It had never entered my childish mind until then that a horrible school-teacher could be a man like other men in private life.

A very tragic happening was that one of my suspenders burst during the Ninth Symphony, and for the rest of the performance I was in mortal fear that my trousers might not "stay put."

After my father's departure we children, of course,

played nothing but sailing off on a ship, again principally by aid of the parlor and dining-room furniture. We read "Robinson Crusoe" and enacted its chapters with great satisfaction to ourselves. It was all good fun to us, but the anguish of parting from the country in which they had grown up and lived for so many years, and the dread of the unknown in a strange land, must have been terrible for my father and mother.

Finally came an enthusiastic letter from my father bidding us to follow him to New York; we accordingly set sail, August, 1871, in a little ship of the North German Lloyd, the *Hermann* from Bremen, my mother, Tante Marie, Frank, myself, and two younger sisters. I was desperately seasick for several days until one Sunday morning, when, as I was lying on a bench on deck, the young captain rudely kicked me off, saying, "Look here, youngster, you have been ill long enough, now brace up," which I did and enjoyed the rest of the trip immensely. The captain was in a very romantic mood because he was to marry a young American girl on his arrival in New York. In the evenings my mother would sing Schubert and Schumann on deck and the captain several times gave us firework displays, rockets, etc., in honor of his approaching nuptials.

When we arrived in New York we found my father anxiously pacing the wharf where he had been waiting, since early morning, for eight hours, to take us in a carriage from Hoboken to a house in East 35th Street which he had rented and furnished completely from top to bottom as a surprise for my mother. The hot and cold water on every floor, the gas and the carpets were a revelation to us, as these modern conveniences were hardly known in Breslau at that time. My youngest sister, Elizabeth (now Mrs. Harry T. Seymour), was born in this house.

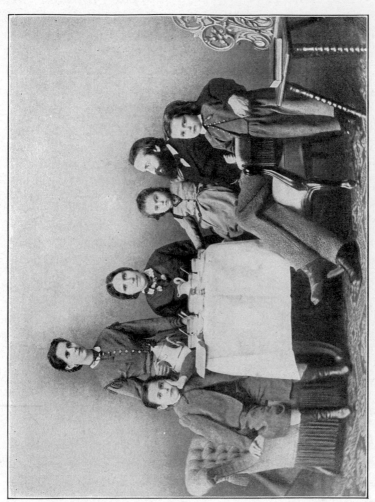

AFTERNOON COFFEE IN THE DAMROSCH HOME, BRESLAU, 1867

Frank, Tante Marie, Mother, Marie, Father, Walter

My brother and I were immediately put into the primary department of Public School No. 40 in East 23d Street, and as we did not know a word of English we were entered in the lowest class, although I had already been in the Sexta of the Gymnasium (High School) and my brother in the Quarta, and I had studied Latin and he both Latin and Greek. But we dutifully spelled out CAT, DOG, etc., until after a few weeks of this we were promoted, and so these promotions went on with lightning rapidity until we had acquired English and could enter a class more appropriate to our years, nine and twelve respectively.

I continued my studies of piano under an old teacher, Jean Vogt by name, and after his return to Germany I studied with Pruckner, von Inten, Max Pinner, and Boeckelman. The last, feeling that I could not raise my fingers high enough from the knuckles, gave me a machine of steel springs which, through rings attached to the fingers, were to lift them higher than nature would permit. Unfortunately this contrivance brought about a weakness in the third finger of my right hand from which I have never quite recovered and which unfortunately, or fortunately, has prevented me from becoming a professional piano virtuoso. But I had acquired a good technic and a singing quality of tone which served me well years after when I began to give recitals at the piano on the Wagnerian music dramas, at which I played the orchestral part on the piano while I recited the text and explained the various musical motifs and their relation to the text.

My first appearance in an orchestra was, I am sorry to say, a rank failure. I was only a boy of fourteen years and my father had prepared a charming operetta of Schubert's, "Der Häusliche Krieg," for a "Summer

Night's Festival" of the Arion Society. In this occurs
a delightful March of the Crusaders with one loud clash
of the cymbals at the climax. It did not seem worth
while to engage a musician at "full union rates" for this
clash and I was, therefore, intrusted with it. At rehearsals I counted my bars rest and watched for my cue
with such perfection that the cymbals resounded with
great success at the proper time and in the proper manner,
but at the performance, alas, a great nervousness fell
upon me and as the march proceeded and came nearer
and nearer the crucial moment, my hand seemed para-
lyzed, and when my father's flashing eye indicated to me
that the moment had come, I simply could not seem to
lift the cymbals which suddenly weighed like a hundred
tons. The march went on but I felt that the entire evening had been ruined by me and that every one in the
audience must know that I had "funked it." As soon
as I could I slipped out of the orchestra pit underneath
the stage and into the dark night, feeling that life had no
joy left for me. I could not bear to hear the rest of the
opera or to meet my father's reproachful eye.

II

BAYREUTH IN 1876—MY DOLL'S THEATRE

In the summer of 1876 Wagner inaugurated the Bayreuth Theatre with the first production of his great "Nibelungen Trilogy." All the old friends and the musicians who had been in the forefront of the fight in the early days when Wagner's genius was not generally recognized, gathered there from far and near in order to be present at what was destined to be a magnificent demonstration of the final triumph of the cause.

My father, naturally, was keen to be there and to rejoice with his old colleagues. He had not returned to Germany since he had left it in 1871 to found a home for his family in the New World. He had never regretted this step, but many bonds of sentiment and many old friends drew him to Europe. Alas, he had no money for such a trip and there seemed no way of obtaining it. There was a lottery formed by a few Wagner enthusiasts the proceeds of which should go to the Bayreuth Fund. The winner of the lucky number was to receive a ticket for the first performance, and my father bought a number, but of course he did not win, and there was the price of the steamship passage to pay and the expenses of maintenance in Europe besides. In his despair he told his old friend Schirmer, the New York music publisher, of his distress and Schirmer immediately said:

"Doctor, you simply must go, and here is a loan of five hundred dollars, which you can repay me whenever you can afford it."

lutely crazy performance, but the audience was hugely
delighted and contributed so liberally that my co-director
and I had a surplus with which to begin preparations for
another play.

Some parents on reading this may think that all this
was a huge waste of time, but I cannot agree with them.
Quite apart from the fact that it taught me a good deal
in the use of the brush, it was a great stimulus to the
imagination and a welcome outlet for the desire all children have to live in a make-believe world of fancy. At
any rate, Gustav Schirmer and I can claim that we were
the first to produce Wagner's "Rhinegold" in America,
and it is possible that this was the germ for my decision
eighteen years later to form the Damrosch Opera Company solely for the purpose of producing Wagner throughout America.

The dolls' theatre was, however, not my only diversion
from my school and musical studies.

At one Christmas my father and mother gave me a very
complete tool chest, with which I fashioned, among other
things, a dolls' house for my sisters and quite a little fleet
of boats. I remember one three-master, about three feet
in length, the wood for which I obtained from a foreman
at the Steinway piano factory, then situated on Park
Avenue. This three-master with all sails set won several
races for me on the pond in Central Park.

In those days, Central Park was considered very far
uptown, and where now the palaces of millionaires flank
its borders, Irish squatters lived in improvised huts around
which goats would gain a meagre livelihood from the
rocks stretching on all sides. These squatters established a kind of lien on the land, which I believe was recognized as having some legal force when the property be-

came more and more valuable and the owners began to grade the land for residential purposes.

Just as in the early days in Breslau, we continued to celebrate Christmas Eve in America in the good old fashion. Weeks before, a delicious atmosphere of mystery and secrecy began to envelop every member of the family. The "front parlor" became taboo for us children. Packages began to arrive and were stored there. The Christmas tree, which was always carefully chosen by my mother and which, according to old regulations, had to touch the ceiling with its top, was brought in in the evening after we had been carefully "shooed" upstairs into our respective bedrooms.

Dozens of sheets of gold and silver paper were cut by us into glittering garlands for the tree and we were, of course, expected to present our parents on Christmas eve with something fashioned by our own hands, or to be able to recite a poem or play a new piano solo. Of all this they were supposed to know nothing until the great day arrived, although they must have heard our dreary practising of it for weeks before.

The celebration was held on Christmas eve, before supper. My father and mother would disappear into the forbidden room to light the hundred candles on the tree and put the last touches on the heaps of presents. Then my father would play a march on the piano and we would all troop in and stand breathless before the tree so beautifully illuminated by the gentle light of the candles. Our presents would, of course, consist mainly of necessities in clothing and underclothing, shoes, etc., which we would have received anyhow, but which gained an added glow because of the occasion. But there were always books, and the tree was crowded with cakes and candies and gay-colored paper flowers and there were toys and joyous singing of Christmas songs and hymns around the tree. Then would come a delicious supper, accompanied by a cup of which Rhine wine and sliced pineapples were the constituent parts.

After supper we children had to recite our verses or play our piano solos, and, alas, these exhibitions sometimes ended in tears, as the exciting events that preceded this contribution to the festivities sometimes blunted our memories and we would get "stuck" in the middle. Then we would cast a frightened glance at my father, who would, perhaps, look rather serious until mother's smile or some joking remark would put him and us in good humor again.

Those wonderful Christmas celebrations of my childhood continued into my married life. Then when my children came, besides participating in my mother's tree, we tried, my wife and I, to bring into our own home on this beautiful day a kind of festive celebration which should pass on to our children and friends that which my father and mother and Tante Marie had so freely given to me.

We have had some wonderfully jolly Christmases. My four children and their cousin, Walker Blaine Beale, took on themselves the loving burden of our entertainment. A play was sometimes written or charades improvised, for which upstairs closets were ransacked for costumes and other paraphernalia in such haste and amid such ruthless confusion that Minna, our old Swedish nurse, who has been in our family since the birth of my oldest daughter, would often throw up her hands in horror at the bedrooms, which indeed looked as if a tornado had swept over them. I remember a delicious take-off on

"Pelléas et Melisande" which my oldest daughter, Alice,
wrote. I had given a number of lecture recitals on the
opera the previous season and it was much in the family
mind. Then another year a drama on "The North Pole"
was written. This was just after the dispute between
Peary and Cook as to the discovery of the pole. There
was a real shiver when we were heralded back to our
transformed parlor. The Christmas tree had quickly
become a lonely pine outlined against bleak areas of
farthest north cotton sheets, stretching in all directions
over "hummocks" of sofas and chairs. Our five children,
for Walker seemed as much our very own in these celebrations as my own four girls, gave us a wonderfully
spirited drama of the conquest of the polar regions!

I can see and hear dear David Bispham laugh, my old
friends Doctor and Mrs. George Harris's enthusiasm,
Margaret Anglin, Julie Faversham. . . . Our happy,
happy Christmases!

The last Christmas party at our home was that of 1916.
Then in 1917 Walker was training at Camp Dix and we
all went out with his mother and spent Christmas Day at
an inn near by to which he could come. There was a
rumor everywhere that his regiment was to embark for
overseas in a few days, although he really did not sail
until May. We all did our best to make it gay in that
hotel dining-room, the rain falling dismally. We were
so proud of our young khaki-uniformed lieutenant! My
Polly played and played, rags, anything and everything,
on the old hotel piano. We did not know it was to be
our last happy Christmas together, but war had already
given to joy a kind of yearning anguish.

My nephew was killed the 18th of the following September, 1918, at Saint-Mihiel. Reconnoitring to assure

the safety of his men, he leaped a fence to join three fellow officers. A shell tore them to pieces. This was in the early afternoon. Walker was taken to a field hospital and died at eleven that night.

We know that he did not suffer very much, and we think we know that he never understood how severely he was wounded, that he never knew that what, as a soldier, he so freely offered had been accepted.

He was his grandfather's, Mr. Blaine's, youngest grandson, only twenty-two, his mother's only son, our brightest and best.

There is no day we do not think of him, but Christmas, the day of giving, is his own especial day.

On a frigid day last winter (January, 1922) travelling with my wife on an untidy, dilapidated post-war train through Germany, on my way to Stockholm to fill an engagement to conduct the orchestra there, we read in an English magazine an article on Tennyson ending with a description of the old graveyard in which lie the bodies of his two grandsons, both killed in the war. "I did not know," I said, looking out over the black wintry flat German country, "that Tennyson lost *two* grandsons in the war!"

"But so did *my* father," my wife said proudly, and she spoke truly, for another nephew, Emmons Blaine of Chicago was no less a war victim than Walker. Unable to pass the physical tests required to enter the army he agonized to find the nation's greatest need behind the lines in which to enlist. He chose shipbuilding and offered himself as a workman at Hogg Island, near Philadelphia. Although never overstrong, he worked early and late, and fell a victim of the terrible epidemic of the "flu," dying at Lansdown on October 9, 1918.

Though Walker had already died in France, we knew only at the time that he was wounded. Of his death we learned four days later. Thus these two cousins, Emmons and Walker, are forever enshrined together in our anguish, in our pride, and in our love.

III

FOUNDING OF THE SYMPHONY AND ORATORIO SOCIETIES OF NEW YORK

In 1873 Anton Rubinstein, greatest of Russian pianists, accompanied by the violinist Wieniawski, came to America by invitation of Steinway and Sons. He dined at our house and expressed wonder that my father had not yet been able to achieve a position in New York commensurate with his reputation and capacity. My father explained to him how difficult the situation was and that the entire orchestral field was monopolized by Theodore Thomas. He told Rubinstein that when he had first arrived in New York he had met Thomas at the music store of Edward Schubert in Union Square and that after the introduction Thomas had said to him:

"I hear, Doctor Damrosch, that you are a very fine musician, but I want to tell you one thing: whoever crosses my path I crush."

Thomas at that time really believed that America was not large enough to contain more than one orchestra, but he lived long enough to see my father surpass him at the head of a symphony orchestra, as founder of the first great music festival in New York and, above all, of opera in German at the Metropolitan.

In 1881 the first symphony orchestra on a permanent basis had been founded in Boston by Major Higginson, and before Thomas's death there were half a dozen great subsidized orchestras actively operating in the United States, a number which has since then increased to twelve. Rubinstein said to my father: "Why don't you begin by founding an oratorio society, and that will lead to other things?"

My father consulted a few devoted friends, and the Oratorio Society of New York was accordingly founded in 1873 and began rehearsals in the Trinity Chapel with a chorus of about eighteen singers, my mother's glorious voice leading the sopranos and my very humble and little self among the altos. The first performance took place in the warcrooms of the Knabe Piano Company the following winter, at which time the chorus had increased to sixty singers. The programme was a remarkable one for that period, containing a capella chorus and accompanied choruses by Bach, Mozart, Handel, Palestrina, and Mendelssohn.

From this small beginning the society developed until it became the foremost representative of choral music in New York, performing, with a chorus of three hundred and fifty voices, under my father's direction, the older oratorios of Handel, Haydn, and Mendelssohn, and such novelties as the first part of "Christus" by Liszt, the Berlioz "Requiem" and "Damnation of Faust," the Brahms "Requiem," Cowen's "St. Ursula," the choral finale from the first act of "Parsifal," and the third act of "Meistersinger."

Indirectly, but logically, the founding of the Oratorio Society led to the founding of the Symphony Society of New York in 1877, which at last gave my father an orchestra with which he could demonstrate his abilities as a symphonic conductor.

The differences between him and Thomas were very

marked. Thomas, who had educated himself entirely
in America, had always striven for great cleanliness of
execution, a metronomical accuracy and rigidity of tempo,
and a strict and literal (and therefore rather mechanical)
observance of the signs put down by the composers.
America owed him a great debt of gratitude for the high
quality of his programmes. My father had been educated in a more modern school of interpretation, and his
readings were emotionally more intense. He was the first
conductor in this country to make those fine and delicate gradations in tempo according to the inner demands
of the music, gradations which are too subtle to be indicated by the composer's signs, as that would lead to exag-
gerations, but which are now generally considered as
necessary in order to bring out the *melos* of a work.

Both conductors had their violent partisans, and, as
they were at that time literally the only orchestral conductors in America, feeling ran very high. My father
was the last comer, and Thomas was well fortified in the
field, with a group of wealthy men to support him. The
first years for my father were very hard and a portion of
the New York papers assailed him bitterly, continuously,
and with vindictive enmity. Again and again dreams of
murder would fill my boyish heart when I would read
one of these attacks in the morning paper.

It was hard work to keep the two societies going and
to enable them to meet the bills for hall rent, soloists,
and orchestra. There was as yet but a small public for
the higher forms of music, and again and again it looked
as if further efforts would have to be abandoned. But
my father persevered and struggled on, making a living
for his family by teaching violin, composition, and singing, and occasionally getting a fee of "a hundred dollars

in gold" as violin soloist or in a chamber-music concert, officiating as musical director in a church and as conductor of the German male choral society, the Arion.

The first production of Symphony No. 1, in C minor, by Brahms became a subject of intense rivalry between the two conductors. Brahms had waited until his fortieth year before writing a symphony, and the work was eagerly awaited in New York, as the reports from Germany proved that it had made a sensation.

My father went to see old Gustav Schirmer at his store on Broadway and asked him whether the orchestral score of this work had yet arrived. Schirmer told him that it had, but that he was in honor bound to give it to Theodore Thomas as he had promised it to him. My father was very much chagrined to think that this prize should thus have escaped him, and he spoke of this very regretfully to a pupil of his in composition, Mrs. James Neilson, member of an aristocratic old family in New Brunswick, New Jersey, and a woman of great beauty and distinction. Mrs. Neilson said nothing to my father but quietly went down to Schirmer's and inquired of the clerk whether the orchestral score of the Brahms symphony had arrived, and when he answered in the affirmative, she asked whether it was for sale. "Certainly," answered the clerk.

She thereupon purchased a copy of the score and sent it up to my father with her compliments. His astonishment was intense, but she did not tell him until weeks afterward how she had obtained it.

He received the score on a Thursday and the first rehearsal for the next concert was to take place on the following Monday. This left but little time to obtain the necessary orchestral parts and Schirmer naturally would not sell him any. He therefore cut the score into three parts and divided them among three copyists, who worked day and night and managed to have the parts ready in time for the rehearsal. Great was the triumph in the Damrosch camp at this victory over the Thomas forces.

Some years later I gave the first performances in New York of the Third and Fourth Brahms Symphonies, but I had no need to resort to strategem to obtain the scores and orchestral parts.

Orchestral conditions were bad compared with to-day. There was no such thing as a "permanent orchestra." The musicians of the Symphony Society, for instance, played in six symphony concerts during the winter, each preceded by a public rehearsal. They also officiated at four concerts of the Oratorio Society, and this was almost the extent of their efforts in that direction. The rest of the time they made their living by teaching, playing in theatres, at dances, and some of them even at political or military processions and mass meetings. If a better "job" came along than the symphony concert they would simply send my father a substitute. Small wonder that occasionally their lips gave out and the first horn or trumpet would break on an important note during a symphony concert. And yet, in spite of this disheartening condition, my father succeeded in infusing the orchestral players with such emotional intensity, and in imparting so lofty an interpretation to them, that the audiences of that day were often roused to the greatest enthusiasm; and I would tuck my arm very proudly into his as we marched home from a concert, even though we knew that the subscription to the concert was not more than eight hundred dollars and the single sale at the box office had not reached the hundred dollar mark.

But all this was changed like a flash in the year 1879 when my father decided to perform "The Damnation of Faust," by Berlioz, until then unknown in America. This concert, which was held at Steinway Hall, in East 14th Street, necessitated the services of solo singers, the New York Symphony Orchestra, the chorus of the New York Oratorio Society and the male chorus of the Arion Society.

The work and the performance made a sensation. All New York buzzed with it, and during that winter, 1879, it was given five times in succession to crowded houses, creating an excitement such as New York had never before seen in the concert field.

I played in all these performances at the last stand of the second violins, as my father considered it of the utmost value to me as a future conductor to be able to follow the conductor's beat as one of the orchestra.

IV

AUGUST WILHELMJ—TERESA CARRENO

In the spring of 1878 Maurice Strakosch, an old concert manager, called on my father and asked him whether he would permit me to go on a Southern concert tour with the celebrated violinist, August Wilhelmj, who was then touring the country under Strakosch management. Mr. Max Liebling, his regular accompanist, had been taken ill and as both Wilhelmj and Strakosch knew that I had accompanied my father a great deal at home, they thought that I could acceptably fill the position at such short notice. I was naturally wild with delight at the idea and prevailed on my father to let me go. I was to receive the, for me, munificent salary of a hundred dollars a week and all my railway expenses.

We set forth the following Monday, the company consisting of Wilhelmj, a soprano singer whose name I have forgotten, and Teresa Carreno, who was then already a great pianist and certainly the most beautiful woman I had ever seen.

Wilhelmj, who was exceedingly lazy, refused even to rehearse with me. Our first concert was in Washington and I was to accompany him, among other things, in the Mendelssohn Violin Concerto. I was naturally nervous about it, and to my delighted astonishment, on the afternoon of the concert, Carreno turned on Wilhelmj, reproaching him for not giving me a rehearsal and insisting that rather than put me to such an unfair strain, she would accompany him in the concerto herself. This was a characteristic act of this remarkable artist and woman, and I shall speak more in detail about my immediate adoration for her in another chapter.

In Washington Baron von Schloetzer, the Prussian minister, who was an old friend of my father's, received me very kindly, and, to my delight, included me in the dinner which he gave in honor of Wilhelmj and Carreno. He was an original and delightful old bachelor and wildly fond of music, although his only accomplishment in that line was a real talent for whistling, his *pièce de résistance* being the "Tannhäuser Overture," in which he would whistle the "Pilgrim's Chorus" and the fluttering accompanying violins seemingly at the same time.

At his dinner he treated me somewhat as an older man would a child, and would tell his butler to my great chagrin to only half fill my glass because I was too young to drink as much as the older people. He had several rare vintages of claret standing on the sideboard and some of these I was not allowed even to taste, all for the same reason.

After dinner both Wilhelmj and Carreno played and then the beautiful Mme. de Hagemann, American wife of the Swedish Minister, sang most delightfully. She has since written charming memoirs of her earlier diplomatic life abroad, especially of the Court of Napoleon the Third just before the Franco-Prussian War, entitled "Courts of Memory."

From Washington we went farther and farther South and my young mind was tremendously impressed by its romantic atmosphere, the luxuriant tropical foliage and the lazy, cheerful life of the "niggers" swarming everywhere.

At Macon, Georgia, Wilhelmj and I stopped at an old

ramshackle hotel in two rooms en suite. We did not wake up until about eleven o'clock the following morning, feeling very heavy and headachy, and on examination found our trunks rifled of whatever valuables they contained. We had evidently been chloroformed. A burly detective was engaged by Wilhelmj to take charge of the case, but of course nothing happened except that Wilhelmj and I purchased revolvers. His was very large and mine very small and this is about the only weapon that I ever acquired, and of course never used.

New Orleans was a real revelation. It was then still an absolutely French city. I was invited to dinner at several delightful Creole families and French was the language at table. The old Creole restaurants were at the height of their glory, and such delicious crabs, pompano, and shrimps I had never eaten before. Alas, their nice sanded floors have been replaced by dancing parquets, and noisy ragtime bands and wretched cooking are but poor substitutes for their past glories.

THE MUSIC FESTIVAL OF 1881

During the summer of 1880 my father conceived the idea of giving a monster music festival in May, 1881, which was to last a week and for which a chorus of one thousand two hundred, of which the Oratorio Society should be the nucleus, was to be trained in sections during the entire winter. He conferred with some of his friends, outlined his project to them, and a Music Festival Association composed of the directors of his Symphony and Oratorio Societies was formed. Other prominent New York citizens were added and a guarantee fund was provided, ample to protect the project financially.

Although I was only eighteen, my father deemed me sufficiently advanced to intrust the drilling of a great portion of this chorus to me, a confidence of which I was very proud.

The entire summer of 1880 I spent in the little New England town of Amherst. A very remarkable Frenchman, Doctor Sauveur by name, had perfected a new system of teaching French and Latin, and Amherst College had turned its buildings over to him for a summer course. It seemed to my father and me that this was an excellent opportunity for me to acquire the rudiments of these two languages.

I accordingly arrived in Amherst armed with a grand piano, reams of music paper, and the orchestral score of the great Berlioz's "Requiem," which my father had selected as one of the works to be performed at the Festival. There was no piano score in existence and, to my joy, my father intrusted me with the task of making one from the original orchestral score.

I obtained a lovely bedroom from a farmer on the main street for the opulent price of two and a half dollars a week, and my grand piano was installed in the parlor, of which I had the entire use for four hours a day to practise. My meals I got at the principal little hotel for six dollars a week and when the genial proprietor saw me consuming my first dinner he said:

"Ef I had known you et that hearty I would have charged you more. I won't make nothin' out of you."

The meals were certainly delicious, and at eighteen one's capacity in that direction is unlimited.

When I arrived in May the college was still in session and I was made welcome by several of the students, among them Lawrence Abbott, now editor of *The Outlook,*

and John Cotton Smith, now rector of St. John's in
Washington.

My days were certainly busy ones. In the morning I
attended the sessions of Doctor Sauveur in French and
Latin and in the afternoon I practised piano and worked
hard at the arranging of the piano score of the Berlioz
"Requiem." Incidentally, I seemed to find plenty of
time for games and fun of all kinds with a delightful
family who had a country place there and where I got
my first real glimpse of American country life, which
is indeed unique and with which no other country can
compare.

As fast as the different numbers of my arrangement of
the Berlioz "Requiem" were finished, I sent them on to
my father who, after revising them, gave them to the
publisher in order to have the piano scores ready for the
rehearsals in the fall. He was well pleased with my work,
especially the "Tuba Mirum," in which he thought that
I had condensed quite cleverly the four orchestras which
Berlioz intended placed at the four corners of the stage
to represent the trumpets of the last judgment.

When I returned to New York in September, my
father intrusted to me Section B of the New York Festival Chorus, numbering two hundred voices and the
Newark Harmonic Society of Newark, New Jersey,
numbering three hundred. He himself drilled the chorus
of the Oratorio Society of four hundred at which I always
played the piano accompaniments, and Mr. Cortada,
an old pupil of my father's, trained a section in Brooklyn
and another in Nyack, New York. I hurled myself at
my task with such vehemence and enthusiasm that by
the time the Festival came along my choruses were letter-
perfect, but I had become voiceless. My vocal cords

had quite gone back on me in justifiable anger at my abuse of them.

The choral works to be performed included the Berlioz "Requiem," Rubinstein's "Tower of Babel," Handel's "Messiah," Beethoven's "Ninth Symphony," and shorter selections. The monster chorus and orchestra numbered fifteen hundred, and a special stage and sounding-board were built at the Seventh Regiment Armory at which the Festival took place. The organ from St. Vincent's Church was transferred bodily, and I was intrusted with the organ accompaniments. An enormous audience of ten thousand people attended every performance, and the public acclaimed my father with much enthusiasm as America's greatest musician. Such happy, happy days!

Among the many memories of this great occasion I can never forget the first rehearsal of the four orchestras and sixteen kettledrums which Berlioz used in the "Tuba Mirum" to depict the Last Judgment. This rehearsal took place in the Foyer of the old Academy of Music in Fourteenth Street; and as the sixteen kettledrums came in like one man just as the fanfare of the judgment Trumpets begins, the effect of these vibrations in a comparatively small room was so tremendous that one by one the orchestra men arose and a murmur began which grew and grew and finally relieved itself in a loud shout of enthusiasm. It was several minutes before my father could continue the rehearsal. I have never witnessed anything quite like it since. We are now so sophisticated by Strauss and the later-day dissonancers that so-called instrumental "effects" neither shock nor stir us. And as regards the dissonances with which some of the ultra-moderns seek to irritate our ears, I have always claimed that the human ear is like the back of a donkey—if you whip it long enough and hard enough, it gradually becomes insensitive to pain.

Theodore Thomas and his supporters were much irritated that my father should have "gotten ahead" of them with so stupendous a musical demonstration, and they immediately proceeded to copy his idea by giving a Music Festival the following year in the same building.

For me, the immediate result of the Festival was my election at eighteen years of age as permanent conductor of the Newark Harmonic Society. This gave me the long-desired opportunity to produce choral works with orchestral accompaniment, and for several years I gave three or four of these every winter, including not only the older oratorios of Handel and Mendelssohn, but more modern works like Berlioz's "Damnation of Faust," Rubinstein's "Tower of Babel," the Verdi "Requiem," and choral excerpts from the operas of Wagner. All of these concerts my father attended, and after each performance he would analyze my conducting, praise freely and enthusiastically where he thought I deserved it, and also show me where he considered a tempo wrong or an entrance of instruments or chorus not properly indicated. My mother and aunt would often lend their lovely voices in the choruses at the performances whenever I thought I needed them, but they would always insist in the most blindly partisan way that my concerts were wonderful and that I was altogether a very remarkable boy.

This year marked my real beginning as a professional musician, and I enjoyed my weekly rehearsals in Newark immensely, although horse-cars, ferry-boats, and trains made the trip in those days a cumbersome one. But after each rehearsal Mr. Schuyler Brinkerhoff Jackson, the president of the society, Mr. Shinkle, the secretary, my dear old friend Zach Belcher, enthusiastic tenor and music lover, Frank Sealey, my pianist and since then for so many years accompanist and organist of the New York Oratorio Society, used to go with me to a nice German beer saloon near the railroad station where, over a glass of beer and Swiss-cheese sandwiches, we waited until train time and discussed the welfare of the Harmonic Society and music in general. Alas, the Volstead Law has ended all such simple and happy foregatherings and the soda-water counter with its horrible concoctions is but a poor substitute for the gentle and soothing beer of Pilsen and Munich.

V

LISZT AND WAGNER

In the spring of 1882 I sailed for Europe. My father wanted me to know his old friend, Liszt, and to hear the first performances of "Parsifal" in Bayreuth. My throat was also still bothering me and the doctor thought that a cure at Ems would be a good thing.

I was naturally overwhelmed at the idea of seeing the great Liszt face to face. His name had been, ever since I could remember, a houschold word in our family. My father and mother had told me so much of his friendship for them, his genius and his triumphs as a piano virtuoso, and of his voluntary relinquishment of all this to devote himself exclusively to creative work, and toward helping the entire modern school of young composers. My father had kept up a desultory correspondence with Liszt during the years he had spent in America, and as soon as I arrived in Weimar I went to the little gardener's cottage in which he lived to pay my respects to the old master. I entered his room in great trepidation, and when I managed to stutter a few words to tell him that I was the son of Doctor Leopold Damrosch, I was amazed at the kindness of his reception. He immediately spoke of my father and mother with such love that I forgot some of my timidity. He asked me about an opera on Shakespeare's "Romeo and Juliet," which my father had composed in the old Weimar days but which he had subsequently destroyed as he was dissatisfied with it. He then asked me how long I expected to stay in Weimar. I said two days and that I was then going to Ems for a cure and then to Bayreuth to hear the first "Parsifal" performances.

A curious change came over Liszt as I spoke. He repeated several times, "Two days, ha, yes, 'Parsifal,' of course, Bayreuth.—'Parsifal,' of course," and then he picked up a box of cigars.

"Well, at least you'll take a cigar before you leave Weimar?"

I said: "No, master, thank you very much, I do not smoke."

"You should then go to-night to the theatre to hear the first performance of Calderon's play 'Above all Magic is Love,' for which your father's old friend Lassen has written the music and which he will conduct."

I assured the master that I would certainly go, but sensing a certain frigidity in the air, and feeling that so unimportant a person as myself must not take any more time of the great Liszt, I withdrew.

That evening I went to the historic little theatre doubly hallowed by the productions and ministrations of Goethe, as well as the memorable times in the fifties when Liszt officiated there and conducted the first performances of Wagner's "Lohengrin" in which my mother had sung *Ortrude*. The theatre was so small that you could almost see every person in it as in a drawing-room, and to my astonishment, in the first intermission, one of the servants of the theatre came to me and asked me if I were Herr Damrosch. When I answered in the affirmative he said that Kapellmeister Lassen wished to see me. I followed him to the stage and was immediately accosted by Lassen whom I had not met before, but of whom I knew, because he and my father had been close friends for many years.

He said: "What did you do to the master this morning?

I came in just after you left and found him in tears. He said, 'a young son of Damrosch called on me this morning, I thought of course he would stay here and study with me, but instead of that he told me he was only going to stay two days. The young generation have forgotten me completely. They think nothing of me and they have no respect for us older men of bygone days. Am I a hotel in which one takes a room for a night, then to pass on elsewhere?'"

Needless to say, I was overcome at such a dreadful development of a perfectly innocent remark of mine. I could not conceive it possible that so small a person as myself should have unwittingly brought about so tragic a result, and I implored Lassen to tell me how I could efface it.   Lassen, seeing my unhappy state, advised me to go the next morning at eight o'clock to see Liszt again and to explain everything to him.   I sat through the rest of the play but actually did not hear a word of it or a note of Lassen's music; I was too occupied with my own misery. I did not sleep all night, but tossed about restlessly and at six arose and wandered about dismally until seven when a frowsy waiter in the dining-room of my hotel, the "Russische Erb Prinz" gave me a cup of coffee.

Punctually at eight o'clock I knocked at Liszt's door and as I entered I saw this wonderful-looking old man with his splendid white hair and deep-set eyes, already at his work-table.   As he saw me his eyebrows arched and said: "What, still in Weimar?"

I came forward and tried to speak, suddenly burst into tears and then managed to stammer out my great admiration for him, how my father had always held him up as the ideal musician of our times, and how he must have misunderstood my words of yesterday if he thought that I intended any lack of respect or reverence for such a man as he. As I reread this it seems quite articulate, but as I told it to Liszt it must have sounded very ridiculous, but nevertheless I suddenly felt his arms about me and a very gentle furtive kiss placed upon my forehead. He led me to a chair, sat down by me and began again to talk and reminisce about my father and mother. He then invited me to come that afternoon to his piano class and I left very much relieved at the outcome of my visit.

I then called on another old friend of my parents and also of Liszt's, Fräulein von Schorn. I found at her house a friend of hers, Baron von Joukowski, a Russian painter of distinction and a highly interesting man, who had become very friendly with the Wagner family and who had designed the Hall of the Holy Grail for the "Parsifal" production at Bayreuth. When I told them of my experience with Liszt they explained to me that Liszt had grown very old, that he felt the modern musical world was forgetting him and that in choosing a sacred text like "Parsifal," Wagner had been, so to speak, encroaching somewhat on his domain. Perhaps even a latent jealousy of Wagner's all-usurping powers was slightly clouding a friendship and self-sacrifice which Liszt had so abundantly given to Wagner all his lifetime. They also told me that Liszt was now surrounded by a band of cormorants in the shape of ostensible piano students, many of whom had no real talent or ambition, but who virtually lived on the master's incredible kindness, abusing it in every way and altogether making the Weimar of that day a travesty on former times.

Bülow confirmed this to me several years later and told me how he had once "cleaned out" Liszt's rooms and bade this unsavory crowd never to return. Liszt had thanked him, but next morning they were all back again.

I attended the audition in Liszt's rooms that afternoon and found that there was indeed a pitiful crowd of sycophants and incompetents assembled, but there were a few exceptions, notably young Eugene d'Albert who was then perhaps fifteen or sixteen years of age and who played wonderfully and to Liszt's great satisfaction. There were a few others who, however, did not play on that afternoon. But another one who shall be nameless, sat down to play the Beethoven sonata in E flat, Op. 31, No. 3, and botched the introduction so horribly that Liszt gently pushed her off the chair and sat down himself saying, "This is the way it should be played," and then the music seemed to just drop from his fingers onto the piano keys, and such a heavenly succession of sounds ravished my ear that I did not think it possible human hands could evoke it. He then said to her: "Now, try it again." And she did, and, if anything, played even worse than before. Again Liszt played the opening phrases, and then, somewhat irritated, he said:

"So, blamieren Sie sich noch einmal." (Now, make a fool of yourself again.) By that time to our relief she felt that both she and we had had enough.

After this I met Liszt several times and he always treated me with uniform cordiality, but every once in a while the memory of our first meeting would come to him and he would make some gently malicious remark, such as "Oh, here comes our young American; like lightning he flashes through the world!"

From Weimar I went to Ems and dutifully took the "cure" for five weeks, drinking the three glasses of the more or less miraculous waters while the band played before breakfast, and watching little girls dressed in white smilingly presenting bouquets of bachelor's-buttons, popularly supposed to be his favorite flower, to old Emperor William, who, accompanied by an adjutant or two, used to take the cure at Ems every summer.

To strangers like myself the place on the promenade at which the French Ambassador, Benedetti, had "insulted" the King of Prussia in 1870 was always pointed out, but this was many years before Bismarck's famous and cynical confession that it had all been a put-up job by him in so altering the famous telegram relating to the King's meeting with Benedetti that, according to Bismarck's memoirs: "It will be known in Paris before midnight, and not only on account of its contents but also on account of the manner of its distribution, will have the effect of a red rag upon the Gallic Bull."

Two summers ago, after an absence of thirty-eight years, I revisited Ems with my wife and daughters. We had motored from Paris to Coblenz on a visit to General Allen, then in command of our Army of Occupation in Coblenz, and from there to Ems was but a short motor ride. We found the town occupied by French troops from Morocco, and our officer guides pointed out with some amusement the stone which marks the place where Benedetti and King William had met in 1870.

In July I went to Bayreuth in high expectation, to hear the first four performances of Wagner's "Parsifal." To a young musician from America such an experience was especially new and exciting. I arrived there a week or two before the first performance, hoping to gain admission to some of the rehearsals. I found this impossible, but I met scores of artists by whom I was cordially received because I was my father's son. Many of his old friends were there for the "Parsifal" performances and I remember with much pleasure the kindly, refined and gentle Herman Levi, General Music Director of the Munich Opera, who had been chosen by Wagner to conduct the Bayreuth performances.

I received an invitation for the first reception held by Wagner and his wife, Cosima, at Wahnfried and dutifully presented myself there with some nervousness, which was allayed somewhat when I found Liszt almost at the door as I came in. He immediately recognized me and not only introduced me to Cosima, but when she said, "Father, you must introduce this son of our old friend, Doctor Leopold Damrosch, to the Meister," he took me into Wagner's workroom where I beheld Wagner surrounded by musicians and in front of him the giant tenor, Albert Niemann, well known later on to Wagner lovers in America as a member of the German company at the Metropolitan for a number of years, and also as the creator of *Tannhäuser* in Paris at the tragic and disastrous performances of 1861.

As we came in, Wagner was joking Niemann unmercifully, saying:

"Look at this man! I invited him to create the part of *Parsifal* for me and he refused because I told him that *Parsifal* must be a beardless youth and he said he would not cut off his beard for any man."

"Why, Meister," answered Niemann, "you know that is not true; I would cut off my nose if it were necessary to sing one of your rôles properly."

Wagner greeted me with kindness, asked about my father, and a few days later sent me, through his publishers, for my father, a manuscript copy of the finale from the first act of "Parsifal" (no orchestral score was

at that time engraved) for performance in New York by
the Symphony and Oratorio Societies. This was a remarkable act of friendship on his part and I was very
proud to be able to carry the precious score back to my
father.

It was to me indescribably touching to note the way
in which Liszt sought to efface himself at Wagner's
house, in order that Wagner's glory should stand forth
alone. When I first saw Liszt there I, following the custom of the young musicians at Weimar and elsewhere,
sought his hand in order to kiss it; but, with a force incredible in so old a man, he pressed down my hand, saying
with his gentle smile: "No, no, not here."

I doubt whether there ever was a musician who worked
so incessantly for the benefit of other musicians as he.
He was constantly seeking, either with his ten magic
fingers as pianist or with his pen as musical critic or propagandist, or with his own money, to save others from want
or to help them to obtain the recognition which he thought
they deserved. It is impossible to name the hundreds
whom he thus benefited—Berlioz, Saint-Saëns, César
Franck, Schumann, Cornelius, and so on, and of course
above all Wagner himself, whose friendship with Liszt
has become historic. Like most friendships, the one gives
much more than he receives, and that one was Liszt, who,
in his admiration for Wagner's genius minimized himself
and what he had accomplished as composer to an exaggerated degree. In those personal qualities that make up
a man's character, Liszt was infinitely the superior.
Wagner's genius as a musician was the greater, but this
brought in its trail an overwhelming egotism and a vanity
which made many of his relations with his fellow men
unfortunate. Liszt gave up all worldly glories and hon-

ors and riches which he might have acquired if he had continued his career as perhaps the greatest piano virtuoso that ever lived, in order to devote himself absolutely to composition and musical propaganda, without any thought of pecuniary rewards. He literally, like his patron saint, Francis of Assisi, took the vows of poverty. When I saw him he lived in most simple fashion, always travelled "second class" and gave what little money he had to others who seemed to him to need it more. Without his never-ceasing support and encouragement, his absolute faith in the eventual triumph of Wagner's music, and without continual financial support from Liszt and from those he constantly urged to help, Wagner could never have carried on his struggle toward the triumphant completion of a Bayreuth and an almost complete realization of his ideals.

The first performance of "Parsifal" made a tremendous impression on me. I was much moved by the noble allegory and the music accompanying the sacred rituals of the Christian Church as presented upon the stage in the scene during the uncovering of the Holy Grail. But I must confess that with each succeeding performance this feeling lessened. The fact that it was not a devotional ceremony but an imitation of one which had been carefully drilled and trained into the performers whose gestures of devotion repeated themselves each time with automatic regularity, gradually began to affect me disagreeably. I was at that time too young to analyze this feeling properly, but, as the years went by, I gradually arrived at the belief that such ceremonials should not be presented on a stage, for if we see a group of Christian Knights partaking of the Lord's Supper, we should have the full conviction that it is a real ceremony and not an imitation. The foot-washing scene between *Parsifal* and *Kundry* also affected me disagreeably. It was too direct an imitation of Magdalen washing the feet of Christ. On the other hand, the Good Friday scene between *Parsifal* and *Gurnemanz* moved me and many others in the audience to tears because it was a lovely and lovable presentation of the divine mercy through the self-sacrifice of the Saviour. Old Scaria, the Vienna bass, who took the part of *Gurnemanz*, sang and acted this scene with convincing tenderness.

I was naturally much interested in the invisible, subterranean orchestra of the Bayreuth auditorium, and as the first noble theme of the prelude literally floated into the darkened hall, the great advantage of an invisible conductor was manifest. The division of the music into bars, which are an essential of the conductor's beat, should be seen only by the orchestra, and I still wish it were possible to educate the public to listen to music with their ears only and not with their eyes. But this theory of mine would find violent opposition from the small but select company of "prima donna conductors" who, at that parting of the ways which comes to every conductor, whether he shall make himself an interpreter of the composers' works or a perverter in order to demonstrate his own "tricks of the trade," have chosen the primrose path because a large part of the public are easily gulled and more easily moved if the conductor "dramatizes" the music through his gestures. By the skilful manipulation of his arms and hands, his hips and his hair, he gives the impression that when the 'cellos play a soulful melody, it really drips from his wrists, and when the kettledrums play a dramatic roll it is really the result of a flash of his eye. There are many people, especially among the gentle sex, to whom admiration for one conductor entails a deep hatred of all others. It would be interesting to note how many of them could pick out their favorite if half a dozen of the prima donnas of the baton were to perform invisibly with an invisible orchestra in quick succession to each other.

The strings of the Bayreuth orchestra were noble and rich in tone, but I was disturbed by many inaccuracies and false intonations of the wind choir, which surprised me all the more as the orchestra was supposed to be composed of the best of every kind from the different opera-houses of Germany. These faults were not noticed or acknowledged by my German friends, and I think that the years have brought more and more of a cleavage in this respect between their orchestras and ours, and that to-day American orchestras obtain, especially in the wind-instrument choirs, greater purity of tone and, without sacrificing elasticity, a greater precision of ensemble.

I have always had a penchant for French wood-wind players and have given them and their Belgian cousins a preference in my orchestra. Generally speaking, a conductor can safely engage a first prize from the Paris Conservatoire in flute, oboe, or bassoon without giving him any further examination.

Where else can one find a flute of such ravishing tone quality as that of George Barrère, who has been first flute of the New York Symphony Orchestra for seventeen years and who was first recommended to me by his great teacher, Tafanel, in Paris? I am happy to say that he is developing many American players and giving to them something of his own luscious and spiritual tone quality, so that he, as well as Mathieu, our first oboe, and

Lettelier, bassoon, are continuing the great traditions of the Paris Conservatoire in this country and imparting their qualities to a group of young American pupils. Germany has produced some great clarinet players, of whom Muhlfeld, for whom Brahms wrote his beautiful "Quintet for Clarinet and Strings," was a fine example. Mr. Lindemann, first clarinet of my orchestra, is another, and his tone is of a peculiarly pure quality. I prefer the tone of the German trombonists to that of their French colleagues. The Germans cultivate a darker and more noble tone quality.

The summer of 1886 I returned again to Germany. I had been invited to conduct some selections from "Sulamith," a cantata of my father's, at the annual meeting of the "Ton-künstler Verein" which took place at the beautiful Thuringian hill town of Sondershausen, the residence of the princely house of Schwartzburg-Sondershausen, where the prince maintained a good permanent symphony orchestra.

Liszt, as venerable founder and president of the Ton-künstler Verein, an association of musicians the original purpose of which was the production and cultivation of the modern school of composition, again received me very kindly and expressed himself as much pleased at hearing my father's work.

At the close of the Festival I accompanied him, together with Baron Joukowski and Fräulein von Schorn, back to Weimar. During the trip Liszt was in a very gay mood and kept us in gales of laughter with a number of outrageous puns and amusing comments on certain phases of the Festival, especially on a long debate between Doctor Rieman, an eminent musical theorist, and another man whose name I have forgotten, on certain theories regarding the science of harmony. This debate, which was wholly technical and very "gründlich" lasted for two hours, during which poor Liszt had to sit in the front row in a room crowded to suffocation and with not a door or window open. I can still see the venerable head of Liszt drooping and dropping every now and then from sheer fatigue, and then the Meister raising it again with that ineffable smile on his face in order to show an interest in the discussion.

When we arrived in Weimar, Joukowski invited us all, together with Lassen, to dinner at the Hotel "Zum Russischen Hof." It was a jolly affair. Champagne was served immediately after the soup and Liszt reminisced so brilliantly and beautifully of the old Weimar days of which Fräulein von Schorn and Lassen had been a part and with which I, too, could claim some connection through my parents, that we all sat spellbound.

During the dinner Liszt asked me if I knew anything of a portrait of his which had been painted under interesting conditions many years before. Liszt occupied rooms at the old Villa d'Este at Tivoli, near Rome, for a month or two every winter. It then belonged to his old friend, Cardinal Prince Hohenlohe. One evening his bell rang, and as his servant had gone out, Liszt took a candle and opened the door. His visitors were Henry Wadsworth Longfellow, the American poet, who had brought a painter friend, Mr. Healy, to introduce to the maestro. Longfellow was so struck with the picturesque appearance of Liszt as he stood in the old doorway in his long black soutane, holding a lighted candle, that he asked Liszt for permission to have Healy paint a picture of him, and he consequently gave Healy several sittings. Longfellow took the painting back with him to America.

I had never heard of or seen this picture, but thirty years later, when Ernest Longfellow, a nephew of the poet, was lunching at our house I remembered the incident and asked him if he knew anything of the whereabouts of the picture. He told me that he remembered it very well and that it was still hanging in his uncle's house in Cambridge. Through the courtesy of the present occupants I was permitted to take a photograph of it and it is reproduced in this book.

It was not until midnight that we accompanied Liszt through the park and the lovely Goethe Garden back to his house. It was a gentle summer night with a hazy moon giving an indescribable glamour to the trees and bushes, and suddenly Liszt laid his hand on my shoulder and said "Listen!"

From the bushes came the song of a nightingale. I had never heard one before and stood spellbound. It seemed incredible that such ecstatic sweetness, such songs of joy and sorrow, could come from the throat of a little bird, and to hear it all at twenty-four years of age and standing at the side of Liszt! Dear reader, I confess that to-day, thirty-five years later, I still thrill at the memory of it.

Alas! That was almost the last time that I saw Liszt. In July I went again to Bayreuth to hear the first "Tristan" performance, and one morning I met him, looking very old and worn, coming all alone out of the church from early mass. A few days later, July 31, he had followed his dearest friend, Wagner, into the beyond.

The following winter, in Liszt's memory (March 3, 1887), I gave the first complete performance in America of his oratorio, "Christus." This work made so profound an impression that I repeated it the following year.

I am sorry that "Christus" has not been performed

since then by our choral societies, as I consider it to be
Liszt's greatest work. Many of its themes are based on
the Gregorian modes. The choruses are set in sonorous
harmonies and breathe a tranquillity which can only be
achieved by a perfect mastery of the subject and the form
in which it is treated. There are two orchestral numbers
—a Pastorale, indicative of the shepherds and the annun-
ciation, "Angelus Domini ad Pastores ait," and the
March of the Three Kings, "Et ecce Stella quam Vide-
rant"—which are brilliantly orchestrated. The march
depicts the three kings of the Orient with their mighty
retinue, the star guiding them to the manger in Bethlehem being indicated by a sustained high A flat in the
first violins in an organ point around which the proces-
sional continues. The trio, or middle part, in a beautiful
unison of the violins and violoncellos, depicts the kings
opening their treasures and presenting gold, frankincense,
and myrrh to the little Jesu.

The entrance of Christ into Jerusalem is characterized
by an atmosphere of exalted, joyous acclaim, and the
setting for baritone of the prayer of Jesus,

> O my Father, if this cup may not pass away
> from me, except I drink it, Thy will be done,

is one of the most moving that I know of in the history of
religious music.

In the last part there is an exquisite but simple setting
of an ancient Eastern hymn, "O Filii et Filiæ." Altogether I cannot understand why, in the dearth of religious
music written by modern pens, "Christus" does not take
its permanent place in the repertoire of choral societies.

Like many other works of the greatest masters, a few
good cuts will add to the effectiveness of this oratorio.

VI

THE FOUNDING OF GERMAN OPERA AT THE METROPOLITAN—DEATH OF MY FATHER

The Metropolitan Opera House was built in 1882 by a group of rich New Yorkers who, feeling themselves shut out by the older aristocracy who owned the old Academy of Music and occupied all the boxes at the Italian Opera seasons of Colonel Mapleson, determined to have an opera of their own. They leased their new house for the inaugural season of 1883-84 to Abbey, Schoeffel, and Grau, a firm of theatrical speculators and managers who had made a name for themselves by the tours of Mary Anderson and other celebrated "stars" of Europe and America.

The Metropolitan Opera stockholders had appointed as architect a man whose reputation had been made in building churches, but who knew nothing of theatrical or operatic requirements, or of the latest developments in Europe in the construction of the stage and modern stage appliances. As a result, the stage arrangements were of the most clumsy description. Great walls, many feet thick, ran beneath the stage from the front to the rear, thereby precluding the possibility of a "transformation" scene in which one set of scenery could sink into the ground while the other descended from above. The parquet floor was placed so low that the orchestra pit, which was supposed to be an imitation (but was not) of the sunken orchestra at Bayreuth, had to be placed still lower and in consequence the conductor was perched on a kind of pulpit high in the air so that the singers could see him.

He had to gesticulate wildly upward toward the singers and downward toward the abyss in which the orchestra fiddled without being able properly to see his gestures. Besides this, the orchestra, being so far from the stage, was almost inaudible to the singers, and this often resulted in the most disastrous dropping of the pitch, especially in the concerted numbers. Years later and at huge expense some of these faults of construction were corrected.

For their season Abbey, Schoeffel, and Grau engaged a large number of operatic stars, including Nilsson, Patti, Sembrich, Trebelli, and many others of distinction, but there was absolutely no artistic head of the enterprise nor any one who had had any real managerial experience with grand opera, and in consequence all these stars stepped on each other's feet and trains and the confusion was incredible. Good performances were an accident, as the principal artists usually deemed it beneath their dignity to attend rehearsals, and the season ended in failure and the bankruptcy of Abbey, Schoeffel, and Grau. Colonel Mapleson, the astute manager of the Academy of Music, rubbed his hands with glee at this downfall of what he called "the new yellow brewery on Broadway." The directors of the Metropolitan were at a loss what to do with their elephant. Their president was James Roosevelt, an uncle of Hilborn Roosevelt who was then president of the New York Symphony Society and who was a stanch and devoted friend of my father's. He suggested to his uncle that my father be appointed as director and that a season of opera in German be inaugurated, as Italian opera was evidently on the wane and Wagner, especially, on the ascendant.

The directors thought well of this scheme and accordingly made an arrangement with my father under which he should become director of the opera for the season 1884–85 and that he should engage a company of German singers of which, however, Madame Materna must be one, as she had sung with great success at the Theodore Thomas Festival of the preceding year and they wanted some name already known in America to head the list of singers.

This meant a complete revolution in operatic affairs, as until then Italian opera had been the only fashionable form of musical entertainment. Opera in German was rather looked down upon and Wagner's genius was as yet too imperfectly known or recognized to exercise much influence on the opera-going folks of that time.

My father was to receive a salary of ten thousand dollars, for which he was to act as manager and also as musical conductor of the season. The salary was certainly not large, even for those days, but my father was glad to get it and at the same time to carry out the dream of his life, the introduction of the Wagner music-dramas to America, and to sweep away forever the artificial and shallow operas of the old Italian school with which Mapleson, Max Strakosh, and others had until then principally fed our public.

He sailed for Europe in May and returned in August with all his contracts made, including Madame Materna, to whom he had to pay a thousand dollars a night, as she had gotten wind of the dictum of the Metropolitan Opera House directors that under all circumstances she must be one of the company.

Among the singers were Marianne Brandt, one of the greatest dramatic mezzo-sopranos and contraltos of our times, and Anton Schott, a typical German "heroic tenor," with whom Bülow had had his famous altercation at Hanover a few years before at a "Lohengrin" performance. Schott had sung Lohengrin's "Farewell to the Swan" out of tune and this had so irritated Bülow, who was conducting, that he turned on the unfortunate tenor and said to him: "You are not a Knight of the Swan, but a Knight of the Swine." Schott, as an ex-officer in a Hanoverian regiment, deemed his honor as an officer insulted, demanded an apology or a duel, and as the irate von Bülow would grant him neither the one nor the other, Bülow had to resign his post as director of the Royal Opera, while Schott remained triumphant in his position.

For the youthful lyric soprano rôles my father had engaged Madame Seidl-Kraus, the wife of Anton Seidl and possessor of a voice of great purity and simple appeal. The coloratura rôles were sung by Madame Schroeder-Hanfstangel, a truly great artist, with the real bel canto of the Italian school, whom Gounod had admired so greatly that he invited her to Paris to sing Marguerite in "Faust" at the Grand Opera.

The other singers possessed both the virtues and the failings of the German Opera School of that time. They were very amenable to ensemble work, carrying out the dramatic side of their rôles with real ability, forming an excellent ensemble, and tireless in rehearsing, but their singing was sometimes faulty and not equal to the naturally beautiful tone emission of the best Italian singers.

The stage manager, Wilhelm Hock, was one of the best in Germany and his management of the movements of great crowds on the stage, as for instance in "Lohengrin" on the arrival of Lohengrin and the Swan, the building of the barricades in "Massaniello," the Coronation

Scene in Meyerbeer's "Le Prophète," was a revelation to
our public. The orchestra was, of course, that of the
New York Symphony Society, and my father infused the
entire ensemble with such an ideal of perfection that
during many of the performances, especially in "Lohengrin," "Le Prophète," "Fidelio," and "Walküre," the
public seethed with excitement and enthusiasm. There
had been an "improvised" performance of "Walküre"
at the Academy of Music under the German conductor
Neuendorf a few years before. The *Brunhilde* had been
sung by Madame Pappenheim, possessor of a glorious
voice, but the rest of the cast had been wofully deficient.
Insufficient rehearsals and ignorance of the music of
Wagner on the part of the conductor had also prevented
this performance from making any impression or giving
any real idea of the beauties of the work.

The performance under my father included Madame
Materna as *Brunhilde,* who had created the rôle in Bayreuth in '76 and who was then at the very height of her
glorious vocal powers; Madame Seidl-Kraus, an exquisite
and pathetic *Sieglinde;* Anton Schott, a vigorous and
highly dramatic *Siegmund;* and Staudigl as *Wotan.*
Staudigl was a son of the famous old Viennese bass with
whom he had studied, singing with such good results that
he made as fine an impression in concert and oratorio as
in opera. The first barytone was Adolf Robinson, who
had begun his career with my father in Breslau and whose
warm impassioned *bel canto* won instant recognition here.

There was no professional opera claque at the Metropolitan in those days such as is now maintained by some
of the singers and conductors who, in rivalry with each
other, foolishly spend their money in the hiring of twenty
to fifty husky men, under a well-trained leader, who stand

at the side of the balconies and family circle and clap with the machine-like regularity of a steel hammer in an iron foundry in order to produce so and so many recalls after an act. In those days this was not necessary. The public applauded wildly and shouted themselves hoarse of their own free will, and the papers almost unanimously pronounced the performances an artistic revolution, and said that such dramatic truth and ensemble work had but seldom before been presented in such a convincing way on the operatic stage of New York.

During the entire winter I lived in a sea of excitement and of joy at seeing my father's genius at last so universally recognized. But my anxiety was also very great. I was with him constantly, from morning until night, and could see that the labor of carrying everything entirely on his shoulders, the effort of organizing an artistic whole out of the many different elements, was overwhelming. The rehearsals often lasted all day and I do not think that I missed a rehearsal or a performance during the entire season. Sometimes I would timidly implore my father to put some of the work, especially the managerial part, on other shoulders, but he would not listen, saying that the responsibility was his and that he could not delegate what he conceived to be his solemn duty as one representing German art in a foreign country to any one else.

In the meantime, the directors, after deliberating on their future course, decided that opera in German had come to stay and offered my father a contract for the following year in which, however, with what they conceived to be real business methods, they reduced his salary to eight thousand dollars but offered him a share in any possible profits. Money matters were to my father always so unimportant as far as he was concerned, that I think he would have signed a contract in which he bound himself to pay eight thousand dollars a year to the Metropolitan Opera House for the privilege of maintaining Wagnerian opera there. He accepted their proposition and was happy in the evident security of opera in German for many years to come. During this winter he would not give up his beloved Symphony and Oratorio Societies, and he always insisted that the weekly Thursday evening rehearsals with the chorus of the Oratorio Society were a rest for him from operatic affairs.

During one of these rehearsals in February 1885 (I think we were preparing the "Requiem" of Verdi) he suddenly complained of feeling ill and I rushed from the piano toward him, and together with some of the singers we carried him to a cab and brought him home.

Pneumonia set in and he was too worn with the gigantic struggles of the winter to withstand it. During this terrible week of illness the opera had to be kept going and I conducted "Walküre" and "Tannhäuser" without much difficulty. They had been so splendidly rehearsed by my father and had been performed several times; I knew them by heart, and artists, chorus, and orchestra gave me the most affectionate and willing assistance. I have therefore never claimed much credit for what many kind friends at that time considered an extraordinary feat.

The season had only one more week to run, but my father had made arrangements for a short tour comprising Chicago, Boston, and Philadelphia.

On February 15 he died and left me numb and overwhelmed by the terrible responsibilities which began to press in upon me. Even at this late date I cannot bear

to write of my loss. Our relations had become so close
and intimate, and during the last years he had so often
leaned on me with such sweet confidence. I had always
looked up to him as my ideal of a man and musician, and
it seemed to me that I could never smile again.

The last performances at the Metropolitan immediately
after his death were conducted by John Lund, a highly
talented chorus master who has since made his home in
America, but there were so many immediate necessities
crowding in upon me that I had no opportunity for in-
dulging in quiet grief. Events moved with incredible
and terrible swiftness. The contracts for the tour had
to be met. My father's estate was technically liable,
although he left literally no money. There was no one to
assume the responsibility of taking the company on tour
except poor me, and I accordingly set forth, together
with the entire company of about a hundred and fifty
members, on a special train of the West Shore Railroad
for Chicago on Saturday afternoon of February 21. We
were to open with "Tannhäuser" at the Columbia Theatre
on the following Monday evening. During this trip the
worst blizzard of the year struck our train. We were
completely snowed in and the road, which was at that
time a rather lame rival of the New York Central, was so
ill-equipped with means to shovel us out that instead of
arriving on Sunday evening, we did not get into Chicago
until Monday at eight P. M., the hour at which the performance was to have begun. My dear brother Frank,
who had come on from Denver to meet me in Chicago
and to discuss future plans, boarded our train a little
while out of Chicago and told me that not only was the
house sold out, but all had determined to wait until we
arrived and chivalrously to "see us through." The

mayor of the city had made an excited speech from the proscenium box in which he was sitting and said that Chicago must help a young man like myself who had so courageously undertaken to carry on the great work of his father.

When we arrived at the station the company were quickly bundled into cabs and omnibuses. Luckily the scenery had been sent on ahead, but the costume and property trunks were on our train, and the work of transferring them and getting out the "Tannhäuser" costumes and properties was agonizing.

Materna and I were the first to arrive at the theatre, and we were marched through the auditorium from the front entrance by the local manager who wished to give this ocular demonstration of our presence. The audience cheered.

Behind the scenes the confusion was incredible. The trunks with the wigs could not be found, nor the trunks with the footwear, and *Tannhäuser* and the other singers of the Wartburg, together with the noble lords and ladies, appeared on the stage in a most remarkable combination of costumes, mediæval and modern. But it made no difference. I began the overture after ten o'clock. The audience cheered themselves hoarse.

The trunk containing Materna's costume as *Elizabeth* was not hurled on the stage until just before the beginning of the second act. It made no difference. When she appeared in all her smiling radiance and sang "Dich Theure Halle" the audience again went mad with delight, and so on until the curtain finally fell at one-thirty in the morning.

Ever since that terrible but wonderful evening I have had a soft spot in my heart for Chicago, and during the many years I have never lost the friendship of that re-markable city. Even to-day, every now and then, an old gray-headed or bald-headed citizen of Chicago comes to me and says: "Do you remember that first performance of 'Tannhäuser' at the Columbia Theatre in February, 1885?"

The success was so great that we extended our season an extra week, during which I produced for the first time "La Dame Blanche" by Boieldieu.

We finished our tour with a week in Boston, where we had a similarly enthusiastic reception, and especially "Walküre" and "Lohengrin" made a profound impression. There I produced (for the first time in America, I think) Gluck's "Orpheus," in which Marianne Brandt gave a glorious and touching impersonation of the title-rôle. It is characteristic of the audacity of youth that I should have given two new performances of operas which were rehearsed and produced while we were on tour, "La Dame Blanche" and "Orpheus." But as the prin-cipal rôles had been sung by most of our artists in Ger-many, these two operas being in the regular repertoire of every German opera-house, the feat was not so extraor-dinary. The performances were good in ensemble and gave great pleasure to the audience.

My farewell performance in Boston was a Saturday matinée of the "Walküre" with Materna as *Brunhilde*. In the morning the orchestra struck. We had made arrangements to send the entire company to New York on one of the large Fall River steamers, but they vowed that they would not go by steamer and insisted on being sent by train. I was equally determined to send them by water. The steamers were palatial, the weather excellent spring weather, and there was no valid reason for object-

ing. When they persisted in their demands I told them
that I would consider them as having broken their contracts, that I would not pay them their salaries for the
week, and would give the "Walküre" performance accompanied on two pianos, by John Lund and myself.
This was, of course, a crazy bluff, but it worked and they
decided to accept passage by steamer.

At the close of the third act of "Walküre," when
Materna as *Brunhilde* had snuggled into the artificially
deep hollow of the rocky couch which sustained her
bulky form and on which she was to begin her slumber of
years until the hero, *Siegfried*, should awaken her, and
when Staudigl (*Wotan*) had disappeared in the flames, I
suddenly noticed, while conducting the beautiful monotony of the last E-major chords of the Fire Charm, that the
grass mats just below *Brunhilde's* couch had caught fire,
and that just as the curtain was descending slowly on the
last bars a Boston fireman with helmet on his head and
bucket in his hand quietly came out from the wings and
poured a liberal dose of water on the flames.   The thing
happened so late and so quickly that there was no panic.
The people went mad with enthusiasm and Materna,
Staudigl, and I had to bow our farewells many, many
times.   Just after one of these recalls I noted the little
fireman standing in the wings and saying: "Be jabbers, I
ought to come out too."

"So you should," I said, and with that took him by
one hand and Materna by the other and thus we dragged
him before the footlights where, with true Hibernian sense
of humor, he bowed right and left with a delighted grin
on his face.

Thus ended my first opera tour.

While I was on tour the directors of the Metropolitan

Opera House met to consider their future policy, and, in
view of the success of the opera in German inaugurated
by my father, they decided to continue on the same lines.
Curiously enough they appointed a young man as director
of the opera who had never had any managerial or musical experience in his life. His name was Edmund C.
Stanton. He was a relative of one of the directors and
had acted as recording secretary for the Board of Directors. He was tall, good-looking, with gentle brown eyes,
always well groomed, of a kindly disposition and the most
perfect and courtly manners which indeed never failed
him and which were about all that he had left at the end
of his seven years' incumbency, at which time the German
opera crumbled to dust as a natural result of his curious
ignorance and incompetency in matters operatic. The
directors at the same time very generously appointed me
as his assistant and as second conductor, granting me a
salary which was large enough to enable me to support
my mother and my father's family decently. This was
naturally a great relief to me and I determined to strain
every nerve to show myself worthy of such confidence
and generosity.

VII

LILLI LEHMANN

In the spring of 1885 I was to accompany Mr. Stanton as assistant director and musical adviser to engage singers for the following season of German opera at the Metropolitan Opera House, but as Mr. Stanton's little daughter became ill and subsequently died, I went over alone and have always been quite proud of the four contracts I had ready for Stanton's signature when he, a month later, arrived in Germany. These were Lilli Lehmann, soprano from the Royal Opera House in Berlin; Emil Fischer, bass from the Royal Opera House in Dresden; Max Alvary, lyric tenor from Weimar, and Anton Seidl, conductor of the Angelo Neumann Wagner Opera Company. These four artists became subsequently the mainstay of the German opera and in America developed to greater and greater power and fame.

Lilli Lehmann, at that time forty years of age, had sung principally the coloratura rôles, and with these had made a great local reputation throughout Germany and Austria. She had sung the *First Rhine Maiden* at Bayreuth in 1876, and an occasional *Elsa* in "Lohengrin," but it was not until she came to America that she began to sing the *Brunhildes* and *Isoldes* which made her one of the greatest dramatic sopranos of her time. Curiously enough, she insisted on making her first appearance in America as *Carmen,* a rôle to which she gave a dramatic, tragic, and rather sombre significance, but in which the

63

lighter, coquettish touches were perhaps not sufficiently emphasized.

She had achieved her pre-eminence as a dramatic soprano only after years of the hardest kind of work, and had only through her indomitable will and energy changed her voice from a light coloratura to a dramatic soprano, and as I was at that period only twenty-three and already occupied a position of considerable responsibility, it took some time before she was ready to concede that I was really a musician of serious purpose who was working day and night to fit myself for the various responsibilities so suddenly thrust upon me.

Conducting is an art with a technic of its own, and good musicianship alone is not sufficient. During a performance the conductor must know how to make his singers and players convey his interpretation, and to do this, a glance of the eye and many different movements of hands and head have to speak a language of their own which his executants must quickly understand and follow. The conductor must also know when and how to follow a soloist with sympathy. This technic cannot be acquired overnight, and I owe to Lilli Lehmann a valuable hint in this connection. As Anton Seidl was the accredited and celebrated Wagner conductor, these operas and any other novelties of importance naturally fell to him, and it remained for me to conduct only such operas as he did not care to assume—Meyerbeer's "Le Prophète," Verdi's "Trovatore," etc., etc. This caused me great sorrow and anguish of heart, as a great part of my training had been in the modern operas. I almost knew the Wagner music-dramas by heart and had received a very thorough training in the symphonies of the classic composers, but for the operas of Meyerbeer and Verdi,

I had a youthful intolerance, and of their traditions of tempi and nuance I knew but little, with the exception, perhaps, of Meyerbeer's "Le Prophète," which had been marvellously performed under my father the preceding year and in which Marianne Brandt had sung the part of the mother with incredible pathos and nobility.

One day, while I was rehearsing "La Juive," of Halévy, Lilli Lehmann turned on me during the intermission and said: "Walter, in those old operas you do not watch the singers enough, you are occupied with the orchestra as if you were conducting a symphony. You give them the cue for their entrances and you look at them instead of at your singers. We need you and you need us. The orchestra have their printed parts before them; we sing by heart and have to rely on the conductor for difficult entrances. Watch my lips when I sing, and you will know when I breathe and you will breathe with me; you will immediately also sense the *tempo rubato* which is such an important part in the proper phrasing of these older operas."

This advice was a revelation to me, and I found to my delight that by heeding it, not only was I able to follow the singers with the orchestra, but even to influence the singers in regard to tempi. At the performance of "La Juive" I must have stared at Lilli like a Cheshire cat whenever she was singing. The music went with remarkable unanimity and elasticity, and at the close of the performance Lilli, who was never very profuse in praise, turned to me and said: "You see, Walter, how well it goes. What did I tell you?"

In this way, slowly and often painfully, I strengthened my grasp of the technic of my craft, and with increased assurance on my part came an increased compliance on the part of the singers to follow my artistic desires as regards the interpretation of their rôles.

But the operas that I was permitted to conduct were still only the left-overs from Anton Seidl's richly laden table, and he was naturally not willing to give up any of his prerogatives to a man so much younger. My first real opportunity came in the year 1890, when Seidl was to conduct an exquisite opera by Peter Cornelius, "The Barber of Bagdad." Paul Kalisch, Lilli Lehmann's husband, was to sing *Nureddin* and Emil Fischer the loquacious Barber. Cornelius had been a devoted and close friend of my father and mother in the old Weimar days under Liszt. Liszt had produced this opera in Weimar in those days, but the Weimar public had rejected it because of what they considered to be its ultramodern tendencies, and because of this, Liszt had resigned his position of Grand Ducal Kapellmeister. I was naturally much interested in our New York production. I had attended almost every rehearsal and had revelled in the exquisite beauties and humor of the work.

Two days before the performance, Seidl became dangerously ill and I was in a fever of uncertainty whether Stanton would postpone the performance or let me conduct it. I found that Lilli Lehmann protested loudly that it would be impossible for me to conduct this work, that it was too difficult and too intricate, and that it needed a conductor of many years' experience and plenty of rehearsals at that. But I seemed to have "good friends at court" and it was decided that I should conduct the general rehearsal that morning for which singers, chorus, and orchestra had been hastily called together, and if all went well I was to conduct the performance. As I walked into the orchestra pit I could see Lilli Lehmann seated all by herself a few rows back, looking at me with what seemed to me baleful and threatening eyes. But as I turned my back on her and gave the signal for the overture, my apprehension left me and I gave myself up completely to the music. The curtain rose and Kalisch began *Nureddin's* lovely song together with his attendants on awakening from his long illness to renewed health and with renewed longings for his beloved *Margiana*. Everything went as if on wings and at the end of the act I saw, to my delight, among the singers who were rushing toward me with affectionate congratulations, Lilli, the stately, telling me that she had not believed it possible, but was now convinced that I had a thorough grasp of the music and could conduct it successfully.

The performance the next day went even better than the rehearsal, and I date from this my entry as a full-fledged opera conductor, and my relations with Lilli Lehmann became artistically more and more fraternal and personally more and more friendly.

In 1897–98 I engaged her to sing *Isolde* and the *Brunhildes* in my Damrosch Opera Company and paid her a thousand dollars a night and all hotel and travelling expenses for two people (her sister Marie travelled with her), and she also insisted that I must pay her laundry bills. But I found that this remarkable woman, having established her right to these perquisites by contract, refused to abuse them, and when she found that I paid quite a large figure for her "parlor, bedroom, and bath" at the Normandie Hotel near the Metropolitan, she was furious; and, saying that she did not see why these rascally hotel proprietors should be enriched by me, she moved to a much cheaper suite at the top of the hotel and she and her sister did a great deal of their laundry in their own bathroom, partly because she wished to save me the expense, and also because she insisted that all American laundries ruined delicate lingerie. Incidentally the elevator boys insisted that she never tipped them, and I sent my manager to her hotel to do this, as otherwise she would not have received adequate service.

So much has been written about her marvellous portrayal of the heroic figures in the Wagner music-dramas that it is hardly necessary for me to add anything to the general chorus of admiration, but I wish to emphasize the fact that by far the greater part of the credit belongs to her for her indomitable will and perseverance, as nature had not given her originally a dramatic voice. It was a wonderfully clear and high coloratura soprano, but by persistent practice she developed an ample middle and lower register and made it equal to the emotional demands of an *Isolde* or a *Brunhilde*.

Her acting was majestic, but in the first act of "Tristan" and in the second act of "Götterdämmerung" her anger was like forked flashes of lightning. I suppose that her technic of acting would be called old-fashioned today, as those were the days of statuesque poses, often maintained without changes for long stretches at a time.

On the forenoon of the days that she had to sing *Isolde* she always sang through the entire rôle in her rooms with full voice, just to make sure that she could do it in the evening. Compare this to those delicate prima donnas who, on the days when they have to sing, often speak only in whispers in order that their precious vocal cords may not be affected.

Having achieved so much through her own energy and triumphed over so many obstacles, she thought that she could similarly transform her husband, Paul Kalisch, from a lyric to a dramatic tenor. How she worked and harassed that poor man! She certainly was the stronger of the two, and while his entire inclination was toward easy and delightful companionship with others of similar inclinations, she forced him to study and to sing for hours at a stretch, but with only partial success as far as his transformation into a real dramatic and "heroic" Wagner tenor was concerned. It simply was not in his nature to become "heroic," and when, as sometimes happened, he committed some blunder, some false entrance while singing *Siegfried* in the "Götterdämmerung," the glances which *Brunhilde* cast upon him on the stage were so terrible, so pregnant with punishment to come, that from my conductor's stand I used to pity the poor man thus compelled to swim around in a pond which was so much larger than he wanted; and often after such a performance I would find him moodily seated all alone at a table in the restaurant of the hotel with a pint bottle of champagne before him and with no desire to go upstairs and face the anger of his *Brunhilde* spouse.

A tragic but rather amusing occurrence in Pittsburgh should here be recorded. The Damrosch Opera Company was playing a week there at the Alvin Theatre. On the night in question we were to give "Götterdämmerung" with Lilli Lehmann as *Brunhilde*. All was well. No singers had sent ominous messages of illness during the day, and I had just sat down to a quiet dinner at the Duquesne Club, previous to the performance, when a telephone summoned me. It was my wardrobe mistress, Frau Engelhardt, an excellent woman, devoted to her work, who had been at the Metropolitan in the old German opera days and who had been with me ever since the founding of the Damrosch Opera Company. She implored me to come to the theatre immediately as something dreadful had happened. I of course left my dinner with but faint hope of eating it later on, arrived at the theatre and found the stage silent as the grave, the scene set for the first act of "Götterdämmerung" and seemingly no one there but Frau Engelhardt, who in greatest agitation begged me to come immediately to Madame Lehmann's dressing-room, where the "something dreadful had happened."

I knocked at her door and heard a tragic and hollow voice call "come in," and as I opened the door a sight indeed terrible met my astonished gaze. There stood Lilli Lehmann, already apparelled in her white *Brunhilde* garb, but covered from head to foot with soot, so black that she seemed more fit for a minstrel show than a Wagner music-drama. Her face was covered with black streaks, especially where her tears had made long and terrible furrows down her cheeks. I could not imagine what had happened, and only gradually and between hysterical bursts of tears, I learned that Lilli, according to her custom, had gone to the theatre hours before the performance and had proceeded to dress herself, only looking into the glass at the last moment to prepare her make-up. She had then discovered the terrible condition of her face and costume. It seemed that the janitor had given the heater in the cellar a special raking which had sent tons of this dreadful Pittsburgh soft-coal soot flying through the registers and into the dressing-rooms where it settled like a pall on everything within reach.

Lilli vowed that it was absolutely impossible for her to sing that night and I was in despair. It suddenly came to me that if I could divert her mind in some way the tension might be eased, and I therefore turned on poor trembling Frau Engelhardt and told her in as angry tones as I could dramatically summon, that she was discharged, that it was her duty to take care of my artists, and to allow such an outrage to happen to the greatest of all of them was something which I could not understand or forgive.

As soon as I denounced our wardrobe mistress in this manner, Lilli pricked up her ears and remonstrated with me at my injustice. She insisted that it was not Frau Engelhardt's fault and that it was very wrong of me to discharge her. It showed that I had no heart and she for one would never hold her responsible for such an occurrence. Slowly I allowed myself to be persuaded and at the psychological moment gently left the dressing-room, giving Frau Engelhardt a comprehensive glance which she understood. I knew that the two women together would soon set matters to right.

Outside the dressing-room I found my faithful Hans, son of my prompter, Goettich. I gave him some money and told him to run to a florist and buy a bunch of the whitest flowers that he could find and to bring them to Madame Lehmann with my compliments. I then returned to the club and finished my dinner.

When I got back to the theatre just before the performance, I found Lilli already on the stage, newly attired in clean white robes, but as she turned toward me I could still discern darkish streaks beneath the make-up of her cheeks, and in her sombre, dramatic voice she said: "Walter, I thank you for the lovely white flowers, but they will never, never wash me clean again." Her singing that night seemed to me more glorious than ever.

From Pittsburgh we went to New York, where I had

arranged with Abbey and Grau to give me the Metropolitan Opera House for a short season of three weeks. As I wanted a special attraction for New York, I engaged Madame Nordica for a few "Lohengrin" performances in which she was to sing *Elsa*, and Lilli Lehmann, *Ortrude*, a part that she had never sung in New York, but whose dramatic possibilities interested her very much and for which she was eminently suited. At first she was furious that I had engaged any other singer for New York. "If I was sufficient to carry on your season out of town, I do not see why you have to engage that —— for New York." But I explained to her my managerial reasons and somewhat pacified her, and as soon as we arrived in New York I arranged for a little rehearsal on the stage of the Metropolitan for Lehmann, Nordica, and myself, in order that all the scenes, especially of the second act, in which their acting together was of importance, might be properly arranged. At this rehearsal Lehmann treated Nordica with icy disdain, but Nordica acted with such clever tact and deference that Lehmann could find no hook upon which to hang her anger, and the rehearsal passed off with outward calmness, although I could feel the volcano trembling beneath. As we passed out into the street in the late afternoon a terrible rain-storm was raging and Lilli saw Madame Nordica approach a coachman in livery who was waiting with opened umbrella to take her to her coupé. Lilli, clad in a long gray rain-coat and old hat, turned to Nordica: "Ha, you ride? I valk!" she said, as she lifted her dress and showed a pair of great boots.

Incidentally my "showman's instinct" had proved correct. Our performances of "Lohengrin" with this combination proved artistically very interesting and the

public flocked to hear them. Nordica's *Elsa* had been
very carefully trained at Bayreuth, and Lehmann's
Ortrude was truly demoniac, worthy to rank with that of
Marianne Brandt's in its representation of concentrated
hatred.

VIII

HANS VON BÜLOW

In 1856 my father and Hans von Bülow, pianist, were struggling to gain recognition and a livelihood in Berlin. Both were idealists and enthusiastic followers of the "new school" in music, of which Berlioz, Liszt, and Wagner were the great representatives. Bülow's letters of that period show that they gave many chamber-music concerts together, both in Berlin and elsewhere, and it is interesting to note that at one of them, together with the violoncellist, Kossman, they performed a trio by "Cesar Franck of Liege," about thirty years before this father of the modern French school of composition became generally known and recognized. It was through Bülow that my father and his achievements as a violin virtuoso and composer became known to Liszt, who invited him, in 1857, to become violinist at the first desk of the Weimar Opera Orchestra, then under Liszt's direction.

The friendship between Bülow and my father remained intimate and fine during my father's entire life, and even beyond, as this chapter will show.

My first recollection of Bülow goes back to 1876, when he came to America at the invitation of the Chickering Piano firm to inaugurate their new Chickering Hall on Fifth Avenue and 19th Street, and to give piano recitals all over the country.

When my father and mother went to Berlin in the

74

sixties for a joint concert with Bülow, they stayed with him and his wife, Cosima. Since then much had happened. Cosima had run away with Wagner, Bülow's most adored friend, and Bülow had nearly died with the shame and misery of it. One evening during dinner at our house my mother asked him about his children, whom she had not seen since those early days, and I can still hear the punctilious courtesy with which he answered: "They are where they should be, and in the best possible hands—with their mother."

The fine intellectuality of his playing, the quality of his phrasing, especially in Bach and Beethoven, created a deep impression on our public which was not minimized by certain eccentricities in his appearance and behavior. He always appeared on the stage for his afternoon recitals attired in the traditional black double-breasted frock-coat and very light-gray trousers, his hands incased in light-brown gloves and holding a high silk hat which was carefully deposited under the piano before he took off his gloves and began to play.

For one of his recitals a young and highly talented soprano, Miss Emma Thursby, had been engaged. She was a protégée of old Maurice Strakosch, an impresario of the old school, shrewd, polished in his manners, who very cleverly advertised the high personal character of the young singer and especially her great "purity," vowing that acquaintance with her, hardened old sinner that he was, had made him a better man.

At the Bülow recital her singing of some German songs by Schubert and Schumann, I think, was received with such enthusiastic applause that she gave an encore, a rather trivial song by Franz Abt. When Bülow, in his dressing-room, heard this "desecration" of a programme composed of works of great masters only, his rage knew no bounds, and when he came out on the stage to continue his own programme, he deliberately took out his handkerchief and carefully wiped the keys of the piano up and down in a noisy glissando scale and then began to improvise on the recitative from Beethoven's Ninth Symphony, "O friends, not these tones. . . ."

Another time he gave a chamber-music concert with my father and they played, among other things, the "Kreutzer Sonata" of Beethoven. Just before going on the stage he turned to my father and said:

"Let us play it by heart."

"With pleasure," answered my father and laid down his music.

"No, no," said Bülow, "take it on the stage with you."

After they had taken their places on the stage Bülow ostentatiously rose, took my father's music from the stand and his own from the piano and laid them both under the piano.

His memory, not only for music, but for all things that interested him, was prodigious and to me uncanny. But it was, after all, human and not infallible, and on this occasion he did lose his place in the last movement of the sonata and my father had to improvise with him for a few bars until, with quick ingenuity, he found the thread again.

I have spoken elsewhere of the terrible responsibilities which were placed upon my shoulders because of the sudden death of my father, and as the years went by I seemed to miss him more and more, not only his wonderful companionship, but the wise counsel with which he used to help me solve my musical riddles. I worked hard and made progress, I think, for my circle of friends and followers grew larger and larger. But I knew no one in this country to whom I could turn in the same way as to my father, or who would have given me of his wisdom so freely and generously as he. Seidl, my associate at the Metropolitan, was not friendly and was completely wrapped up in himself, and besides, he had, to my thinking, only one specialty, the Wagner music-dramas. As a symphonic conductor he was completely without experience when he first came to America and his interpretation of the classics lacked foundation and real penetration, in spite of the noisy acclaim which a certain part of our public gave him because of his undoubted genius as a Wagner conductor.

A lucky chance brought me a clipping from a German newspaper announcing that Hans von Bülow would spend the summer of 1887 in Frankfort, where he would teach a class of advanced pianists and devote the entire receipts toward building a monument to his old friend, Joachim Raff, who had spent his last years in Frankfort as director of the conservatory.

I immediately determined to go to Germany and ask Bülow if, in view of his old friendship with my father and my need of the help of some great musician, he would be willing to let me study with him the interpretation of the Beethoven Symphonies in especial, and such other works as it would interest him to analyze for me.

Bülow was at that time considered the foremost conductor of Germany. He had taken a little mediocre orchestra of fifty, belonging to the Grand Duke of Meiningen, and through his supreme genius had galvanized it into a marvellous instrument. Under his guidance this little orchestra had created a sensation all over Germany and Austria and a special *tour de force* was their playing of certain symphonies entirely by heart without any music before them.

When I arrived in Frankfort I found that Bülow was living at the Schwan Hotel, and with much trepidation I told him what I wanted of him. He seemed very much touched and claimed that it was the first time in his experience that a musician who, as he put it, "was already prominent in opera, symphony, and oratorio" thought he could learn anything from him. In the warmest, I may say most affectionate terms, he promised me every possible help and advised me to take rooms in the same hotel. This I did, and I can truthfully say that the entire summer during which I was with him in closest companionship, not only in his rooms and during the lesson hours for the pianists, many of which I also attended, but on long walks to the museums, the parks, and the suburbs of Frankfort, his almost paternal kindliness, his wisdom, and his comments on things artistic, literary, political, and personal were a revelation to me. So many stories were current about his biting comments and brusque behavior toward people who excited his enmity, that I was amazed to find him throughout so companionable and so gentle in all his relations toward me. He had a heart most tender and sensitive, but life had dealt this idealist so many hard knocks that he incased his heart in a shell with which to protect it from further onslaughts.

He went through all Beethoven's nine symphonies with me, bar by bar, phrase by phrase, and I still have the scores in which he made certain notations of phrasing or illustrated changes in dynamics of certain instruments in order to bring out the undoubted intentions of Beethoven more clearly. He virtually analyzed the symphonies for me in the same way as in his edition of the piano sonatas, and at the close of our three months together he gave me a copy of his own score of the Ninth Symphony with all his own annotations, many of which were based on the analysis made by Wagner during his historic performance of that work at the corner-stone laying of the Bayreuth Fest-Spielhaus.

During these three months of intensive study I received so much from him that was new to me, such a wealth of ideas regarding interpretation and the technic of the conductor's art, that it took me years to digest it properly and to learn how, instead of merely copying slavishly, I could make it my own and accept or reject parts of it, according to the methods of analysis taught me by him.

During our stay in Frankfort a little Prince of Hesse, whose mother, the Landgravine, was a "Royal Highness," being a niece of the old Emperor William, invited von Bülow to give a Brahms recital at his palace. Bülow immediately insisted that I, too, must be invited, which accordingly I was. When I accompanied him he introduced me to the various exalted personages assembled, and the Landgravine asked me if I were not "the son of the great Doctor Damrosch." I politely answered: "Yes, your Royal Highness."

"Was he not a friend of Rubinstein?" she continued.

"Yes."

"He played the viola, did he not?"

I said: "No, your Royal Highness, the violin."

"No," she said, "the viola."

This taught me that royalty must never be contradicted, even if they know "facts" about your own father of which you are not aware.

would not hear of it and bravely went on the stage to
begin his programme.

Unfortunately, owing to the summer heat, the windows
of the aula were open wide, and during the music the cries
of the children playing below, the rumbling of carts over
the rough pavements of the mediæval streets, came up
in constant clangor.

Bülow began, faltered, began again and stopped—ran
from the stage and returned to begin again.   But it was
no use.   The noise continued and the recital had to be
called off, and after a nervous crisis accompanied by
great weeping, we got him back to the hotel and to bed,
Bülow heaping curses on the little professor on whom he
blamed everything, the glaring sunlight, the cries of the
playing children, and the noise of the carts.   The recital
for the following day was, of course, cancelled, and we
arranged everything for taking Bülow back to Frankfort.

In the morning when I called at his rooms I found him
punctiliously attired in his frock coat, high silk hat, and
brown glacé gloves, and in answer to my evidently astonished gaze, he said: "We must not leave without paying
our farewell call of ceremony on the Greek professor."
I trembled at the outcome, but a carriage with two horses
and a liveried coachman was already waiting in the courtyard of the hotel to take us up the hill to the old mediæval tower of the university in which the professor lived.

We were ushered into a wonderful circular library, the
books covering the entire inner wall of the tower, and
while we were waiting for the professor, Bülow ran
around the room like a dog on the scent, examining the
titles of the various books on the shelves.   Suddenly he
pounced on one, pulled it out and began to turn the leaves
quickly until he got to a certain page at which he held

the book open just as the old professor entered, trembling from head to foot. I was rather apprehensive of the meeting between the two men, but to my astonishment, Bülow advanced, book in hand, and with a low bow handed it silently to the gentle amateur impresario, pointing to a certain place on the opened page. The professor read it, blushed, and looked with a kind of dumb apology at von Bülow, who then took up his hat and, with another low bow, left the room, followed by me, still completely mystified by this silent ceremonial, the meaning of which I could not understand.

During the drive back to the hotel, Bülow chirped up considerably. Now and then he chuckled and finally, as if the joke were too good to keep, he turned toward me and said:

"Do you know what quotation I gave to the Greek professor? It was from one of the Greek philosophers to the effect that 'it is not wise for a man of learning to mix himself up in the practical affairs of life.'"

Perhaps some learned reader of this may be able to tell me who the Greek author was. Bülow never told me.

On our long walks Bülow would often reminisce about the past and would tell me enough stories to fill a book. Two of them I shall tell here.

Bülow was spending a winter in Florence and was invited to conduct a performance of Beethoven's Ninth Symphony with the local orchestra. In those days Italy had literally no symphonic orchestras, and the players, recruited from the opera-houses, had but little routine for concert music of symphonic importance. The men were willing and eager, but even such a routined conductor as Bülow found it difficult to make them understand certain rhythmic subtleties in this most intricate of all

Beethoven's works. In the scherzo there comes a place where the kettledrum has to enter rudely with a repetition of the first bar of the main theme:

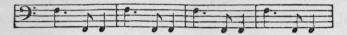

This rhythm the kettledrum player simply could not grasp, no matter how patiently Bülow endeavored to instil it. He tried it slow, he tried it fast. Bülow got more and more excited and irritable, and finally, as a last resort, he fairly shouted to him on the rhythm of this theme the Italian word for kettledrum. At the top of his voice rose the word:

"Tym—pan—y! Tym—pan—y!"

A delighted smile broke over the face of the kettledrum player.

"Ah, capisco, capisco," he shouted, and immediately proceeded to put his newly won knowledge to the practical proof.

Bülow told me that at one time he had adopted the habit of jotting down any strange or incongruous names that he found on the signs of shops in the various cities of the various countries that he visited. In a small little German town he found over a greengrocery, the name of "Seidenschwanz." This appealed to him and he tucked it away in his memory, determined to find a given name to add that would, by its very contrast, fit it. For months he cudgelled his brains, but in vain, until one night in Venice he jumped up from his bed, shouting: "I have it. *Caligula Seidenschwanz!*" The name of the most cruel of Roman Emperors coupled with that of the little greengrocer!

Next morning he proceeded to an engraver and had visiting cards printed bearing the mysterious name of:

Caligula Seidenschwanz.

Shortly after, whenever Doctor Hans von Bülow paid a call on any one, instead of presenting his own card, he left that of Herr Seidenschwanz, thereby completely mystifying his friends.

I told this story years after while dining at the house of my dear friends, May Callender and Caro de Forest. Lilli Lehmann was one of the guests, and when I finished she jumped up and said:

"Walter, that is a very remarkable story, but it is absolutely true, as I happen to know. I was coloratura soprano at the Berlin Royal Opera at the time when Bülow paid us a visit one night when we performed Meyerbeer's 'Prophète.' He was so disgusted with the performance that he wrote one of his indignant and cynical letters to a Berlin paper, in which he compared the Royal Opera to a circus, and then added insult to injury by apologizing to Herr Renz, owner of the greatest circus in Germany, saying that he meant no insult to him, as he had always been a great admirer of the Circus Renz. This letter aroused the old intendant, Baron von Hulsen, to such fury that he forbade Bülow further entrance into the opera-house and at the same time induced the old

Emperor to withdraw the title of 'Pianist to His Majesty, the King of Prussia' from von Bülow."

Lilli Lehmann then continued to narrate that the morning after the performance she received a large basket of flowers in which a card had been tucked, on which was written "To the only bright spot in yesterday's performance. In admiration, *Caligula Seidenschwanz.*"

Until that evening, when I explained the origin of the name, Lilli Lehmann had not known that the flowers had been sent her by von Bülow.

At the close of the summer session Bülow invited me to go with him to the Cologne Musical Festival. He told me that he had written to Brahms about me and wanted me to meet him, and I would also hear a fine performance of the Brahms "Requiem." Needless to say I jumped at such an opportunity.

My father, who with that wonderful liberal attitude of his did not share the narrow attitude of other Wagnerians who hated Brahms, had been among the first to introduce his music in America and had given the first performance of the Brahms Symphony No. 1 in C minor in America. Bülow had become a similar propagandist for Brahms in Germany. I considered him the last great composer of modern times, doubly interesting because the great genius of Wagner, whom he admired greatly, left him untouched as far as his own creative work was concerned, and he is, perhaps, the only great modern composer whose works can show no influence of the Wagnerian school. To conduct his symphonies is to me still one of the greatest joys of the winter, and I continue to marvel how little the years have aged them and how noble in conception and rich in subtleties of feeling they continue to express in an unbroken line the highest ideals of the Beethoven symphonies.

In the hurly-burly of a festival, I had but little opportunity to see much of Brahms, who was there only a very few days, and I was too young and unimportant to claim any attention from him; but I was grateful to Bülow for the opportunity of meeting him, and can still see his wonderful and kindly eye turned on me as Bülow told him some nice things about me.

During our stay in Cologne I had an experience so curious, so extraordinary, that I must especially assure my readers that it is true in every particular.

One morning Bülow announced to me that he was going to cross the river in the afternoon to visit the widow of an old friend of his, Madame B——, who lived in a villa in Deutz. He asked me to accompany him, and we accordingly called on a rather attractive young widow, attired in the deepest mourning, who welcomed us very graciously. Her husband, a Belgian pianist of distinction, had been professor of piano at the Imperial Conservatory in St. Petersburg and had there married a young Russian pupil of his.

After chatting awhile, she proposed that we go into the garden for a cup of tea, and we followed her, accordingly, to a small stone building in the middle of the garden that looked like a chapel, but which, to my horror, I discovered, as we entered, to be a mausoleum. In the centre stood a sarcophagus on the top of which reposed a coffin, with a glass top, in which lay the body of B——! A footman in livery followed us with a samovar and the teacups.

It seems that the lady had thus endeavored to demonstrate her love for her departed husband. I confess that I became almost ill and hurriedly left the mausoleum to smell the roses in the garden, but Bülow punctiliously and courageously stuck it out and had his cup of tea under these unique conditions.

Many years after I heard through Mrs. Franz Rummel, whose husband had been a favorite pupil of B——, that his widow was again happily married and that B—— had been properly buried underground.

In 1889 I induced Mr. Leo Goldmark, brother of the Viennese composer, who was interested in music and the musical affairs of New York, to bring von Bülow to America for another visit, and more especially to give his Beethoven sonata cycle.

Bülow brought his second wife with him and the visit was a great success in every way. She had been a young actress of talent at the Meiningen Court Theatre and he had married her while he was conductor of the orchestra there.

The Beethoven recitals were given at the Broadway Theatre which was crowded to the doors, and press and public greeted the old master with such friendly enthusiasm that he was very much touched and became very enthusiastic about America. He also conducted my orchestra in a memorable concert at the Metropolitan Opera House in which he demonstrated his marvellous powers as a conductor. Among the works on the programme was the "Tragic Overture" by Brahms. Just before beginning the rehearsal of this he called out to the orchestra librarian, Russell, by name: "Where is the contrabassoon? Why is there no contrabassoon engaged?"

In vain were Russell's protests that he had not been told to engage a contrabassoon, but suddenly Bülow's anger subsided and he began the rehearsal. During it, as was his custom, he conducted without any orchestral score before him. His memory of what the individual instruments had to play was indeed remarkable, although

I always felt that he enjoyed showing it off a little at rehearsals.   After the rehearsal was over he called Russell to his side and, slipping him a five-dollar bill, whispered: "Do not say anything; it was my mistake, there is no contrabassoon in the Brahms Overture."

IX

ANDREW CARNEGIE AND THE BLAINE FAMILY

In the spring of 1887 I sailed for Europe to spend the summer in study with Hans von Bülow, and on the steamer I met Andrew Carnegie and his young wife Louise. They were on their wedding trip and on their way to Scotland, where Mr. Carnegie had rented "Kilgraston," a lovely old place near Perth. He had known my father and had invited him a few years before to a dinner given in honor of Matthew Arnold who had been in America on a lecture tour. Mr. Carnegie spoke of my father with great affection and respect, and expressed his delight that I had taken up my father's work. He invited me to come for a visit to Scotland after my studies with von Bülow were over.

In the late summer, I accordingly sailed in a small steamer from Hamburg to Leith and was received with great friendliness by Mr. and Mrs. Carnegie at Kilgraston. Among their guests were James G. Blaine, his wife, and two of their daughters. My acquaintance with this remarkable family soon ripened very fortunately for me into close friendship and resulted finally in my marriage to Margaret, one of the daughters—but I am progressing too fast.

Mr. Blaine had been defeated for the presidency in 1884. Since that time he had been occupied in completing his book "Twenty Years of Congress," and in the spring of 1887 he and his family were taking a year's holiday abroad.

Because of my youth and the exigencies of my profession, most of my life had been spent among musicians and those interested in music. This was the first time that I came into personal relations with a great statesman, at that time the foremost in our country, and I found to my amazement that, although an atmosphere of great dignity surrounded him, he was absolutely simple and gentle in his contact with other people.

His wife, a woman of singular strength of character, with a highly original mind and an absolute devotion to her husband and his ambitions, was in many ways as remarkable as he. Her knowledge of and interest in literature—poetry, history, memoirs—was very comprehensive, and the discussions thereon, which were constant at Mr. Carnegie's table, interested me immensely and opened new worlds to me.

The two daughters, Margaret and Harriet, high-spirited and sharing the interests of their parents, gave them a devotion and love so partisan and intense in its character that it seemed at first to attract me toward them almost more than anything else. As a boy I had suffered agonies at seeing my father misunderstood and often attacked by men not worthy to tie his shoe-strings, and here I found similar conditions but on a much greater scale, as Mr. Blaine's career had been national and his triumphs and defeats had enlisted the sympathies or execrations of millions of American citizens. Music had entered but little into the lives of the Blaine family—although since then my wife has become enthusiastically devoted to it—and I was really delighted that for the first time in my life I was compelled to establish relations from a purely human standpoint and without the assistance of any of the "romantic glamour" of my profession. At this time, however, I got but a glimpse of the Blaines, as they stayed only a week after my arrival, but there were delightful rumors of a four-weeks coaching trip from London to Scotland which Mr. Carnegie was planning for the following summer and for which we were all to be invited.

Mr. Carnegie was at that time a generous supporter of Gladstone and the Liberal Party, and several of its leaders came to Kilgraston to visit him, among them John Morley, who impressed me immensely and for whom at his own and the Carnegies' request, I played excerpts every evening from Wagner's "Nibelungen Trilogy," explaining the music and the text, as Mr. Morley had never heard the music before. I was very proud of being able to interest so fine a mind as his in Wagner's music, and like to think that my Wagner lecture recitals, which in later years I gave all over America, had their origin in these informal talks in Scotland for Morley and the Carnegies.

Incidentally, Mr. Carnegie became more and more interested in the New York Symphony and Oratorio Societies and consented to become their president and chief financial supporter. The more intricate symphonic works did not appeal to him, but he had a natural and naïve love for music. Because of his study and intimate knowledge of Scotch literature, poetry especially, together with an intense affection for the country of his birth, he particularly loved the folk-songs of Scotland, and in a high, quavering, and somewhat uncertain voice could sing literally dozens of them from memory. To me these folk-songs were a revelation, and I still think that they have a variety and charm beyond those of any other race.

I even adore the Scotch bagpipes and am almost in sympathy with the Scotsman who says that his idea of heaven is "twenty bagpipers a' playin' t'gither in a sma' room and each one playing a different tune."

On our long walks and fishing excursions together, Mr. Carnegie talked continuously and freely regarding his many plans to better the world through liberal benefactions. He had already begun the founding of free libraries all over Great Britain and America, and would often tell me of his own great poverty as a child and the difficulty of obtaining the books and education which he craved. His imagination would kindle at the opportunities which his libraries would give the youth of to-day, and a constant optimism as to the future of the world seemed to direct all his plans.

The poor salaries paid to our teaching profession would especially arouse his ire, as he considered that the entire future of America lay in the hands of its teachers and that, therefore, the greatest minds of the country should be enlisted in the work and suitably rewarded. As the reader knows, this conviction finally culminated in his remarkable and comprehensive scheme of pensions to college professors who had served their calling a certain number of years.

As he would unfold to me his various dreams and plans, he became really eloquent. His little hands would clinch, and for a moment even his fishing-pole and a possible trout at the other end would be forgotten, especially when he talked of his greatest aversion—war—and of its hideous uselessness in settling any disputes.

As a boy he had had hardly any school education, but

he had inherited the Scotch passion for books. He had read omnivorously and, what is better still, remembered what he read. Burns and Shakespeare he knew by heart and could quote very aptly to clinch a point in his arguments.

His sympathy for suffering, especially that caused by poverty, was very great and expended itself in practical help in every direction. The hard struggles of his early youth had made him very understanding, and many widows left destitute received immediate help from him and the children were put through school and placed in business through his assistance.

His attitude toward religion was very curious. In those days he professed to be an agnostic, but he had old Scotch prejudices in favor of a "Scotch Sunday." He despised theology and yet was really religious, but he did not care to define his God or to explore the mysteries or possibilities of a future life. His prejudices were as unyielding as the pig iron which he manufactured at his Homestead works, and no argument would move him if his mind was made up.

While Mr. Carnegie had a real admiration for music in its simpler forms, this never crystallized into as great a conviction regarding its importance in life as that which he had regarding the importance of science or literature, and though always generous in its support, his benefactions never became as great as in other directions. He could understand that a library, a school, or a hospital could not and should not be self-supporting, but I could not convince him that music should fall into the same category. He always insisted that the greatest patronage of music should come from a paying public rather than from private endowment. He built Carnegie

Hall in order to give New York a proper home for its musical activities, but he did not look upon this as a philanthropy, and expected to have the hall support itself and give a fair return upon the capital invested.

In the spring of 1888 I again sailed for Europe with the Carnegies, and on arriving at the Metropole Hotel in London we found the rest of the coaching party already assembled—the Blaine family, Mr. Henry Phipps a partner of Mr. Carnegie's, and Mrs. Phipps, Gail Hamilton (Miss Dodge), a cousin of Mrs. Blaine's well known as a writer; also a young Universalist clergyman, Doctor Charles Eaton, who was the pastor of Mrs. Carnegie's church.

We left the Hotel Metropole June 8, in the morning, on top of Mr. Carnegie's four-in-hand. There was a great crowd of people to see us off and wish us "Bon voyage," among them John Morley and Lord Rosebery. All the men of our party looked very sporty in high gray-top hats which we had hurriedly acquired at a hatter's in the neighborhood that morning.

I had been appointed treasurer of the tour by Mr. Carnegie, "with no salary but all the usual perquisites," as he put it.

The coachman, a stout, good-natured Scotsman of real ability, drove his four-in-hand with such skill and care that when we arrived in Invernesshire four weeks later, his horses were in even better condition than when we started.

It was certainly an ideal way to travel, and the pace was leisurely enough for us to see and enjoy the exquisite countryside of England and Scotland. Every night we stopped at a different inn but always carried our lunch in hampers, and at noontime halted at some picturesque nook by the bank of a river or on some grassy meadow in the shade of the trees and enjoyed our meal in lazy fashion.

The discussions between Mr. Blaine and Mr. Carnegie at these picnic luncheons were certainly fascinating to listen to, and especially illuminating to an American musician whose horizon had perhaps been bounded too exclusively by his own ambitions and the problems of his own art. Mr. Blaine knew England, its history, and its great families far more intimately than any Englishman I have ever met. It is well known that he never forgot anything, and whenever we stopped either for luncheon or at an inn for the night, he would immediately proceed to add to his immense store of knowledge by questioning the local farmers, field workers, or innkeepers regarding the economic or political conditions of that part of the country.

An amusing opera-bouffe element of the entire coaching trip was added by the constant but furtive appearance and disappearance of four American newspaper reporters who had been sent by their respective papers to "shadow" Mr. Blaine because the Republican convention for the presidential nomination was about to be held in Chicago, and it was eagerly hoped that Mr. Blaine would accept the nomination again. He, and through him we, of course, knew that nothing was further from his mind, but in the dusk of evening, when we would arrive at our inn for the night, these four reporters, having travelled by train, would already be there and try directly or indirectly to obtain "inside information" regarding Mr. Blaine's intentions. The reporters included Stephen Bonsal for the *New York World* and Arthur Brisbane for the *New York Sun*. The latter, wishing to combine pleasure with business, would sometimes scorn the train and hire a high dog-cart.

Our itinerary took in all the cathedral towns of the east coast of England. We were bound by no time-tables and, therefore, had every opportunity to see and study the mighty Gothic churches of Cambridge, Ely, Peterborough, York, and Durham.

I had agreed to conduct a concert in London on the 19th of June, and so very reluctantly said a temporary good-by to our party at York. This concert was given by Ovide Musin, an eminent young Belgian violinist, who wished to perform a concerto of my father's which he had played in New York about eight years before under my father's own direction. I had an excellent London orchestra of seventy-five players and also gave Beethoven's Seventh Symphony and the Liszt Hungarian Rhapsody Number One. It was my first experience as a conductor in England, and as the concert passed off very well I was much elated, especially when, just before catching my train for Durham to rejoin the coaching party, I read some complimentary criticisms of the concert in the *London Times* and *Telegraph*.

It was raining when I left the railroad station in Durham to walk to the road along which Mr. Carnegie's coach was to appear. I well remember my thrill of joy when I heard a merry fanfare played on the coaching horn by one of the footmen—whom, by the way, I always envied for his virtuosity on this instrument—and shortly after, at a turn of the road, I saw the coach appear with everybody on top attired in gray rain-coats and waving a friendly welcome. My wife has always insisted to my children that on this entire trip I wore a double-breasted frock coat which had done previous duty at my matinée concerts in America, but I think this is a gross slander and not based on fact.

We crossed the border into Scotland and of course stopped at Walter Scott's home and also visited the ruins of Linlithgow Castle, in which Mary Queen of Scots was born. And here the four reporters, who had been as constant as leeches and as inevitable as death and the taxgatherer, solemnly entered the ruins and gave Mr. Blaine a telegram which they had just received announcing Benjamin Harrison's nomination at the convention. As Mr. Blaine had expected this for weeks, the news did not excite him greatly. He bade a friendly good-by to the four young sleuth-hounds, several of whom have since achieved fame in their profession, and we continued our journey farther north until we arrived at Mr. Carnegie's home, Cluny Castle, on the evening of July 3.

It was bitter cold and the wind was whistling shrilly over the Dalwhinny Moors as we first caught sight of Cluny, but an American flag was floating proudly over its turrets, and inside warm fires and a delicious dinner were awaiting us.

Then began a summer of delights for me. Mr. Carnegie had a piper who, according to old Scotch custom, would walk around the outer walls of the house every morning to awaken us. My room was in the bachelor quarters and had a little fireplace in which a peat fire smouldered comfortably. The smell of peat and the sound of the piper as he drew nearer and nearer to my window and then again receded in the distance are always inseparably associated in my memory. In the mornings I usually worked at my studies in counterpoint and composition, but from luncheon on it was nothing but delightful entertainment or listening with keenest interest to discussions of all kinds—political, economic, poetical. Miss Dodge was a most stimulating person. She had a mind that would accept nothing without analysis or proof, and the verbal duels between her and Mr. Carnegie were fascinating, for, although she was not Scotch, she, as much as Mr. Carnegie, typified the story of the two Scotsmen who meet each other and one says: "Where are you going, Donald?" "Oh, just doon to the village to contradict a wee."

Occasionally I would accompany Mr. Carnegie to some lonely loch among the hills to fish for trout, but I have never developed into a very ardent disciple of Izaak Walton. I used to get more pleasure from lying on my back watching the marvellous Scotch sky with its low-hanging clouds framing the hills in their loving embrace, with perhaps now and then just a speck of blue shining through, than from the catching of the "finny monsters." These, however, rarely measured over six inches in length, although I certainly enjoyed them the following morning, when we had them for breakfast, rolled in oatmeal flour and deliciously fried.

In the evenings I had to contribute my little quota toward the house-party by playing Beethoven and Wagner on an excellent Broadwood piano.

During all this time I was amazed at the extreme simplicity and gentleness which characterized Mr. Blaine's demeanor toward all with whom he came in contact. Here was a man who at that time was the most loved and the most execrated American, and yet he had in him absolutely nothing of the "prima donna" manner of many of those in my profession who have achieved fame. His dignity, however, was innate and unconscious, and during the many years that I knew him and knew him intimately

I have never seen any one who dared to presume on his simplicity and general cordiality of manner by undue familiarity. His power of abstraction from his surroundings was remarkable. He enjoyed working in the room in which his family were talking, laughing, and disputing on all manner of subjects, while he would sit in a corner concentrated on some problem of his own and work it out, absolutely oblivious to what was going on about him.

The Blaine family left Cluny all too soon, and not only I, but the entire household felt their absence keenly.

Other guests followed, among them John Morley, with whom I went on long and to me very interesting walks. He seemed a very lonely and perhaps a disappointed man. He was married, but childless, and told me once that the great regret of his life was that he had no son, as he would like to have brought him up and educated him according to a theory all his own as to what an Englishman's training really should be. How many men have had such dreams and how few, if any, can really control the future of their children!

In March, 1889, Benjamin Harrison was inaugurated President and Mr. Blaine became his secretary of state.

I was, as usual, terribly busy that winter with the opera, concerts, and Wagner lecture recitals, and there were times when Washington seemed very far away, but Margaret Blaine had good friends in New York whom she visited occasionally, also a sister, the wife of Colonel Coppinger of the United States army, who was stationed at Governor's Island in New York harbor. Whenever she stayed with Mrs. Coppinger I was a very frequent passenger on the little ferry-boat which seemed to me maintained by our beneficent War Department for the sole purpose of enabling young men like myself to reach this picturesque though antiquated military fortress.

Mr. Carnegie was absolutely unconscious of my aspirations regarding Margaret Blaine, and the following summer he suggested a visit to Bar Harbor, where Mr. Blaine had built a summer home. I accepted with an alacrity which he mistook as springing only from the same source as his own desire to see again the friends who had contributed so much toward the delights of the coaching trip and Cluny Castle. When I afterward told him of my hopes and that they had received some encouragement during our Bar Harbor visit, he was very much put out and vowed that if he had ever suspected anything of the kind he would never have taken me with him. He told me that he had hoped I would not think of marriage for many years, but would remain as a kind of semi-attached musical member of his household, which at that time consisted only of himself and his wife. Of course I listened to his many arguments absolutely unconvinced, and obstinate though he always was, he found his equal in me. I must confess, however, that when he saw how much in earnest I was, he not only completely receded from his position, but accepted my engagement and marriage with absolute good humor and approval.

My engagement to Margaret Blaine was announced in October of the following year at the wedding of her brother, Emmons, to Anita McCormick, of Chicago.

Mr. Blaine had bought the old Seward mansion on Lafayette Square, very near the White House, and Mrs. Blaine, who had a remarkable flair for harmonious house furnishings and decorations, proceeded to make it into a dignified and charming house, the special feature of which was a large drawing-room on the first floor, created by changing two rooms into one.

I have told elsewhere how in those days I was compelled, because of my youth, to confine myself at the Metropolitan to the conducting of such operas as "Le Prophète," "La Juive," and "Trovatore." Seidl, my older colleague, completely monopolized the Wagner operas, which I was of course particularly anxious to conduct. Against "Trovatore" I had at that time a particularly strong and unreasonable aversion, although it was partly justified in that we did not have a cast in our German Opera Company that could do justice to its Italian atmosphere or its vocal demands.

Whenever good luck would have it that the Saturday matinée was a Wagner opera, I would ask for and obtain from Director Stanton the permission to leave for Washington on Friday night, as this would enable me to spend Saturday and Sunday with my fiancée. On one of these Fridays, just after I had received my permission, my brother Frank came to me and urged me to take the first train to Washington that I could catch, as he had just heard that the tenor who was to sing in "Siegfried" on Saturday afternoon was ill, and that in all probability the opera would be changed to "Trovatore." I quickly took the hint, and when the message came that I was to conduct "Trovatore," I was nowhere to be found and Anton Seidl was compelled to conduct it. He was furious, as he had no greater love for it than I, and my brother told me afterward that he conducted the entire opera with a black scowl on his face, which was bent low over the score and from which he never lifted his eyes once to give a sign to singer or orchestra.

During the following winter, tragedies began to overwhelm the Blaine family. Walker, the eldest son, a young man of great talent who had inherited much of his father's personal charm and who had become a great help to Mr. Blaine in the State Department, died, to be followed shortly after by the oldest daughter, Mrs. Coppinger.

These two tragedies, following so closely upon each other, were the first break in that perfect family circle, and this affected Mr. Blaine's spirit and health to such an extent that I do not think his vitality ever recovered from it.

I was married to Margaret Blaine on May 17, 1890. I should like to write much more than a chapter about the thirty-two wonderful years of our married life, but as my wife has sternly forbidden me to even mention her name in these memoirs, this chapter must close with the best left unsaid, though the most deeply felt.

X

THE DAMROSCH OPERA COMPANY, 1895-1899

With the return of Abbey, Schoeffel, and Grau in 1891, Wagner virtually disappeared from the stage of the Metropolitan Opera House as their entire energies were turned toward producing operas of the French-Italian School. It was a natural reaction from the seven years of opera in German and the pendulum swung far to the other side. A company of truly great singers had been assembled by the new managers; the audiences revelled in their *bel canto*, and as Abbey, Schoeffel, and Grau assumed the entire financial responsibility of the enterprise, the directors of the opera-house were also well satisfied. They had become tired of the growing deficits of the German opera.

The head and controlling spirit of the firm was Henry Abbey, a magnificent and honorable gambler in "stars" whom he paid so liberally that, while he sometimes gained large profits, he many times lost more heavily. The chances of profit were too small and generally it was too much like the roulette tables at Monte Carlo, with the odds in favor of the stars.

John Schoeffel was not much more than the hyphen between Abbey and Grau. I never could see that he did anything except, perhaps, arrange for the advertisements of the opera company when it visited Boston, where he lived as lessee of the Tremont Theatre.

The actual direction of the opera season, the arranging of the repertoire, the engagement of the artists, and the handling of them was in the hands of Maurice Grau, who had developed into a first-class opera manager. He claimed but little knowledge of things artistic, but he was astute and had a real flair, up to a certain point, for giving the public what it wanted. He was honorable in his dealings with the artists and in a grudging way (which operatic artists often have) they liked him, although they tortured him incessantly. He used to sit in his office like a spider from morning until night, working out repertoires, quarrelling with the singers or placating them, and altogether having no interests in life beyond that—except, perhaps, the national game of poker, in which he and a small group of cronies used to indulge—and a great affection for his little daughter.

With the exception of "Lohengrin," which had sporadic performances in the Italian language, poor Wagner was virtually boycotted, and with my great adoration for him I chafed under this condition more and more.

The winter of 1893–94 I had been asked to arrange something original in the way of an entertainment for a charity in which I was interested, and as Materna, Anton Schott, and Emil Fischer were at that time in America, I conceived the idea of giving a stage performance of the "Götterdämmerung" at Carnegie Hall. Materna was old and fat, but her voice was still glorious; Anton Schott still made a personable *Siegfried*, and Emil Fischer was at the height of his vocal and histrionic powers. The scenery, though simple, was well improvised and part of it specially painted, and the weapons and other properties were borrowed from the Metropolitan Opera House.

The success was so remarkable that we repeated the work several times and added "Walküre." This seemed to me conclusive proof that the American public were more than ready for the return of Wagner, and I called on Abbey and Grau to suggest that they include a certain number of Wagner performances in German in their repertoire. They threw up their hands in horror at the idea, saying that Wagner spelled ruin, but as they were very kindly disposed toward me (I had conducted many orchestral concerts for some of their instrumental stars) they suggested that if I wanted to be foolish enough to give Wagner performances myself, they would gladly rent the Metropolitan Opera House to me in the spring and on easy terms. Almost irresistibly I was drawn into the resolve to take their suggestion seriously, although it was made laughingly and sceptically as to its outcome. I consulted a number of devoted friends who shared my optimism and finally decided to make the plunge, and, in order to finance my mad scheme properly, I sold my house on West 55th Street.

At the home of Miss Mary Callender and Miss Caro de Forest, both of them true friends and music lovers, a "Wagner Society" was formed, the purpose of which was to help the sale of subscription seats for my venture and to spread the propaganda for the project in every way. At the first meeting of this society so many seats were subscribed for that the success seemed assured, and, besides this, the directors of the Metropolitan Opera House, although they were entitled to the free use of their boxes, suggested to me very generously that as Abbey and Grau would charge a nominal rental of five hundred dollars a night for my performances they would pay me that amount for the use of their boxes, so that I should have the house virtually rent free.

Abbey and Grau, who looked on me as a kind of foolish boy who was plunging madly toward destruction, told me with equal generosity that I could have whatever of their enormous stock of costumes and properties might prove of use for the Wagner operas.

About this time I received a letter from Mr. William Steinway, then the head of the house of Steinway & Sons, and a great lover of music, asking me to come down to see him, as he was very much interested in my project for the return of Wagner to the Metropolitan. I did so and found him at his desk crippled with gout but very cheerful and happy over my venture, for which he prophesied great success. He suggested, however, that while he realized that the idea and the venture were entirely mine, and that I was entitled to every credit and advantage from it, it would be a very generous act on my part if I invited Anton Seidl to share the conducting of the Wagner operas and music-dramas. He pointed out that Seidl was looked on by the American public as a great Wagner conductor, and his co-operation would show that I intended to found my project on the broadest and most generous lines. He said that if I would agree to his suggestion, he would arrange a meeting for Seidl and myself at his office for the following day, and I could be sure of his heartiest personal and financial support.

I thought well of his idea, and, while Seidl and I had never been on cordial personal terms during the old German opera days, nor afterward when we went our separate ways as concert conductors, I felt that the project might be much strengthened by a combination, and accordingly met Seidl, together with William Steinway, in the latter's office the following day. I outlined my project to Seidl, told him of the support I had already gained, of my arrangement with Abbey and Grau, and that I was financing the scheme myself, but that, with full admiration for his work in America during the years of German opera after my father's death, I should be glad to divide the Wagner operas with him. I showed him a list of the eight I intended to produce. They were, as I remember, as follows:

"Rhinegold"
"Walküre"
"Siegfried"
"Götterdämmerung"
"Tristan and Isolde"
"Meistersinger"
"Lohengrin"
"Tannhäuser"

I suggested to him that he should pick out the four which he preferred and that I would conduct the other four. Steinway pronounced this offer extremely fair and generous and urged Seidl to accept it, but Seidl said he would have to think it over and would notify Steinway of his decision.

The next day he called on Steinway at nine o'clock in the morning and told him that he had come to the conclusion that he would not divide the conducting of the Wagner operas with any one and, therefore, preferred not to have anything to do with the venture. Steinway was furious, and when he told me of this he said: "I am now with you heart and soul and here is my check for twenty-five hundred dollars for which I will take subscription seats for your season in different parts of the house."

I arranged for a season of eight weeks at the Metropolitan and a tour of five weeks which should take us as far west as Kansas City, as this Far Western outpost had immediately put in a generous bid for three performances.

I went abroad that spring to engage my artists and succeeded in gathering a notable company of Wagnerian singers: Rosa Sucher, of the Berlin Royal Opera for the *Brunhildes* and *Isolde;* a young singer of twenty-three, Johanna Gadski, who sang for me in Berlin, for *Elsa* and *Elizabeth;* Emil Fischer, of the Dresden Royal Opera, for *Wotan* and *Hans Sachs,* and Max Alvary, the handsomest and most dramatic of *Siegfrieds* and a truly knightly *Tristan.* He had studied the latter rôle at Bayreuth and had sung it there at the first performances. At Bayreuth I also found a highly gifted English singer, Marie Brema, who was then almost unknown but who was the possessor of a rich and expressive mezzo-soprano. Her talent for acting was remarkable and her vocal range so great that I thought I could use her not only for *Ortrude* and *Brangäne,* but, if necessary, for the *Brunhildes* as well.

A great deal of the scenery for "Tristan" and the "Nibelung Trilogy" as well as for "Tannhäuser" I had especially painted in Vienna by the firm of Kautsky and Briosky. They were at that time at the head of their profession, and such beautiful foliage as, for instance, in the forest scene of "Siegfried," had never before been seen on an American stage. Our New York painters gathered around it in amazement when it had been unpacked and properly mounted and hung.

Such an expert on naval matters as William J. Henderson, the eminent music editor of the *New York Sun,* deservedly criticised the architecture and rigging of the ship that bore *Tristan* and *Isolde* across the Irish seas to Cornwall. Vienna, the home of my scene-painters, is not a seaport, and the gorgeous tent of *Isolde's,* and the sails and mast, while very picturesque, completely hid the course of the ship from *Tristan* at the helm, and if he had not been an operatic sailor, who knew exactly where the ship was going to land at the end of the act, he undoubtedly would have sent it crashing against the white-chalk cliffs of England instead of guiding it safely into the harbor of Cornwall.

In the meanwhile, the subscriptions for seats at our New York office had gone up by such leaps and bounds that the financial success of my "crazy venture" was assured before the box-office opened for the single sale of tickets.

I had chosen "Tristan" for the opening performance. It was in 1895. The general rehearsal had gone well and an immense audience filled every available space of the opera-house and greeted me warmly as I appeared on the conductor's stand. I was just about to begin the prelude when a whisper reached me that the English horn player was not in his place. It was old Joseph Eller, who had played in the Philharmonic under my father many years before. He had, incredible to relate, forgotten his instrument and, discovering this only on his arrival at the Metropolitan, had rushed home but had not yet returned. Imagine my agitation! Everything was ready, the lights turned down and the audience expectant, and I finally did not dare to wait any longer. I assigned the English horn part to the third French horn player and we began the long-drawn sighs of the violoncellos of the introductory bars of the prelude. To my great relief I saw Eller slip into his place a few minutes later, and the performance moved well and dramatically toward a triumphant close, in which Alvary, especially, distinguished himself by his marvellous acting and impassioned singing in the scene preceding the arrival of the ship bearing *Isolde*. Sucher invested *Isolde* with a gentle, womanly dignity, but vocally she was no longer quite in her prime and did not, I think, equal Lilli Lehmann or Klafsky and Ternina, whom I brought to America the following year.

To re-enter the Metropolitan on such a Wagnerian wave after German opera had been so ignominiously snuffed out five years before, was a great triumph and satisfaction for me, more especially because my father had laid the foundation eleven years before.

I produced the other Wagnerian operas in quick succession, and as the houses were sold out for every performance the profit was considerable.

Madame Marie Brema proved herself such a valuable member of the company, both as *Ortrude* and *Brangäne*, that I felt it would be wise to give her the opportunity to sing *Brunhilde* in "Walküre" as well. I, therefore, quietly began to train her in that rôle. Unfortunately, during a rehearsal which I had with her alone on the stage, Madame Sucher happened to saunter in and, hearing the familiar music coming from my piano, she suddenly beheld another woman singing *Brunhilde*. She gave me one indignant but comprehensive glance and then majestically sailed off the stage. A few hours later I received a letter in which she announced to me that she wished to return to Germany on the next steamer, as she had not been accustomed until then to have "her" rôles sung by another as long as she was in the company.

This was the first letter of the kind that I had received during my short career as opera impresario, but it was but the prototype of many similar ones that followed each other like snowflakes in a storm during my various opera seasons.

I, of course, immediately sent Madame Sucher a large bouquet of roses and wrote to her that, quite apart from contractual obligations, I could not understand how she would want to leave America after she had "sung herself so gloriously into the hearts of my countrymen." I do not know whether my letter or the roses had any effect, or whether wiser counsels prevailed, but she stayed with me and continued her work with great good nature and even endured the hated sight of having Marie Brema sing *Brunhilde* at several of the subsequent performances.

In Kansas City we ended our stay with a matinée performance of "Siegfried," Madame Sucher as *Brunhilde* and Max Alvary, the handsome, as *Siegfried*. My readers will remember the great scene in which *Brunhilde* is awakened from her slumber of years by the kiss of *Siegfried*, who bends over her in that delightful but difficult position for a long time until a certain bar in the music denotes that the kiss is ended. The house was crowded and the greater part of the audience were women. Suddenly, while I was conducting the exquisite music accompanying the extended kiss, some one in the gallery inclined to facetiousness imitated very distinctly the smacking sound of kissing, and, to my horror, little ripples of feminine laughter rose and fell, awoke and died, to be renewed again. Alvary was wonderful. He raised his handsome head, gazed with calm eyes at the audience until a death-like silence reigned and then, with equal calm, returned to his previous occupation. It was certainly a triumph of man over woman, or rather women, and at the end of the act they greeted this young god with special and adoring enthusiasm.

The entire profits of my first venture as owner and director of an opera company for thirteen weeks amounted to about fifty-three thousand dollars. (Alas! I did not retain this quickly gained fortune a long time.)

I had again planted the flag of Wagner firmly in American ground and naturally did not wish to see it pulled down again. I therefore called on Abbey and Grau and—as I had no desire for managerial honors, the artistic side of it only interesting me—begged them to add a German department to their really splendid galaxy of French and Italian artists and to let me take care of it for them. But at that time they did not seem ready to alter their traditional operatic scheme, and my suggestion did not meet with a favorable response. I then decided that I would go on myself. My first season had taught me a great deal. I had acquired a considerable stock of scenery, costumes, and properties, and I knew where I could still further improve the artistic personnel of my company. I thought that by arranging for a longer season of five months I should be able to give my singers and orchestra better contracts financially and also introduce the Wagner operas over a greater territory.

All my friends except one urged me to go on with the work. The one exception was Andrew Carnegie who said, with that canny business acumen which made him one of the world's richest men:

"Walter, you have made a great success, artistically as well as financially; your profits have been enormous. But such a success rarely repeats itself immediately. You rightly divined the desire of the public for a return of Wagner opera, but this current has drawn into it many people who have come for curiosity only, and to whom Wagner is still a closed book. Many of these will not come back another time. Be contented to rest on your laurels."

Of course I would not listen to such good business advice and accordingly engaged a company of singers for the following year, who made a really remarkable ensemble. Among the newcomers was Madame Katherine Klafsky whose overwhelming impersonations of *Brunhilde*, *Isolde*, and especially of *Fidelio*, still vibrate in my memory. This last opera gave me such joy to conduct that, although it never drew within a thousand dollars as much as any of the other operas, I would insist on keeping it in the repertoire. This proves conclusively that the artist in me was much stronger than the impresario and that I really had no business to engage in the latter occupation.

Fidelio (*Leonore*), in the second act, liberates her husband from his shackles in the prison, and he says to her, "O, my Leonore, how much hast thou done for me!" She answers, "Nothing, nothing, my Florestan," and the orchestra begins a soft murmur, upon which the two voices rise in an ecstatic duet of love. Klafsky gave this scene with such tenderness that the entire orchestra, as well as myself, were by this time almost choking with emotion, and it was all that I could do to lift my baton to give the signal for the beginning of the duet.

Madame Ternina, another newcomer, was prevented by illness from appearing in Chicago, but in Boston she created a genuine sensation. The public divided itself into two factions, the one extolling the almost elemental dramatic vehemence of Klafsky, who fairly poured out her glorious voice, while the other proclaimed Ternina the greater artist because of her more intellectual conception and a certain noble artistic reticence.

Part of the summer of 1894 I had spent in beginning the music of an opera on Hawthorne's "The Scarlet Letter." The subject had always fascinated me and I had years before prepared a dramatic scenario for which

I finally induced Hawthorne's son-in-law, George Parsons Lathrop, to prepare a libretto. I completed the composition of the music the following summer and decided to produce it during the season 1895–96 with the Damrosch Opera Company in Boston, where the scene of the original novel is laid, in the old Colonial days of Governor Endicott.

I gave the rôle of *Hester Prynne* to Johanna Gadski. David Bispham played *Roger Chillingworth*, and Barron Berthold sang the clergyman, *Arthur Dimmesdale*.

The first performance took place February 10, 1896. American audiences are proverbially kind to authors on first nights, and Boston was especially interested in this opera because of Hawthorne's novel. The scenery presented old Boston in very picturesque fashion, and I had spent a good deal of time with my stage manager and costumer in the different Boston collections of Colonial belongings in order to give a correct picture of that period. Early portraits were consulted for the "make-up" of Governor Endicott and other old Boston celebrities, and the "company of ancient and honorable artillery" who appeared in the last act carried an exact copy of the banner which still hangs, I think, in Faneuil Hall.

Gadski gave a very touching impersonation of *Hester*, and Bispham fairly revelled in the fiendish machinations of *Roger Chillingworth*. The artists and composer received numberless recalls and the members of my company united in presenting me with several charming mementos of the day.

Mrs. John L. Gardner, who had already in those days become a real and loyal friend and supporter, and who has, according to her wonderful capacity for friendship, continued as such during these many years, sent a huge laurel wreath to the stage for me, the centre of which contained a large scarlet letter "A"! The reader may imagine what jokes were cracked at my expense about that very prominently displayed letter.

The music was, I think, well written and orchestrated, but so much of it had been conceived under the overwhelming influence of Wagner, that I am afraid Anton Seidl was right when, after hearing the work in New York, he confided cynically to his friends that it was a "New England Nibelung Trilogy."

Reviewing the work critically myself after these many years, I would say that it showed sufficient talent and musicianly grasp to warrant a composer's career, but life and its exigencies willed otherwise, and all the "might have beens" are but idle speculation.

An evil star seemed to shine over that winter's opera season from the financial standpoint. The entire country was suffering from a severe financial depression and my company was large and expensive. I had to travel continually, and during the entire five months carried a company of one hundred and seventy people, including an orchestra of seventy men, as I considered so large an aggregation my solemn duty as a Wagner disciple and propagandist.

As Abbey and Grau finally decided to embark on a German opera department of their own, adopting my suggestion when it was too late for me to combine with them, they very naturally shut me out of the Metropolitan Opera House and I was compelled, for my New York season, to lease the old Academy of Music which had become a house for cheap theatrical productions and had lost its high fashionable estate of other years.

My seasons in Chicago and Boston had been profitable,

but many cities in the South, with the exception of New Orleans, which gave me a wonderful welcome, could not pay expenses, as the theatres were too small and my company too large and literally too good.

In New Orleans we played an entire week at the old St. Charles Theatre. The dressing-rooms for the chorus were in the cellar and just before the first performance the women of the chorus ran shrieking up on the stage, vowing that they would not return, as rats as large as good-sized rabbits were scampering around the cellar. I could not believe them until I went down and saw those horrible creatures with my own eyes.

Our last performance was to have been on Saturday night, but on that day I received a petition signed by a number of citizens asking whether we could give them a "Fidelio" performance with Madame Klafsky on Sunday morning. As our train was to leave at three P. M. on that day, we had to begin this performance at eleven o'clock in the morning. The announcement that this extra performance was to be given was made only the night before and in the Sunday morning papers. By eleven o'clock the house was sold out.

I took the company as far west as Denver and everywhere virtually introduced for the first time the "Trilogy," "Tristan," and "Die Meistersinger" to the public.

I remember a performance in Providence, Rhode Island, where, in default of a theatre, the armory had been adapted for us by an improvised stage which was, however, so low that the orchestra could easily see what was going on. The opera was "Lohengrin," and just before the scene in the last act, when *Godfrey*, the little brother of *Elsa*, appears in place of the magic swan to rush into the outstretched arms of *Elsa*, the stage-manager suddenly discovered that the little ballet girl who always assumed the rôle was not present. What to do? In the emergency he grabbed Hans, son of my prompter and at that time a kind of assistant to everybody as call-boy, assistant librarian, etc., etc. He was only fourteen and small of stature but with the excessive length of arms and legs characteristic of that age. By some painful process he was forced into the costume of *Godfrey* and pushed on the stage just in the nick of time. I suddenly noticed a commotion among my orchestra, and as I followed their astonished but delighted gaze I saw the uncanny apparition of Hans as a counterfeit *Godfrey* standing on the stage evidently frightened out of his wits. Gadski, who sang *Elsa*, with great presence of mind, stretched her arms wide and not only welcomed, but extinguished him beneath the voluminous folds of her cloak and I doubt whether the public realized that the real princely brother had not made his appearance.

When we finally arrived in New York, I had already lost a great deal of the large profits of the year before, and this loss was further increased by my season at the Academy of Music.

During the New York season my wife and I stayed at the stately old house of our dear friends, Sophie and Tina Furniss, on Fifth Avenue and Fortieth Street. With characteristic kindness, they not only took a large proscenium box for every performance, but, having heard that affairs had not gone well financially, insisted that we must be their guests for the entire New York season, in order, I suppose, that I should not have to incur the extravagance of an hotel.

These elderly ladies, together with a married sister, Mrs. Zimmermann, were the daughters of an old East

India merchant who, in the earlier part of the nineteenth century, had amassed a fortune. Their house was full of lovely old furniture and mementos of a bygone age and they dispensed within its walls a very generous and dignified hospitality.

An old colored coachman named Brown had been with them for forty years. He always, together with a young colored footman, sat high up on their carriage in great state and solemnity. The young footman having been sent away in disgrace during our stay, Brown was instructed to procure another boy to take his place. A week elapsed and the new boy had not been found, and when Miss Sophie said to him: "Brown, why haven't you gotten us a new boy? Are they difficult to find?" he answered:

"No, Miss Sophie, there's plenty o' boys, but ah find it so hard to ma'ch mah colah."

He evidently was a great stickler for unanimity, not only in the color of the livery but of the skin as well.

Miss Sophie, the oldest of these three delightful ladies, had an incredible vitality, and although bodily infirmities and advancing years did their best to curb her, she remained active, cheerful, and undaunted until the end. Almost every night during my opera season of six weeks she would hobble from the carriage to her proscenium box, supported by her cane on one side and the footman on the other, and she listened to the Wagnerian music-dramas with unflagging attention. Not even the length of "Götterdämmerung" or "Meistersinger" would phase her, and after the performance, during supper, she would proudly repeat, while her eyes fairly snapped with laughter, some remark of mine that I had made two years before at their country place in Lenox, during my delivery of a series of explanatory recitals on the "Nibelung Trilogy."

Another fellow guest was Doctor Sturgis Bigelow, an enthusiastic admirer of Madame Ternina's art, who had come to New York especially to be present at all of her appearances. She was to have made her farewell to America in the "Götterdämmerung" and Doctor Bigelow had ordered enough flowers from half a dozen of the florists of Broadway and Fifth Avenue to fill the entire Academy, but unfortunately Madame Ternina became ill and her place had to be taken at the last moment by her rival, Madame Klafsky. Doctor Bigelow had no desire to present the floral testimony of his adoration to this rival singer, and therefore proceeded on the difficult task of cancelling his many orders, but as many of the wreaths and lyres had already been prepared, his bill for "damages" was quite large.

Before Ternina sailed for home she told me that she intended to stay away for a few years. I had paid her five hundred dollars an appearance which was a fair honorarium at that time, as she was absolutely unknown and therefore had not yet developed a sufficient "drawing power" to warrant a higher fee, but she said she would not come back to America until she could command a fee of a thousand dollars. This decision she adhered to, and when she did return a few years later, Maurice Grau cheerfully paid her the thousand dollars and she was immediately proclaimed one of the greatest *Isoldes* of our time.

My New York season opened on March 4, 1896, with Beethoven's "Fidelo." The audience was a distinguished one, containing a great many of the old Academy habitués. Grand opera had not been given there since 1888,

when the tenor, Italo Campanini, had brought over an
Italian opera company.

Of Klafsky I have already spoken, but my new barytone, Dimitri Popovici, also made a sensation. I had
found him in Bayreuth, where he had sung *Telramund* and
Kurvenal.

I produced my own opera, "The Scarlet Letter," during the second week, and the reception accorded it was
more than cordial. As the Symphony Society of New
York wished to present me with an exquisitely bound
copy of Hawthorne's "The Scarlet Letter" as a memento,
Richard Welling, the secretary and an old friend, suggested to Anton Seidl, who was in the audience, that
he be spokesman, but as he refused Welling presented
the book to me himself.

While the balance-sheet of the five months' season
showed a "loss of forty-three thousand dollars," the
larger part of my gains of the year before, I cannot say
that my wife and I were very much cast down. Youth is
optimistic, and the loss of money is, in itself, not such a
dreadful calamity if one still has enough to pay one's
debts; and all this time I was adding to my experience
and artistic stature.

After a long consultation with my wife we both decided that the conditions under which I had worked that
disastrous winter were not normal, and that we could
well risk another season. Two factors influenced me
greatly in this decision: one, that a group of Philadelphia citizens had come forward and desired me to consider their Academy of Music as my artistic home, and said
that they would give every possible assistance to a regular
season there, and the other was that Abbey and Grau
frankly confessed to me that they had made a mistake

in not accepting my offer of a combination. They had not been fortunate in the choice of their German singers and had lost a hundred and fifty thousand dollars on their German operas, which was nearly four times as much as I had lost. Grau suggested for the following season an interchange of certain artists, and if I would occasionally lend him Madame Klafsky, whom he admired greatly, he would in turn give me Madame Calvé for a few performances of "Carmen." This arrangement seemed admirable to me, as I was beginning to feel that Wagner opera alone was not sufficient to give a well-balanced opera season, and that for a longer season Philadelphia would demand a more varied repertoire.

For the following season of 1897–98 affairs moved much easier for me. The Philadelphia committee gave me a guarantee for a regular opera season at the Philadelphia Academy of Music. This assured me a home and a permanent place for my large store of scenery, costumes, and properties. Rehearsals also were thus made easier and, for my New York season in the spring, Abbey and Grau again rented the Metropolitan Opera House to me.

I had re-engaged Madame Klafsky, but to our great sorrow she died, and the problem of finding a successor was a serious one. Madame Gadski, who had charmed our audiences with *Elsa*, *Elizabeth*, and *Sieglinde*, was rather young for the heavy dramatic rôles, although I had begun to train her in the "Walküre" and "Siegfried" *Brunhildes*. I began negotiations with Lilli Lehmann and was successful in obtaining her wonderful services for the following year—but of this I have written in detail in another chapter.

The financial results of this season were quite satisfactory, but I was beginning to chafe more and more under the unsympathetic task of manager. To rehearse singers and orchestra from morning until night was a pleasure, because there was an artistic ideal to be achieved and because there were all manner of musical difficulties to be overcome. That was part of my work as a musician and conductor, and the fatigues and worries connected with this were easily endured. But the managerial duties annoyed me, and the constant intrigues among the singers, directed sometimes against each other and at other times against the management, often seemed to me unbearable.

In the spring of 1898 Madame Nellie Melba, the golden-voiced, told me that she would like to join my company for the following winter, and suggested that her manager, Mr. Charles Ellis, well known as the manager of the Boston Symphony Orchestra, form a partnership with me, the company to be called The Damrosch-Ellis Opera Company, half of the repertoire to be devoted, as before, to the Wagner operas and the other half to the performance of French-Italian operas with herself as the principal singer. We were to pay her fifteen hundred dollars a night, ten times a month, guaranteed. The suggestion seemed to me reasonable and advantageous, and arrangements were made accordingly. This combination aroused great indignation on the part of Mr. George Haven, the president of the Metropolitan Opera House. Mme. Melba had been one of the principal singers there for several years and he felt that it was an act of ingratitude on her part to leave the Metropolitan, and on mine to take her into my company, as I had myself been associated with the Metropolitan during so many years while he was president. I did not think that his anger was justified, as a great deal of water had flowed down-stream since those days; and, as Melba, for reasons of her own, had definitely decided to sever all connections with the Metropolitan, I could not see why I should not make her a member of my company. But he could not, or would not, see my side of the controversy, and vowed that as long as he was president of the Metropolitan I should never set foot in it again in a professional capacity. This vow, however, was subsequently not adhered to, as I not only gave performances there later with my own company, but during the seasons of 1900–01 and 1901–02 officiated again as conductor of the Wagner operas for Maurice Grau, who had then become the sole director and lessee of the Metropolitan.

The combination of Wagnerian operas with the operas of the French-Italian school, of which Melba was the glorious star, proved successful from a popular and financial standpoint, and the season showed a handsome profit for Ellis and myself, although a great part of this was dissipated by a spring tour in which Melba, supported by a small company of singers, chorus, and orchestra, toured the Western cities. This tour was managed by my partner, Ellis, and I did not accompany them, as my services as conductor were not needed for the French operas. I had by that time definitely decided to give up all further connection with opera as manager and devote my future life absolutely to purely musical work as a symphonic conductor and, as I hoped, also as composer. The harassing occupation of "managing" singers proved increasingly distasteful to me, and I felt that I was too good a musician and artist to waste my time with such things in which the only advantage could be a possible pecuniary gain.

I found that many singers were like children with no

NELLIE MELBA

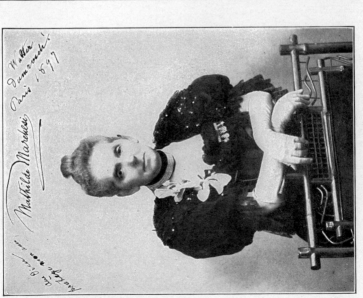

MATHILDE MARCHESI

clear conception of right or wrong. Their constant life
in close proximity to each other at rehearsals and performances often begets an exaggerated conception of
themselves and their importance to the world. They
think that as their contact with the public is only over
the footlights, where they receive enthusiastic acclaim for
their artistic representations, the public literally exists
only for the purpose of hearing them sing, and they
willingly ignore the fact that the public may have other
interests, such as family, finance, politics, or religion to
claim its attention. As it is important for a manager
not only to maintain a balance in his ledger but to seek
the best results that a disciplined ensemble may attain,
he cannot always be in harmony with all the individual
desires and demands of his artists. He must often cast
his opera in opposition to their personal pride, and I have
letters to-day from several of the greatest artists of my
company insisting that they must leave or break their
contracts because I had wounded their deepest sensi-
bilities in putting so and so in the rôle which they claimed
for their very own.

I found that some of them even indulged in occasional
efforts at petty blackmailing. One of my tenors, who
shall be nameless, had a clause in his contract that he
should not be called upon to sing *Tristan* the day after a
very long railway journey. We had played in Cleveland, giving a "Lohengrin" performance in which, however, the other tenor had appeared, and took a night
train in comfortable sleeping-cars in one of which my
tenor occupied a drawing-room to Pittsburgh, which is,
as my reader is aware, a distance of only 150 miles or so.
As we left Cleveland my friend the tenor appeared in my
drawing-room, and, calling attention to the clause in his

contract relating to *Tristan* and a "long" railway trip, insisted that he could not sing *Tristan* the following day in Pittsburgh without endangering his voice. But if I would pay him five hundred dollars extra he would take the great risk of injuring his voice and would agree to sing. Naturally I was furious and told him politely but firmly what I thought of him, and then sent for my other tenor and told him that his rival was trying to blackmail me and I suggested to him that if he would sing *Tristan* for me in spite of his having sung *Lohengrin* the night before, I would consider it as a performance outside of his guarantee. Needless to say he jumped at the opportunity of gaining an extra six hundred dollars and at the same time "putting one over" on his hated rival. I then went to bed and slept soundly on a pillow made downy by a deed well done.

Next morning I received word from tenor No. 1 that he had changed his mind, was feeling very well, and would sing, but I very haughtily told him that it was too late and that I had already made other arrangements.

So far this story seems a wonderful example of virtue triumphant and vice defeated, but, alas, life's problems do not always work out that way! During the day my dramatic soprano who was to have sung *Isolde* became hoarse and the opera had to be changed, so that all my carefully reared structure of righteousness and meting out of punishment to the guilty one fell to the ground with a very dull thud.

This is only one of many such instances, some of them childish and others really wicked. But the most unmoral thing about it is that when the culprits were great artists, no matter how much they enraged me by their wickedness, after they had appeared again triumphantly as *Siegfried* or *Isolde* I would often become so enthusiastic over their work that their slate would be washed clean and I was ready to forgive them again and to begin anew. Such is the power of art, and a grateful public will always be willing to remember only the artistic uplift which they have received from the artist and forget his personal weaknesses.

Naturally my strictures apply only to certain of the singers. There were many who were always honorable in their relations with me. Among the most devoted of the members of my company I should mention the singers of the chorus. Many of these had been at the Metropolitan in the German opera days. Their salaries were small, but if one of their number fell ill or suffered other misfortune, none so quick as they to help, and they always endured the hardships of travel with great good humor and unfailing courtesy and decency toward me.

Among other reasons that impelled me finally to give up the opera was the realization how comparatively seldom absolute artistic perfection can be obtained at a stage performance. There are so many people concerned in it that it is almost impossible always to obtain a cast which is thoroughly satisfactory, and one "second rater" can spoil an ensemble. Still another problem was the question of stage illusion. I gave this a great deal of attention and study, and spent a great deal of money on scenery and lighting. I examined the best inventions in this direction in the opera-houses of Germany and imported many of them. I was the first to bring over the very clever swimming-machines used in Dresden by the Rhine Maidens in "Rhinegold." But Wagner's demands on the stage are so extraordinary that a real illusion is not often possible. His music excites the imagination and is often all sufficient. One can see the glorious flames crackling and burning around the sleeping *Brunhilde* when one hears an orchestra of a hundred playing the music of the "Fire Charm," but how seldom does a stage performance enhance this illusion! The *Brunhilde* may be too big and too fat, or the light of the flames may too clearly show that the scenery is but painted canvas and pasteboard after all, and our sophisticated eyes know only too well how the plumber's steam-pipes convey the steam that is intended to simulate the smoke of the flames from the boiler in the cellar. It sometimes seemed to me, after striving in vain to carry out Wagner's ideal of a union of all the arts in order to produce a new and perfect art form (the "music-drama"), as if this great genius had really committed a gigantic mistake, and as if the very artistic illusion and semblance of verity was destroyed by the scenic paraphernalia.

Of course there were performances over which a happy star seemed to shine and which now and then gave us complete satisfaction and happiness. But the static quality of scenery became to me more and more a hindrance to an imagination ready to soar on the wings of the music.

I carried on my opera company for another year in conjunction with Mr. Charles Ellis, and then definitely resolved to cease all managerial activities and to confine myself absolutely to purely musical work. It took me some time to arrive at this decision, as opera work has also a very fascinating side, and I had made real friends with many of my singers.

I had found Ellis to be a delightful partner. He had had years of experience as manager of the Boston Symphony Orchestra, and his equable temperament and fair-mindedness had made him many friends. I sold to him my share in all our scenery, costumes, and properties as he wished to continue operatic work with Madame Melba as his principal star, and I agreed to conduct a limited number of Wagner performances for him in Philadelphia during the following season.

After the four hectic years I had spent with the Damrosch Opera Company I was glad of such an opportunity to take stock of the past and cogitate on the future.

My wife and I rented the old Butler place in Westchester County, near Hartsdale—a lovely old mansion surrounded by dark pine forests and with the little Bronx River trickling through—and there we spent most of the winter until May. I wrote a violin sonata there and enjoyed the tranquillity of a life freed from operatic worries and excitements.

In 1900 I was once more tempted into the field of opera, but this time it carried with it no managerial or financial responsibility.

Maurice Grau was at that time the lessee of the Metropolitan Opera House. Abbey had died a few years before and the directors, who had gradually realized that it was Grau who had been the real "man behind the gun," gave him and a small group of financial backers the lease of the Metropolitan Opera House. Grau invited me to return to the Metropolitan as conductor for the Wagner operas. He had at that time a strong group of Wagnerian singers. At the head was the inimitable Jean de Reszke, together with his brother Edouard. Grau had also taken over from my company Madame Ternina, David Bispham, and Madame Gadski. The latter had been a member of the Damrosch Opera Company for the entire four years of its existence. She was only twenty-three when I first engaged her, possessor of a lovely voice, and an indefatigable worker. There were weeks on our Western tours when she would appear on five successive days as *Elsa, Elizabeth, Sieglinde,* and *Eva.* She was a hard student and her voice developed more and more. During her last year with me she added the "Walküre" and "Siegfried" *Brunhildes* to her repertoire, studying them with me, partly on the trains while travelling, partly in the hotels and theatres of the various cities we visited. When she went into the Grau Company, she added the "Götterdämmerung" *Brunhilde* and *Isolde,* thereby completing the entire circle of Wagner soprano parts, except *Kundry.*

Jean de Reszke, like Lilli Lehmann, turned to the Wagnerian rôles in the high noon of his operatic career. He had made his fame in the French-Italian operas, but Wagner attracted him irresistibly.

I remember that during one of the seasons of the Damrosch Opera Company we were playing in Boston at the Boston Theatre while the Abbey and Grau Company were performing in the huge Mechanic's Hall. Jean and Edouard de Reszke attended one of my "Siegfried" performances with Max Alvary in the title rôle. They applauded their colleague vociferously, and after the performance Jean lamented to me that he was compelled to sing nothing but *Fausts* and *Romeos* and *Werthers,* while it was the ambition of his life to sing Wagner. The memory of his extraordinary impersonations of these rôles later on is too vivid to need comment from me. Illness kept him away from America one year, and when he returned I was again at the Metropolitan as conductor of the Wagner operas. It was a joy to work with this man. Great artist, courteous gentleman, and generous colleague, and (what is most valuable to a conductor) indefatigable at rehearsals. His return was like the triumphant entry of a victorious monarch. He was a marvellous mimic, and used to give us delicious imitations of the various artists of the company coming into his dressing-room to offer their congratulations after his first reappearance.

De Reszke would first depict the French tenor colleague who in polite, reserved, and even patronizing accents would say:

"Vraiment, mon cher, vous-avez chanté très bien ce soir, très bien, je vous assure!"

Then would come the German barytone in a double-breasted frock coat and punctiliously polite manner, saying:

"Erlauben Sie mir, Herr de Reszke, Ihnen meine grosse Hochachtung aus zu drücken für den wirklich ausgezeichneten Genuss den Sie uns heute Abend bereitet haben."

He was followed by the Italian barytone, who would rush in impulsively and, kissing Jean on both cheeks, would exclaim:

"Caro mio, carissimo!" followed by a flood of Italian words.

Then came the real climax of the scene. Enter the electrician who, thrusting a "horny hand of toil" into that of de Reszke, would exclaim in real "Yankee" accents:

"Jean, you done fine!"

Edouard de Reszke, the huge bass brother with the heart of a child and an imperturbable good nature, was an equally good mimic. But his wonderful stories and impersonations were of a decidedly Rabelaisian character and will not bear repetition here.

With these two well-corseted but un-Corsican brothers, Madame Ternina or Madame Nordica, Madame Schumann-Heink, and David Bispham we gave performances of "Tristan" which came as near perfection as I ever hope to witness.

Madame Nordica had been for years a so-called "utility" singer at the Metropolitan. She had been trained in the French-Italian repertoire, and while her voice was beautiful she had not yet achieved full stardom, perhaps because she was American born and lacked the European cachet, which at that time was more important than it is to-day. She was not by nature musically gifted and was able to learn a rôle only by the hardest and most painful work of endless repetition and rehearsals. But her ambition was boundless—she bided her time and, like Lilli Lehmann, gradually worked herself into the Wagner repertoire. Realizing its advertising value, she offered herself to Madame Cosima Wagner for the "Lohengrin" production at Bayreuth. She meekly accepted every instruction given her there during the months of preparations, no matter how meticulous or artificial some of them seemed to her, and the success which she obtained there launched her successfully on her career as a Wagner singer. I trained her in the *Brunhildes* as well as *Isolde* and was amazed at the way in which she achieved through hard work what nature gives to others overnight.

I remember her coming to Philadelphia to sing "Götterdämmerung" with my company. She arrived the previous day and I found her still very uncertain in the second act, which is rhythmically very difficult. I sat down with her at eight o'clock that evening and we went over that second act again and again until about four o'clock in the morning.   It was ghastly but wonderful. At ten A. M. I gave her an orchestral rehearsal and in the evening she sang the rôle with perfect assurance and with hardly a mistake.

One performance of "Tristan" which we gave with the Grau Company in Baltimore at the Lyric Theatre, which has perhaps the best acoustics of any auditorium in the country, still stays vividly in my memory.   At the close we were so elated that all concerned kissed each other ecstatically after the last curtain fell.   Those are the rare moments that make one forget the many times perfection in opera seems impossible to attain.

XI

ARTISTS

I have written elsewhere of my first visit to Europe after my father's death, when the directors of the Metropolitan Opera House made me assistant to the director, Edmund C. Stanton.

I had gone over to engage German singers for the coming season, and Emil Fischer, bass from the Dresden Royal Opera, was one of those whose contract I had ready for Stanton's signature when he arrived a month later. Emil Fischer had become discontented with his life in Dresden and in signing with us broke his contract with the Royal Opera, and according to an arrangement which all the directors of the various German operahouses had with each other, this prevented him from ever again appearing on the stage of a German operahouse. He remained in America and became one of the main props of the Metropolitan Opera House Company, and later on of my Damrosch Opera Company.

His voice was a beautiful *basso cantante* of great range and vibrancy. His tone production was perfect, and his powers as an impersonator equalled his singing. He will always remain in my memory as the greatest *Hans Sachs* I have ever heard. He imbued the part with a nobility and at the same time with a delightful humor that no other *Hans Sachs* has quite equalled.

As a man he was a delicious mixture of childishness, vanity, generosity, and kindliness, but I do not think that any emotions of life touched him very deeply.

In dress he was always extremely fastidious, inclining toward a somewhat flamboyant love of extremes. His neckties were rather vivid, his trousers perhaps a shade lighter in gray than the most harmonious taste would demand. He had a highly developed chest, of which he was so inordinately proud that he never buttoned the upper part of his waistcoat, as if to demonstrate that no waistcoat could be cut large enough to encompass his manly proportions.

Of the value of money, as far as saving it was concerned, he had no idea, and his constant effort was directed toward hiding from his wife the fact that he had money in his pocket. She was a buxom lady somewhat older than himself who, in her youth, had been a *tragedienne* in one of the smaller German court theatres. She must have played such parts as *Medea*, and continued the rather exaggerated and gloomy articulation of her words into private life and through all the years that followed her final exit from the stage. Whenever she told me: "My Emil is not well to-day. I have made for him a plate of beef soup into which I have boiled four pounds of beef," it boomed upon my ears like Shakespearian blank verse or like a Greek tragedy of Sophocles. I think that she annoyed Emil excessively, and that he was happiest when he could get away from her no doubt excellent control and find enjoyment among a circle of boon companions.

I recall that when he was a member of my opera company I paid him two hundred and fifty dollars an appearance, with about twelve appearances a month guaranteed, but he insisted that in the written contract I should make it only two hundred dollars an appearance and give him the other fifty in cash. He used this subtle method in order to have about six hundred dollars a month spending money of which his wife should know nothing. It was I who had to endure the complaints from her, which ran something like this: "I do not know why my Emil is so badly paid while all the others get these enormous salaries. My Emil sings better than any of them and he has to be content with only two hundred dollars an appearance!" And I would sit by feeling very guilty, and yet, from that horrid loyalty which one man has for another, not daring to exculpate myself by condemning him.

At one time in Chicago I accompanied him into a haberdasher's shop as he wished to buy a necktie. He selected one the price of which was two dollars and a half, and then superbly handed the astonished clerk a five-dollar bill, saying grandiloquently: "You may keep the change!"

He was a great gourmet, and every now and then would give a banquet at his house to his fellow artists, with interminable courses and all manner of wines. Needless to say he did not save anything from his earnings and there came years, as he grew older and his voice left him, when he had to turn to teaching. But he never changed his habits and his appearance was just as carefully gotten up as in former years. Finally came the time when he was really in want, and I assisted Mr. Flagler, who was also an old admirer of his, in getting up a benefit for him at the Metropolitan Opera House. The directors very generously gave the use of the house, many of the stockholders bought their boxes, and the climax of the performance was the appearance of dear old Fischer in his greatest rôle of *Hans Sachs* in the third act of "Die Meistersinger." A very good sum was realized with which we bought an annuity for him. He was then, I believe, seventy-four (his wife had died several years before), and a ten-year annuity seemed to us the best way of taking care of him without giving him an opportunity to squander his money. He was delighted, and the first thing he did on the strength of his new wealth was to marry a young lady from the chorus, who, however, I believe took excellent care of him until he died.

During the second year of the Damrosch Opera Company, while we were in St. Louis and just the day before Fischer was to sing *Hans Sachs*, a telegram arrived saying that his wife was very ill and was not expected to live more than eight hours. Frau Alvary insisted that I must make him go to New York to see her. He did not want to go. He had not been on particularly pleasant terms with her, he knew he could not arrive in time to see her alive, and besides that he knew also that I had no substitute to sing *Hans Sachs* for him and that the cancellation of the opera would cost me about five thousand dollars. But Frau Alvary, who seemed quite ready to insist on reasons of sentiment when her own purse was not concerned, so bedevilled us both that I finally, being still young and sentimental, decided that he should go. I was therefore compelled to change the programme at the last moment and to substitute single acts from different operas, which, of course, was a very costly change, as the audience in St. Louis had especially looked forward to the first performance of "Die Meistersinger."

The news of a possible change of programme had travelled fast, and on that morning I received a visit from a young singer, Gerhardt Stehmann, who a year before had come to St. Louis with a little German opera company which had promptly stranded, leaving him without a job. He had, however, continued to live there, acting in occasional German plays and teaching Latin, as he was a man of excellent education. He asked me if I could not give him a place in my company. I found him to be an excellent singer, but above all a man musically so gifted that he could learn an entire rôle in a few hours. He learned the entire third act of "Die Meistersinger" overnight, so that I was able at least to present that to my St. Louis audience. I immediately engaged him as a permanent member of my company, and he remained with me until its dissolution three years later, when he returned to Germany and was grabbed by Mahler for the Imperial opera at Vienna, where he has been ever since. He literally knew and sang every bass and barytone part in the Wagner operas and music dramas. His *Beckmesser* in "Die Meistersinger" was a masterpiece of delineation, and no one could depict this nasty, carping, jealous, and vain person in so convincing a fashion as he. But if the exigencies of the moment demanded it, he was just as able to sing *Hans Sachs, Pogner, Kothner,* or any other of the good old burghers of that opera. In "Tannhäuser" he was equally at home as *Landgrave* or *Biterolf,* but his most remarkable feat of learning a part quickly was performed in New York one spring. The German composer, Xaver Scharwenka, was at that time living in New York as piano virtuoso and teacher. He had, years before, composed an opera which he was anxious to perform, and William Steinway and others asked me if I would let him have my opera company for this purpose, so that he could conduct it himself at an extra performance. I agreed and a good cast was selected. The tenor part was to have been sung by Ernest Krauss, a rather conceited heroic tenor who, not finding the part to his liking, pleaded hoarseness only the day before the performance. There was, of course, no substitute, and it seemed as if the performance would have to be cancelled, which would have been a cruel experience for the composer. To my astonishment Stehmann appeared and said very simply: "Give me the part and I will learn it for to-morrow night." When I interposed, "But this is a tenor part and you are a bass barytone," he answered: "Give it to me. I think I can transpose a few of the high notes and can at least save the performance." Scharwenka, overjoyed, gave him the part and he sang and acted it the following evening without a mistake—a truly remarkable feat.

I grew very fond of him, not only because of his musicianly qualities but also because as a man he was so simple and honorable, and I was glad to hear later on that he had made an excellent position for himself in Vienna.

This summer of 1922, I visited Vienna again after many, many years. I felt that the war should be completely over for us and that we should seek in every way to reestablish cultural relations with our former enemies.

I found Stehmann still at the Vienna opera, now no longer called Kaiserliche but Staats-Oper. It was a joy to see him again, but the war had brought to him also great misfortune! He told me that from his savings, while a member of my opera company and from subsequent savings in Vienna, he had bought a house with several acres of land in the Austrian Tyrols. With tears in his eyes he showed me photographs of this property. The house was charmingly situated in a picturesque valley with the Tyrolean Alps beyond. After the war this territory was taken over by Italy; and that government, wishing to drive out the Austrians and settle the land with Italians, had compelled Stehmann to "sell" his property for a sum fixed by them. He had no choice and the

price which he received amounted to about thirty-seven
thousand five hundred kronen, which happened to be the
amount I had paid that morning for a pair of shoes—at
the present valuation about three dollars and seventy
cents! The Poles claim that Bismarck pursued the same
policy in Posnia when Prussia endeavored to suppress
Polish national aspirations, by forcing them to sell their
lands to the Prussian Junkers.

I was sorry on arriving in Vienna not to see once more
the venerable old singer, Marianne Brandt, but she had
died, aged eighty-four, during the previous winter. In
1884–85 she had been one of the main props of my father's inaugural German opera season; and her emotional
intensity in "Fidelio" and as the mother in "Le Prophète" had made a deep impression on our public. Nature had not endowed her with beauty of face or figure,
and she always insisted: "I have been a virtuous woman
all my life because I am so ugly that no man would ever
look at me."

Wagner had invited her to Bayreuth to sing the part
of *Kundry* in "Parsifal," but whether because of her lack
of beauty or because, as she thought, of terrible intrigues
on the part of Madame Materna, she sang the rôle only
once and always remained exceedingly jealous of Madame
Materna, whose rather amplitudinous charms, she insisted, had completely hypnotized Wagner.

She simply adored my father and his single-minded
idealism, and the spirituality of his character appealed to
her to such an extent that she was willing to undergo any
amount of work and to sing any rôle which he wanted of
her, whether it were a star part or one of the Valkyries
in "Walküre." After his death she was inconsolable, and
always went on the anniversary to Woodlawn Cemetery

to deposit a wreath on his grave. She also sought to demonstrate her veneration for his memory by helping me in every way possible, both as superb artist and as one well versed in the practical side of operatic life through years of experience in Vienna and at the Royal Opera in Berlin. She always called me "Mein Sohn," and her encouragement and faith in my future as a musician during many trying times can never be forgotten by me.

She had a delightful sense of humor, but also a very quick temper, and I remember her telling me one day that she had received a notice from the New York Post-Office Department that a registered letter was awaiting her down in the General Post-Office at City Hall. She went there and inquired at the proper window for her letter.

"Yes," said the official, "we have it here. Have you got some document to prove that you are Marianne Brandt?—a letter, a bank-book, or a passport?"

"I have none of these things, but I am Marianne Brandt and I want that letter."

"I am sorry, madame, but the rules are strict, and you will have to bring some one to identify you."

By this time Brandt was in a state of high indignation. "You will not give me the letter? I will prove to you that I am Marianne Brandt!" And then she proceeded with full voice to sing the great cadenza from her principal aria in "Le Prophète." Her glorious voice echoed and re-echoed through the vaulted corridors of the post-office. Men came running from all sides to find out what had happened and finally the agitated official handed her the letter, saying: "Here is your letter, but for God's sake be quiet!"

She finally retired from the stage to her old home in

Vienna and gave of her art with both hands to a group of devoted pupils. During the war I heard from one of them that, owing to the destitute condition existing in Vienna, she was in real want, but she promptly returned the check we sent her and in a very sweet letter addressed as usual to "Mein Sohn" assured me that she did not need any money, that she did not expect to live much longer, and that she thought she could hold out without receiving any alms from her friends. We did succeed, however, in sending her food which she shared with others.

One of the singers whom I engaged for the Metropolitan Opera House during my first visit to Germany and who afterward achieved great fame was Max Alvary, a young lyric tenor at the Weimar Ducal Opera House. He was the son of the well-known German painter, Andreas Achenbach, of good education, gentlemanly bearing, and a refined artistic taste. He was also exceedingly good looking. As a singer he was very uneven, although he had studied with the Italian master, Lamperti. At first we paid him only a hundred dollars a night, but after he had sung minor rôles for a few months Anton Seidl chose him to create the part of *Siegfried*, and in that rôle he made a success so instantaneous as to place him immediately in the front rank of German opera-singers. No one else has given *Siegfried* such an atmosphere of boyish innocence and picturesque beauty. The women, bless them, simply worshipped him, from the sixteen-year-old schoolgirl to the matron of mature and more than mature age, and this success repeated itself when he appeared as *Siegfried* in Germany, Austria, and England. He made a great deal of money and spent it lavishly. His armor and helmet in "Lohengrin" were

specially made for him out of silver after a design which
he had drawn himself. The stuffs for his costumes were
often specially woven for him. He reached the climax of
his career when he was chosen by Cosima Wagner to sing
Tannhäuser and *Tristan* at Bayreuth. At that time this
shrine for the Wagnerite had already become, under the
guiding and autocratic hand of the widow of Wagner, a
highly artificial product. I saw several of these performances and was frankly amazed at the apparent degenera-
tion since the days of Wagner. Alvary, who had a great
sense of humor, gave most entertaining descriptions of the
rehearsals, and how, for instance, in slavish imitation
of certain rhythms in the orchestra, *Tannhäuser* and
Wolfram had to execute a kind of minuet opposite each
other in order to fill in the instrumental introduction before *Wolfram* begins his famous plea to *Tannhäuser:*
"Als du im kühnen Sange uns bestrittest."

In the spring of 1891 Carnegie Hall, which had been
built by Andrew Carnegie as a home for the higher musical activities of New York, was inaugurated with a music
festival in which the New York Symphony and Oratorio
Societies took part. In order to give this festival a
special significance, I invited Peter Iljitsch Tschaikowsky, the great Russian composer, to come to America
and to conduct some of his own works. In all my many
years of experience I have never met a great composer so
gentle, so modest—almost diffident—as he. We all loved
him from the first moment—my wife and I, the chorus,
the orchestra, the employees of the hotel where he lived,
and of course the public. He was not a conductor by
profession and in consequence the technic of it, the
rehearsals and concerts, fatigued him excessively; but he
knew what he wanted and the atmosphere which ema-

nated from him was so sympathetic and love-compelling that all executants strove with double eagerness to divine his intentions and to carry them out. The performance which he conducted of his Third Suite, for instance, was admirable, although it is in parts very difficult; and as he was virtually the first of great living composers to visit America, the public received him with jubilance.

He came often to our house, and, I think, liked to come. He was always gentle in his intercourse with others, but a feeling of sadness seemed never to leave him, although his reception in America was more than enthusiastic and the visit so successful in every way that he made plans to come back the following year. Yet he was often swept by uncontrollable waves of melancholia and despondency.

The following year in May I went to England with my wife, and received an invitation from Charles Villiers Stanford, then professor of music at Cambridge, to visit the old university during the interesting commencement exercises at which honorary degrees of Doctor of Music were to be given to five composers of five different countries—Saint-Saëns of France, Boito of Italy, Grieg of Norway, Bruch of Germany, and Tschaikowsky of Russia.

The proceedings proved highly interesting and enjoyable. As each recipient of the honor stepped forward in his doctor's robe, the orator addressed him in a discourse of orotund Latin phrases, praising his many virtues and accomplishments, and these phrases were constantly interrupted by the clatter of facetious remarks and requests from the undergraduates in the balcony, all this according to old established custom. Sometimes the uproar became so great that the presiding officer had to arise and demand "Silentium."

Among the other recipients of degrees on that occasion was Field-Marshal Lord Roberts, Baron of Kandahar, who, in his scarlet uniform beneath his doctor's robe, received of course the most uproarious welcome. At that time no one dreamed that twenty-three years later he would go around England uttering solemn warning against the inevitability of war with Germany and bidding England gird on her sword and prepare, only to be laughed at as an alarmist and publicly reprimanded by politicians for seeking to arouse such feeling against a "friendly power."

In the evening a great banquet was given in the refectory of the college, and by good luck I was placed next to Tschaikowsky. He told me during the dinner that he had just finished a new symphony which was different in form from any he had ever written. I asked him in what the difference consisted and he answered: "The last movement is an adagio and the whole work has a programme."

"Do tell me the programme," I demanded eagerly.

"No," he said, "that I shall never tell. But I shall send you the first orchestral score and parts as soon as Jurgenson, my publisher, has them ready."

We parted with the expectation of meeting again in America during the following winter, but, alas, in October came the cable announcing his death from cholera, and a few days later arrived a package from Moscow containing the score and parts of his Symphony No. 6, the "Pathetique." It was like a message from the dead. I immediately put the work into rehearsal and gave it its first performance in America on the following Sunday. Its success was immediate and profound. We gave it many repetitions that winter and I have played it since in concerts all over the United States. Other orchestras have cultivated it with equal assiduity, and in fact for me the time came several years ago when I cried a halt and let the work lie fallow, as it had evidently been over-played and its high-strung rhythms had excited the nerves of executants and audiences so often that they were in danger of being overstrained.

Ignace Paderewski made his first appearance in America in 1891, and I conducted his first five orchestral concerts. He came under the auspices of Steinway and Sons, and they told me that the gross receipts for the first concert were only five hundred dollars! His playing as well as his personality, however, immediately took our public by storm, and I do not think that since the days of Franz Liszt there has been any other travelling virtuoso in whom the man was as fascinating as the artist. People who have wondered how it was possible for him when the Great War began to throw himself so fully equipped at every point into the struggle to achieve national unity for Poland, do not realize that he was, consciously or unconsciously, preparing himself for just this opportunity all his life. He had always dreamed of a united and independent Poland. He knew the history of his people, their strength, and their weakness. It is said that one day he played before the Czar who, congratulating him, expressed his pleasure that a "Russian" should have achieved such eminence in his art. Paderewski answered: "I am a Pole, your Majesty," and, needless to say, was never again invited to play in Russia. His mind is one of the most extraordinary I have ever come in contact with. All the world knows what he has achieved in music—his inspired interpretations, his prodigious memory, and the subtle range of colors of his musical palette, but not so many know of his interest in literature, philosophy, and history, and it took the Great War to demonstrate that as orator and statesman he ranks as high as musician. I heard him make a speech on Poland during the Exposition in San Francisco in 1915 before an audience of ten thousand, in which he gave so eloquent a survey of Poland's history and of her needs and rights, as to rouse the people to a frenzy of enthusiasm, and I am convinced that Poland owes her national existence to-day to his statesmanship and to the sympathy which his personality created among the Allies at the Versailles Conference. I believe that Colonel House pronounced him to be the greatest statesman of the Conference, and it was only the cynical Clemenceau who said to him: "M. Paderewski, you were the greatest pianist in the world and you have chosen to descend to our level. What a pity!"

When he first came to America, his English was very incomplete but even then he demonstrated his grasp of it in unmistakable fashion. One evening he, my wife, and I dined at the house of very dear mutual friends, Mr. and Mrs. John E. Cowdin, in Gramercy Park. Cowdin had all his life been an enthusiastic polo player, and after dinner Paderewski and I admired some handsome silver trophies that he had won and that were placed in the dining-room. I said: "You see the difference between you and Johnny is that he wins his prizes in playing polo while you win yours in playing solo."

"Zat is not all ze difference!" Paderewski immediately exclaimed in his gentle Polish accents. "I am a poor Pole playing solo, but Johnny is a dear soul playing polo."

He is highly gifted as a composer, and besides a very

interesting and spiritual symphony I remember with keen pleasure his opera "Manru," which Maurice Grau brought out at the Metropolitan Opera House in 1902 and which I conducted. I cannot remember ever having worked harder toward achieving a successful première. The orchestral parts, which had been copied in Germany in a great hurry, arrived so full of mistakes that the first rehearsals were an agony of constant stopping and correcting, and these corrections went on during the entire time of preparation, and I believe that I still found two inaccuracies at the rehearsal just preceding the general rehearsal. Again and again I took some of the worst parts home and worked late into the night going through them meticulously myself, and comparing them with the orchestral score in an endeavor to bring order out of chaos. The opera received a warm welcome, but the libretto was lacking somewhat in dramatic interest; and the music, with all its genuine charm and warmth, was not able to successfully combat this lack.

I think that if Paderewski had been willing to sacrifice his marvellous career as a piano virtuoso (and that would have been a great sacrifice) he would have become one of the greatest composers of our time. It does not seem easy to unite the two careers, as they are essentially at war with each other. Liszt, the only man with whom I can compare Paderewski, recognized this fact, and at forty years of age resolutely turned his back on virtuosodom, with its life in the public glare, its excitements, crowds, and emoluments, in order to devote himself to composition. He settled in the little town of Weimar, living a life of poverty, and never again touched the piano for personal gain. Only now and then he would play in public in order to gather funds for the Beethoven monument in Bonn or for some great charity. And yet it is universally conceded that even he stopped too late and that, great as is the sum total of his contributions to creative art, he would have been still greater and able to express himself more genuinely if he had never been "the greatest pianist of his generation."

It is difficult to define the charm with which the artists of Poland seem to be imbued almost beyond any other race. It is more than a social gift. It is not the result of calculation but seems to be a combination of kindliness of heart and good breeding. Madame Marcella Sembrich has it to a supreme degree, also Jean and Edouard de Reszke, also Tim and Joe Adamowski, Paul Kochanski, and my old friend Alexander Lambert, and if the new state of Poland were composed only of such of the Polish elect as I have just mentioned it would soon become the ideal republic of the world. On the other hand, a country composed exclusively of musicians might not make a contented population, as it is well known that we need an audience to listen to us, and musicians, rightly or wrongly, have the reputation of never being willing to listen to each other.

I do not, however, mean to imply that the Poles are the exclusive possessors of personal charm. For instance, I do not know of any man who has it in greater degree than my old friend Charles Martin Loeffler, who was born in Alsace, received his musical education in France, was violinist in the private orchestra of a Russian grand duke in Nice, and, at the age of sixteen, came to America. My father immediately became very fond of him, and on Sunday afternoons, when we always had chamber-music at home in which my father played first violin and Sam Franko second, Martin Loeffler would play the

A priori I shall always say: There must be Opera in English—but at present there cannot be, as nobody knows how to sing in it. The performance however was admirable. Amato was superb and so was the orchestra, chorus and old Herty! Hats off to him too! Kindest regards to Mrs. Damrosch in which Elise joins me. Believe me, dear Walter, as ever and more proudly than ever,

Your friend

CH. M. LOEFFLER.

In 1891 I was asked to give a concert for the Orthopædic Hospital in which my friend, Mrs. John Hobart Warren, was always much interested, and in casting about for some sensational feature which would draw the public I conceived the idea of having Eugene Ysaye and Fritz Kreisler play the Bach concerto for two violins. Ysaye was then at the very zenith of his career and Kreisler had just come to America as a young violinist of great attainments and charm, and still greater promise for the future. The performance of the Bach concerto proved all that I had hoped, and after the concert Ysaye had supper with me at the old Delmonico's in Madison Square. Ysaye is not only a remarkable artist but one of the most brilliant conversationalists I have met, and during the supper he proceeded in the most fascinating way to analyze himself and Kreisler. He said: "I have arrived at the top and from now on there will be a steady decrease of my powers. I have lived my life to the full and burned the candle at both ends. For some time I shall make up in subtlety of phrasing and nuance what my technic as a violinist can no longer give, but Kreisler is on the ascendant and in a short time he will be the greater artist." It is not for me to say whether Ysaye's prophecy has come true, but no one who has heard him in his prime can forget his truly gigantic conception of the Beethoven concerto, for instance, and the mastery with which he poured out the golden flood of his music.

In 1909 I gave a Beethoven cycle at which I performed all the Beethoven symphonies and other smaller works of his in historical sequence. We had engaged Ysaye to play the Beethoven Violin Concerto, but, to my astonishment, he sent word only a week before that he must first play a violin concerto by Vitali, as he had to get his fingers into proper condition before playing the Beethoven. I remonstrated with him and explained to him that in a Beethoven cycle I could not possibly give a concerto by Vitali, even to oblige Ysaye, and suggested that he play the Vitali concerto to himself in the greenroom before the concert, but he refused to accept this amendment and I was ever so reluctantly compelled to cancel his appearance in the cycle. This caused a coolness between us which lasted several years and which I regretted exceedingly. But time is a great peacemaker. We happened to meet again quite casually a few years later, and by tacit consent this little contretemps was completely buried and we are as good friends as of yore.

Perhaps the most important and interesting great musician of France whom I have known was Camille Saint-Saëns, whom I met in 1908 when he came to America on a concert tour. He was at that time seventy years of age. His extraordinary vitality and the fluency of his playing amazed us all, and America outdid itself to honor this venerable *grand maître*. I had the great pleasure of conducting all of his concerts in New York at which he played his five piano concertos, an extraordinary feat for a man of his age. We had heard so many stories from French musicians of his "nasty temper" at rehearsals and his caustic comments on this or that phrasing in his symphonies or concertos that we were all very agreeably disappointed in finding him genial, cheerful, and grateful for what we were able to give him. He even insisted on playing the organ himself at my performance of his Symphony No. 3, which is dedicated to the memory of Liszt. I have always considered this to be his greatest work in that, with all the clarity of form and diction which is a special characteristic of his style, there is also a deep emotion which rises in the last movement to a triumphant and thrilling climax.

I saw him again in Paris during the war in the summer of 1918, and reminded him of a visit which my father had paid to him in 1876.

"That was not the first time I met your father," he quickly rejoined. "I remember very well meeting him in Weimar in 1857 while I was visiting Liszt."

In 1920 my second daughter, Gretchen, was to be married to the son of Judge Finletter of Philadelphia. The young people had met at Chaumont, France, where Finletter had been stationed at General Headquarters after the armistice and while Gretchen and her friend, Mary Schieffelin, were there as war workers. My daughter agreed enthusiastically with my suggestion that the wedding should be in Paris after my European tour with the orchestra was finished, and this to them highly important event was carried out with great success on the 17th of July, the ceremony being solemnized at the American church and the reception held at my hotel, the "France et Choiseul," in the Rue St. Honoré. As I had come to this hotel for so many years, Monsieur Mantel, the *directeur*, and all the employees from the chef down, helped on the affair with an enthusiasm which can only be found in a country like France, where all festivals of family life are treated with tremendous importance. All the reception-rooms down-stairs and the greater part of the courtyard, which had been charmingly framed in with laurel-trees and filled with inviting-looking little tables, had been placed at our disposal. All the employees of the house—including Leonie, François, Pierre, Adolph, Theo, Félice, Madeleine, Michel, and Louis, all of whom I had known during the war and even before—wore large white boutonnières and ribbons in honor of the occasion; and at four o'clock about a hundred French and American friends began to arrive from the ceremony at the church. Among these was my old friend Madame Nellie Melba, who had come over from London for the purpose, and "*le grand maître*" Camille Saint-Saëns, whom all the hotel employees immediately recognized and treated with great and fond deference.

As Saint-Saëns entered the courtyard he turned to me and said, rather testily: "Mon cher ami, pourquoi est-ce que vous n'avez-pas donné une de mes symphonies dans un de vos concerts à Paris ce printemps?" For a moment I was nonplussed what to answer. We had given three concerts in Paris and I had devoted one to the "Eroica" of Beethoven, and the other two to the César Franck D Minor, the Mozart "Jupiter," and the Dvořák "New World" symphonies, but Albert Spalding, my soloist, had played the Saint-Saëns Violin Concerto, so that his name had been represented on our programmes. Suddenly the right answer came to me: "Cher maître, don't you know that during the war I played your great Symphony No. 3 at a gala concert on the Fête Nationale at the Salle du Conservatoire for the benefit of the Croix Rouge, and here is Monsieur Cortot who played the piano part and

here Mademoiselle Boulanger who played the organ."
(Both of them were luckily standing by my side as Saint-
Saëns entered.) He was completely pacified and was
carried off in triumph to the buffet by a crowd of adoring
French musicians in order to offer him some refreshment.
Henri Casadesus told me afterward that when Saint-
Saëns arrived at the buffet he said: "I am thirsty."
"Here is some champagne," said Casadesus. "No.
That is too cold," "Well, here is chocolate." "No.
That is too hot," whereupon he took the glass of cham-
pagne and poured it into the chocolate and drank it
down with evident relish. Pretty good for a man then
eighty-two years of age!

Saint-Saëns had always preserved a great adoration
for Liszt, who had been one of the first musicians to be-
friend him in his early days, and his admiration for Liszt's
music had remained much greater than for that of Wagner.
In fact, during the war the majority of the French musicians were furious at his chauvinistic attitude toward
Wagner.

It is told that when Saint-Saëns was still a very young
man he was calling on Liszt and the servant asked him to
wait a few minutes as Liszt was engaged in another room.
Saint-Saëns, seeing a manuscript orchestral score on the
piano, sat down and proceeded with his marvellous
musicianship to read and play it at sight, when suddenly
the door opened and Liszt and Wagner rushed in, amazed
at hearing the intricate harmonies of Wagner's "Rhein-
gold" so marvellously reproduced. Wagner had just
brought the score to Liszt in order to show it to him.

During the winter of 1920–21 I accepted the co-editor-
ship for a series of music readers to be used in our public
schools, and as I had agreed to invite a small group of

distinguished French and English composers to contribute some songs for this publication, I requested Saint-Saëns to honor us with two. He readily complied, and in the summer of 1921 invited me to come to his apartment as he had the songs all ready. When I called, he immediately sat down at the piano and from his very neatly written manuscript played them for me, begging me to observe that he had made the accompaniment exceedingly simple in order that "the American school-teachers should not be too much puzzled by it." For one of the songs composed in honor of the aviators of the war, he had even written the words himself, and for the other he had taken words by La Fontaine.

He called at my hotel in August of 1921. He seemed to me to have grown more feeble, but seeing on my piano an edition of Beethoven's piano sonatas, edited by von Bülow, with which I always like to travel as I find the playing of these sonatas very agreeable and restful between the inevitable irritations of travel, Saint-Saëns suddenly bristled up and became very angry at a certain rather complicated fingering which Bülow had given to a piano passage, as his fingers had not been adapted by nature to rapid playing.

"This is the way it should be played," said Saint-Saëns, as he sat down at the piano and proceeded to let his fingers, though still clad in gray lisle gloves, run up the keys with incredible swiftness, like little gray mice. This extreme dexterity never left him. I had heard him but a month before at a musical given by Widor in his honor and in which Saint-Saëns played the piano part in his own "Septet with Trumpet." His fingers literally ran away with him, and every time there was a quick passage, he accelerated the tempo to such an extent that the other players simply had to scramble after him as best they could.

He died last winter at eighty-four years of age, and all Paris, governmental, artistic, and scientific, united in giving him imposing and significant obsequies. The respect which the young men of France have for their old masters is something exceedingly sympathetic to an American observer. Whenever Saint-Saëns appeared among them they would hover around with eager deference, flushing with pride as he would say something to the one or the other. In fact, Widor, who is perhaps ten years younger than Saint-Saëns, always insisted on treating him as if he, Widor, were a young, deferential schoolboy in the presence of his great master. Indeed, they reserve the words "*grand maître*" only for their very choicest men of the arts and the learned professions.

With Lillian Nordica I made a joint tour through New England, giving Wagner concerts. As she had by that time arrived at true prima donna estate she had a private car in which she lived and in which I also had a room. The poor lady arrived on the first day with an attack of bronchitis so acute that she could hardly speak. Her voice sounded like the croak of a raven. I have never seen any woman in such abject despair, walking up and down the little dining-room of the car like a caged tigress, every now and then touching a note on the upright piano which had been placed therein, and trying her voice. She was clad in a wrapper, and tears and misery had ravaged her comely face so that it was hardly recognizable. I, of course, thought that she would not sing that evening, but at seven she disappeared into her room and an hour later emerged clad in a magnificent toilet, with her diamond tiara on the top of her head and her face wonderfully made up. When she appeared before her audience with whom she was an old favorite, her manner had all the regal but smiling charm of yore. Her voice? Well, that is another story.

During that entire week this tragi-comedy would repeat itself every day. Her bronchitis never left her, and from my room I could hear this poor woman, as she entered the dining-room, touch the piano furtively and try to sing a few notes. It was agony, and I have hated private cars ever since, and am quite content to occupy a drawing-room or a berth in a regular sleeping-car when I travel. It is certainly more cheerful.

When we finally arrived in New York, where we expected to give two Wagner concerts, lo and behold, the clouds suddenly lifted. Nordica was her old self, and while the diamond tiara could not have looked more regal nor the smile have been more ingratiating than at Worcester, Massachusetts, her voice had again regained its old charm and the cry of the Valkyrie and *Isolde's* Liebestod brought back to the memory of her audiences the happy days when Nordica, Schumann-Heink, and Jean de Reszke had electrified them at the Metropolitan.

Madame Nordica was, however, not the only American artist with whom I came into frequent professional contact and who had achieved an eminence equal to that of the best of Europe. David Bispham became a member of my opera company in 1896. He came of an old Quaker family in Philadelphia, into whose lives music had never penetrated. How Bispham got his intense musical temperament is one of those mysteries that the laws of neither heredity nor environment can explain.

He was a man of some means, and finding the local atmosphere in which he lived uncongenial to his evident artistic needs, he went to Europe. He had a vibrant barytone voice, studied singing with Lamperti, and gradually began to make successful appearances on the stage, especially in England. In my company he achieved especial successes as *Telramund*, *Kurvenal*, and *Beckmesser*, also as *Roger Chillingworth* in my own opera on Hawthorne's "Scarlet Letter." He adored a part in which he could "act." In fact, he sometimes overacted. His musical memory, especially in his later years, was not always to be relied on, but the more he forgot the words the more intense his acting became, and as *Chillingworth*, in which rôle he really never quite learned the text, he fairly contorted his body in giving expression to the sinister machinations and revengeful desires of that demon.

As a man he was of a singularly delightful, almost childlike disposition. The things of this life rarely existed for him as they really were. He saw them through the glass of his own exuberant imagination. The mysterious, the extraordinary, always fascinated him, and he therefore often became the prey of designing people who took easy advantage of his trusting nature. He was a most generous colleague and more free from jealousy than most operatic singers. Rehearsals, no matter how long, were to him as the breath to his nostrils, and he would often spend hours before his glass in the dressing-room making up his face for some character part in close imitation of a famous picture he had seen at the Uffizi in Florence or the Royal Gallery in London. He loved to enact a villain, but, on the other hand, his doglike devotion to *Tristan* as *Kurvenal* often brought tears to our eyes.

My wife and I became very fond of him and, later on, when he and I joined the Metropolitan Opera House Company, again under Maurice Grau, we would often take our meals together on the long Western trips to and from California.

He was exceedingly irascible if servants did not carry out his orders properly, and he would berate them in his very resonant voice with a distinctness of utterance worthy of the *Comédie Française*. One morning we were seated at breakfast in the dining-car of our train when the colored waiter brought him his coffee, which was so weak that a drop of the so-called cream turned it a bluish gray. "Take away that coffee!" Bispham thundered. "It is not fit to drink. It is too weak!"

"Oh, no, sah!" expostulated gently the waiter. "Dat coffee am all right. It's de cream what's too powerful strong!"

At that time leather suitcases were just making their first appearance and I had bought one and carried it about with me. Bispham noticed it and said, in his extreme Kensington English, which he had carefully acquired over there: "Walter, that is a very nice bag you have there. I think I will buy four of them, each one a little smaller than the other, so that I can put them all inside each other."

"Why," I said, "David, aren't you going to pack anything else inside of those bags?"

"Ha, ha, ha!" laughed David. "Walter, you are always having your little joke!"

Whenever my opera company came to Boston the supers, when an extra group or crowd of knights or peasants, etc., were necessary, were always taken from Harvard University. This became a source of enormous revenue to the doorkeeper at the stage entrance. Our stage-manager paid him twenty-five cents for each super, but he not only pocketed this money himself but charged the students anywhere from fifty cents upward, according to the popularity of the opera, for the privilege of hearing it from the stage. In consequence we often had the most wonderful athletic specimens that the ardent pursuit of sport produces among college men, delighting our eyes as the curtain rose, and the knights and nobles in the second act of "Tannhäuser," for instance, clad in magnificent robes, would march in and solemnly listen to the contest of song in the castle of the Landgrave of Thuringia.

But they were not all athletes, and I remember one real student among them. The curtain went up on the first act of "Lohengrin" and, to my amazement as I looked up from my conductor's stand, I saw one of these college boys, dressed in the armor and cloak of one of King Henry's knights, calmly standing at the foot of the throne, large spectacles on his nose, busily following the action of the opera from a libretto which he held in his hand and close to his eyes.

Another time a much more terrible occurrence took place, but very much "behind the scenes." I was in Boston with the Grau Opera Company and, at a Saturday matinée, "Carmen" was given with Madame Calvé in the title rôle. I did not conduct that opera, and happened to saunter on the stage after the third act. I found the whole company in a state of only half-suppressed merriment. While Madame A—— was singing *Micaela's* air on the stage, in which she implores *Don Jose* to leave *Carmen* and return to his old mother, one of these young wretches from Harvard had crept into her dressing-room, and in order to have a triumphant souvenir to hang up in his rooms at college he had stolen her— No, not her stockings, but another important part of her wearing apparel. Madame A——, on return-ing to her dressing-room, had discovered the theft. Her maid had told the wardrobe mistress, the wardrobe mis-tress had told the stage carpenter, he had repeated it to the stage-manager, and so forth and so on, the whole company revelling in it, especially as Madame A—— was herself of New England parentage and was considered an exceptionally proper young person.

XII

ROMANCE

"At last!" my readers will exclaim. "All these reminiscences about musicians are well enough, but it is their love-affairs that we are interested in. Think of Beethoven and the Countess Giucciardi, of Berlioz and Miss Smithson, of Liszt and the Countess d'Agoult, of Wagner and Madame Wesendonck. Musicians are so romantic, so different from ordinary men. They wear their hair longer; they affect delightful eccentricities of conduct and of clothes; the ordinary humdrum of life does not touch them, and they live only in the higher and rarer atmosphere of art and poetry." Therefore woman, who is so much more spiritual than man, sometimes thinks in her unguarded moments that true happiness can only be found by falling in love with an artist or, better still, having him fall in love with her.

Without venturing to place myself in the same category as the great musicians mentioned above, I nevertheless propose in this chapter to give a full and detailed account of all my love-affairs—all, or at least of as many as can be crowded into the confines of a chapter. I have lived a great many years and my life, like that of other artists, has been full to the brim of all kinds of interesting and fascinating happenings, and in order that my readers may gain a true picture I shall begin at the very beginning, promising to tell the truth, the whole truth, and nothing but the truth.

Terrible as it may seem, I have to confess at the outset

that I began my life as a gay *Lothario* at the tender age of eight. My family were then living in Breslau, Silesia, and the rear of the house in which our apartment was situated opened on a large courtyard, upon which several other houses faced. This courtyard naturally became the playground of all the children who lived around it. We were particularly intimate with one family, the children of which consisted of an elder brother, already in the university, who affected the appearance and manner of the great German poet, Friedrich Schiller. He was supposed to have great poetical talents, and it was darkly rumored that he had already written two tragedies. I was greatly in awe of him, but his younger brother, who was a boy of my own age, was my classmate in school— the gymnasium, as it was called. And then there was a sister, little Lorchen, seven years of age, with blue eyes and many blond curls. I had played with her and her brother for several months before I suddenly discovered that her curls were beautiful, like spun gold, and that there was something particularly ingratiating in the blue of her eyes. I had an intense desire to put my arms around her, but, strange to say, the consciousness of this filled me with such anger that instead of giving way to it I took the first opportunity to slap this darling little child most unmercifully. To this day I cannot explain my unnatural depravity, and I wish that I could now—over fifty years later—meet little Lorchen again to tell her that this slap was my only way of letting her know how much I loved her. Alas, she never knew, and as we emigrated to America soon thereafter, I never had the time nor the opportunity to overcome my shyness and to place my love at her feet in proper fashion.

I cannot remember any new passions from then on

until my sixteenth year. Lorchen's picture soon and completely faded from my memory. I was tremendously taken up, first with learning English, New York school life, my musical studies, playing marbles, flying kites, and building ships to sail on the pond in Central Park. But when I was fifteen a little Frenchman came to New York and presented himself to my father with his two little daughters, Louise and Jeanne, who were both pianist prodigies. Louise was fifteen and little Jeanne only twelve. The latter was truly remarkable, and her playing made quite a stir in New York at the time. But I was singularly drawn toward the older sister, Louise. Their mother had died when the children were very young and Louise had quite taken the mother's place and watched over Jeanne with a maternal solicitude and tenderness truly remarkable in so young a girl. She played exquisitely herself, and I can still hear the velvety touch of her fingers in the A Flat Etude of Chopin, but in her adoration for her younger sister's more brilliant talent she completely effaced herself, and it was only with difficulty that one could get her to play if her sister was present. They lived in a little French boarding-house and I used to love to go there in the evening, and while Jeanne would play for us in most brilliant fashion Louise would sit at a table in the centre of the room and, under the mellow light of a centre lamp, would darn stockings or deftly refashion some dress which Jeanne was to wear at her next concert. Louise had the gentlest of brown eyes, and her face and bearing breathed a tranquillity and sweetness rarely found in the agitating nervous life of to-day. She was not talkative, but when she spoke her eyes would smile and crinkle up in very ingratiating fashion.

I had certainly outgrown the slapping age, but had not yet developed the courage to declare my adoration. I seem to have been quite content to sit next to Louise, and to look into her gentle eyes, or watch her deft fingers as they pleated and sewed and did all those clever things which women's fingers alone know how to do. That spring, alas, the father and his daughters returned to France and I have never seen them again.

But so inconstant is youth that the following year I fell madly in love with Madame Teresa Carreno, of whom I have already written in an earlier chapter. I was sixteen and she was twenty-four, radiantly beautiful, brilliantly educated, and a remarkable linguist, speaking English, German, French, Spanish, and Italian with equal fluency. But for me her eyes spoke a language even more eloquent than her tongue, and it was small wonder that I was bowled over completely. On my first concert tour, her beauty, her exquisite playing, and the languorous half-tropical charms of the South through which we were touring was a combination I could not withstand.

But my schoolboy adoration received a severe shock when, on the last day of our tour, a handsome and very robust Italian barytone, by the name of Tagliapietra, came to meet her and I found that she was madly in love with him. They were married a short time after.

She, too, seems to have been unconscious of my adoration. Thirty-two years later, at a dinner given at the Hotel Plaza in honor of my twenty-fifth anniversary as a conductor, she was present and in my speech of thanks I humorously referred to her as the *grande passion* of my early youth. She afterward told my sister: "I never knew that Walter had felt like that about me!"

To proceed with my confessions. The following year

I met—but, alas, this chapter is already overcrowded and I shall have to continue the (to me) so fascinating recital of my various romances in my next book of memoirs, which I expect to publish in about twenty years.

XIII

THE ORATORIO SOCIETY OF NEW YORK

My father had always considered that a study of the oratorios of Bach and Handel was a highly important foundation for the young musician, and I had spent many hours with him in studying their scores and imitating their form in my own counterpointal work. Bach's "St. Matthew's Passion" and Handel's "Messiah," "Samson," and "Judas Maccabæus" I knew virtually by heart. My father also believed the development of amateur choruses to be a very strong factor in the musical growth of a people. Under his inspiration the chorus of the Oratorio Society constantly grew in numbers and technical proficiency; but it suffered from the great dearth of men singers, especially tenors. The terribly one-sided condition of musical development in our country, proceeding almost exclusively on feminine lines, showed itself markedly in this branch of the art. Many of the men singers who in one way or another had been cajoled or coerced into joining a choral society, had often to be drilled in their parts like children, though without a child's quickness of perception. The result was that the labor of training was incessant and the mistakes of one year repeated themselves inevitably the next. In rehearsing such oratorios as Handel's "Messiah" or Bach's "St. Matthew's Passion," for instance, a good routined conductor could always prophesy beforehand what mistakes the chorus was going to make.

During my father's time the sopranos in the Oratorio

Society were of overwhelming power and quality; but this was largely because my mother, when we came to America, gave up all solo singing in public and devoted herself enthusiastically to leading the soprano choir. Her voice was phenomenal in its strength and quality, and when, as in some fugal chorus of Handel's, the sopranos finally enter on the main theme, her triumphant voice would carry everything along with it. She always sang by heart, her beautiful, deep-set eyes fixed on the conductor, and when this conductor happened to be her own husband or son there was a devotion and a love in them that I can never forget.

To maintain a choral society in a huge city like New York is doubly difficult because of the many temptations and distractions that beset its members in so large a metropolis and threaten the regular attendance at rehearsals. I have always felt, therefore, that the many splendid performances which the society has given, in its long existence of forty-nine years, are especially to its credit. The rehearsals with these amateur singers, however, demand from the conductor ten times the energy, patience, and vitality that are necessary with an orchestra composed of trained professionals. And yet there is a charm in working with devoted amateurs. My father loved it, and even during the harassing labors of founding and maintaining the German opera at the Metropolitan, he always turned to the regular Thursday-evening chorus rehearsals of the Oratorio Society as a change and rest. I confess that I have similarly enjoyed the almost primitive study necessary with an amateur chorus after a day spent with my orchestra, and I look back with the deepest pleasure on the many years during which I conducted the Oratorio Society.

Smaller cities should be able to develop choral societies far more easily than New York. Toronto, Canada, has always been an example of what can be accomplished in that direction. There are four choral societies of high merit there, among which perhaps the Mendelssohn Choir, founded by Doctor Vogt, ranks highest. The English have an inherited love and talent for choral singing, and in Toronto the weekly rehearsal is the one "dissipation" of the week, and is eagerly looked forward to by the singers. I have heard the Mendelssohn Choir repeatedly on their visits to New York and have been thrilled by the beauty and volume of their tone and the precision of their singing.

I have written elsewhere of the great musical festival which was projected and conducted by my father in May, 1881. For the great chorus of twelve hundred, which was its outstanding feature, the four hundred singers of the Oratorio Society formed the backbone, and I was intrusted with the drilling of two other sections of the festival chorus. As I had been the accompanist and organist for years at all the rehearsals of the Oratorio Society and had officiated as conductor of the Newark Harmonic Society for three years after the festival, I was technically well equipped to take over the directorship of the Oratorio Society when it was offered to me after my father's death in 1885.

I conducted the last concert of that season, Bach's "St. Matthew's Passion," and found that the affection and reverence which the chorus cherished for my father made them help me devotedly in my difficult beginning.

For the following season I cast about to find a new work to mark my entry into this field, and decided that a concert performance of Wagner's "Parsifal" would in-

terest the New York public. The sacred character of
the work, the importance and beauty of its choral portions,
and the fact that as yet its music was almost unknown
seemed to me to invite such a performance, even though
Wagner had conceived it for dramatic representation and
with a stage-setting. He had intended the work for performance only in Bayreuth, but in 1882, when it was first
produced there, he himself had given me an orchestral
score in manuscript of the choral Finale from the first
act to present to my father, so that he might produce
it in concert form in New York.

During a visit to London in the spring of 1886 I called
on the London representative of the publishers of "Parsifal" and asked whether an orchestral score of the complete work could be purchased. He told me it could, but
that its purchase would not entitle me to a performance
of the work, and that if I used it for a performance I
would have to pay a fine of fifty pounds. I told him I
was quite ready to pay such a fine as I wanted it for a
concert performance in New York, and promptly bought
an orchestral score and had the orchestral parts copied
from it.

Owing to my connection with the Metropolitan Opera
House I was able to give the work an exceptional cast.
Kundry was sung by Marianne Brandt, who had sung it
in Bayreuth at one of the first performances. Max Alvary was cast for the title rôle, and Emil Fischer for
Gurnemanz. Alvary became ill shortly before the performance and his part was taken by another young
tenor of our company, a Mr. Kraemer. The choral portions were sung by the Oratorio Society with thrilling
effect.

This was the first performance of "Parsifal" outside of

Bayreuth, and it made a sensation but also aroused quite a controversy in the newspapers as to its fitness for the concert room. Good and weighty arguments can be produced on both sides. At a performance in concert a great deal is lost to many people, especially to those whose imagination cannot function without the stimulus of scenery, costumes, and dramatic action; but at that time this was the only opportunity for American music-lovers, who could not make the long trip to Bayreuth, to become acquainted with the music. To many listeners the choral portions, especially those centring in the religious ceremonies in the Hall of the Holy Grail, were just as impressive, if not more so, than in a scenic representation. To-day, and generally speaking, I would rather hear the music from "Parsifal" with my eyes closed. My imagination, stimulated by the music, can paint the scenic and dramatic investiture far more idealistically than any actual stage representation, but I do not claim this as a truth for all, but only as my individual preference.

We gave two concert performances at the Metropolitan Opera House (public rehearsal and concert), and over three thousand people listened with rapt attention at each rendition.

Years after, in 1903, when the then director of opera at the Metropolitan, Heinrich Conried, announced his intention of giving a stage performance of "Parsifal," I received a letter from Madame Cosima Wagner, saying that she had heard that I possessed the score and orchestral parts of the work. She begged me not to give them to Mr. Conried, as the *meister* had left absolute directions in his will that stage representations of this work were to be reserved for all time for Bayreuth. She had heard

that I had given a concert performance and wondered
how I had gotten permission.

I wrote to her and explained how I had obtained the
score and had sent the "fifty pounds fine" to the publishers, according to my agreement with them. I then
received another letter from her, as follows:

DEAR MR. DAMROSCH:

Thank you very much for your kind lines and the expression of
your feelings for Parsifal, which, of course, is never to be given out
of Bayreuth; but concerning the production at concert, there has
been made a very limited choice of fragments, which is not to be
extended. The choice, done by the master, is as follows:

1. Prelude, close of the first act,—nothing of the second.
2. Verwandlungsmusik—close of the third act.
3. Amfortasklage
4. Charfreitagszauber

I am astonished that for £50 you got the allowance (permission)
to execute the whole Parsifal in concert and I will ask the publisher
(about it).

Concerning the performance on the stage, I still hope that the cultivated part of the public at New York won't agree to it.

Receive, dear Mr. Damrosch, with my best thanks, my kindest
regards.

C. WAGNER

Bayreuth, 6 Juli, 1903.

Conried, however, obtained his parts elsewhere, and
gave a stage performance that winter. Since then the
copyright on "Parsifal" has run out and it has been produced all over the world.

During my search for modern works I endeavored also
to keep alive the interest in the old oratorios. I owed
much to them, and their dignity and genuine expression
of religious feeling had been a most important factor in
my early and earliest education. As a boy I sang alto in
the Oratorio Society chorus and at sixteen was promoted

to the dignity of accompanist at rehearsals. At this work I became quite an expert, and if my father stopped at a certain place to correct the chorus, I would, of course, know beforehand what he wanted, and would hammer out the right note for the altos or the tenors—it was usually the tenors—or would resort, even while they were singing, to all manner of expedients, such as playing the critical intervals an octave higher in order to keep up the pitch or to define them more clearly. As both my mother and Tante Marie sang in the chorus, there would be the four of us going home together after a rehearsal, discussing this or that point which needed more drilling, or a weakness that needed bolstering up, or we would express mutual enthusiasm over some chorus particularly well sung that evening. Naturally the refrain after almost every rehearsal was: "How can we get ten more first tenors?" America did not seem to grow them, and as even basses were not as plentiful as they should have been, it seemed almost as if the future American composer should write choruses for women only. If at the voice trial of new applicants, which usually took place before or after rehearsal, that *rara avis*, a tenor, was found, we glowed with delight and speculated as to whether he would really turn up at the next rehearsal and become a regular member. It cannot be claimed that tenors are to be found in profusion even to-day, but there has been an immense development in the quality of choral singers. Their voices are better trained, they read better at sight, and the general increase of interest in music manifests itself very strongly in this direction.

In 1892 I gave a Handel festival in honor of the one-hundred-and-fiftieth anniversary of the first performance of Handel's "Messiah" in Dublin under his own direction, in 1742, followed by the one which King George II and his court attended, and when the crowd was so great that the management requested the gentlemen not to wear their swords nor the ladies their hoop-skirts, in order to enable as many as possible to hear the work of "Mr. Handel." At this performance, when the Hallelujah chorus began, with its mighty climax, "King of Kings, Hallelujah! Hallelujah!" King George, overcome with emotion, arose and remained standing until the end. Naturally the entire audience rose in imitation of their royal master, and Great Britain has continued this custom ever since. As this was a fitting homage both to the Almighty and to the composer who in this chorus so marvellously voiced man's adoration for him, my father introduced the custom at his own first performance of the "Messiah," in 1874, and the Oratorio Society audiences have followed it to this day.

An interesting account of the kind of orchestra Handel may have employed is given in a description of a memorial service of the "Messiah," sung in Westminster Abbey shortly after his death. I decided to reproduce such an orchestra as far as possible at our festival performance. The main characteristics consisted in the doubling up of the string parts in the choruses with oboes and bassoons and in duplicating the trumpets and kettle-drums in the choral climaxes. The effect of this was most remarkable. I had placed an additional oboe with every three violins and an additional bassoon for every three violoncellos, with a few contrabassoons and contrabass clarinets to strengthen the double basses and to take the part of the serpent—an instrument which has become obsolete. The doubling up of trumpets and kettle-drums in the climaxes did not make them sound louder, but more full.

For the first time in my experience the sound of the orchestra was not completely buried in the avalanche of tone from a large chorus of three hundred and fifty voices. The orchestral accompaniments supported and supplemented the chorus in a way that perhaps only a very large and mellow church organ might.

In Handel's time he himself usually sat at the organ and filled in with masterly improvisations many of the harmonies for which in his score he had written only the bass, with figures indicating the harmonies which the organist should improvise. Since then various musicians have endeavored to supply these harmonies in permanent fashion by writing them for other instruments in the orchestra, principally for clarinets and bassoons. As most concert-halls are but poorly supplied with organs, these arrangements offered a kind of substitute, and the one most in use was that of Robert Franz. He was a German composer of very lovely songs, and a great admirer of Handel, but, curiously enough, his arrangements were very bad and not in keeping with the Handelian spirit. Mozart also had written accompaniments to supply the missing harmonies for a performance of the "Messiah" in Vienna at a hall in which there was no church organ. His additions, especially in the air "The people that walked in darkness," are of such transcendent beauty that when I proceeded in my work of restoring the Handelian orchestra to its original form my courage failed me completely as I came to this air. It was as if one master had found a painting by another and had encircled it in a frame of such beauty as to enhance the value of the original picture. I could not bear to disturb it, but the clarinets and bassoons of Robert Franz were thrown out by me with great gusto.

Another novel and interesting feature of our festival was a scenic stage performance of a charming pastoral of Handel's "Acis and Galatea." This proved to have dramatic qualities which in their appeal seemed way beyond that of the many Italian operas which Handel has written. The cast was excellent. The part of *Galatea* was sung by Madame de Vere, a charming coloratura singer; the shepherd *Acis* by William Rieger, one of our best young concert tenors; and *Polyphemus*, the giant, by that master artist, Emil Fischer. The scene represented a landscape of classic beauty, and all the participants were clad in very charming Greek shepherd costumes. The scene in which *Polyphemus*, coming upon the shepherd lovers, lifts a huge rock and in jealous rage kills *Acis*, was done with such dramatic intensity as to thrill our audiences. The performance was a real event, as this work had perhaps not been given in its dramatic form since the time of Handel; but, curiously enough, it roused but little interest, for, whereas all the other performances of the festival were crowded to the doors, we had but half an audience at our two performances of the pastoral. It came about twenty years too early, and I think that to-day, especially if given under the auspices of the Metropolitan Opera, it would arouse wide-spread interest.

This spring (1922) I was in Munich and the town was in great excitement over the approaching performance of Handel's "Acis and Galatea" in dramatic form. Their conductor, Bruno Walter, said to me: "We are very proud of this stage performance, as it is the first since Handel's time." He was amazed and, as he told me, much chagrined when I informed him that I had given it in New York nearly thirty years ago. He gave it a beautiful performance. I had costumed my singers in classic Greek, but the Munich stage director had given the work an additional and rather piquant flavor by dressing the singers and dancers as in Handel's time, when all performers, in no matter what age their plays were supposed to take place, wore the costumes and huge periwigs of their own period.

In the summer of 1898 we were much excited by the dramatic accounts of Admiral Dewey's victory in Manila Bay, and it seemed to me fitting to celebrate it by composing a "Te Deum" for soloists, chorus, and orchestra. In order to give my "Manila Te Deum" an appropriate character, I used several of the bugle-calls of the American army and navy as a *cantus firmus*, around which I wove the fugal developments of the voices of the chorus. In the last chorus, "O Lord, in thee have I trusted; let me never be confounded," I used the "Star-Spangled Banner" in similar fashion.

The work received its first performance at a concert of the Oratorio Society, December 3, 1898, and marked the introduction of my brother as regular conductor of the society. The following spring I was invited to conduct it at a Dewey celebration in Chicago, and on February 6, 1900, I directed it again at a special performance given in Carnegie Hall, the proceeds of which were to be used toward the building of an arch in honor of Admiral Dewey. This arch, however, was never built, and the several thousand dollars which resulted from our concert were finally donated by the Dewey Arch Committee to a philanthropic purpose. Our two guests of honor at this performance were Admiral Dewey, in a box on one side of the hall, and Theodore Roosevelt, at that time Governor of New York, in a box on the other side. Roosevelt was

to make an appropriate address, and as the victor of
Manila Bay was present and the entire occasion was one
of jubilant admiration for our navy, we expected one
of Roosevelt's most flaming patriotic addresses on the
glories of the American navy. But, alas, that evening
his mind was completely occupied with things nearer
home, and after a few very courteous remarks about my
music, he launched forth into a terrific speech on the
Street Cleaning Department of New York and the
"duty of every citizen to vote at the primaries"!

In 1892 I gave the first performance in America of
Saint-Saëns's opera of "Samson and Delilah." This
work is admirably adapted for concert performance, and
many portions of it are far more effective in this form than
on the stage. The music is lovely and of great melodic
simplicity, and many of the choruses are written in oratorio form. At stage performances the dramatic climax
of the second act, in which *Delilah* appears jubilantly at
the door of her palace, shaking *Samson's* red wig triumphantly at the admiring high priest and soldiers, is really
an anticlimax, and excites our risibilities much more
than our sorrow that the God-given strength of the
mighty soldier has left him.

From my father I have inherited a deep admiration for
Hector Berlioz and have conducted many performances
of his greater works—the "Damnation of Faust," the
"Requiem Mass," "Romeo and Juliet," and the first
rendition in America of his "Te Deum."

Another novelty which I produced with the Oratorio
Society in 1889 was the "Missa Solemnis" of Edward
Grell. This work created a sensation. Its composer
was virtually unknown except locally in Berlin, where he
had been a teacher of counterpoint and composition in the

first half of the nineteenth century. He had lived himself so completely into the style of the Italian masters of the seventeenth and eighteenth centuries that modern harmonies simply did not exist for him, and his "Missa Solemnis" is conceived absolutely in the manner of the early masters of ecclesiastical music. It is written for four choruses of four parts each and four solo quartets. There is absolutely no accompaniment, and the purity of these sixteen-part harmonies without any admixture of instruments produces truly celestial effects. The four choruses which are generally used antiphonally with the solo quartets, produce thrilling climaxes, and the *Benedictus* especially gives an impression of ecstatic beauty.

I have written elsewhere of my first performance of the "Christus," by Liszt. I also produced "St. Christopher," by Horatio Parker, distinguished American musician and composer. This work, however, did not prove as effective as his "Hora Novissima." It seemed to fall between two stools, as it was neither an opera nor an oratorio.

I gave, of course, many renditions of the oratorios of Handel, Haydn, and Mendelssohn, and inaugurated the custom of an annual performance of Bach's "St. Matthew's Passion" during Holy Week. I am happy to say that I succeeded in "popularizing" this mighty work, so that now it draws a huge and devout audience whenever it is given. But, generally speaking, the interest in the older oratorios is waning, not only in New York but all over the country. The ears of our audiences have lost pleasure in the simpler harmonies of Handel and Haydn, and, accustomed to the richer orchestration of to-day, find the accompaniments of the Handelian orchestra thin and archaic. Something of the simple and naïve reli-

gious faith that inspired the old oratorios has also gone,
and the composer has not yet been found who can voice
the faith and aspirations of to-day. It is a pity that the
old oratorio form should therefore be neglected. I think,
however, that it is not dead but only sleeps, and will
awaken again.

In 1898 I retired as conductor of the Oratorio Society,
owing to the pressure of my operatic and orchestral work,
and my brother Frank was elected as my successor. He
is two years older than I and has always shared my love
and enthusiasm for music in an equal degree. He studied
the piano as a boy, but had always insisted that his talent
was not great enough to warrant making music his profession; and therefore, at the age of seventeen, he with
great courage determined to go out West and begin a
business career. Arrived in Denver, Colorado, with one
hundred dollars in his pocket, he proceeded, in the manner
of our American young men who have no intention of becoming a burden on their parents, to earn his own living.

He began at the very bottom and slowly worked his
way upward, but suffered intensely during his first years
in Denver from the almost total lack of music there. He
had drunk of it in such generous quantities in New York
that it had become a larger part of his very life than he
had realized; and in order to satisfy his need he founded
a choral society with which he gave some of the old
oratorios, and with characteristic audacity he supplemented this with an orchestra composed of a handful of
professionals then playing at the Denver theatres and a
few amateurs. The citizens of Denver, realizing that he
was a real musician in spite of his modest estimate of
himself, urged him to give up business and turn altogether to music.

At the time of my father's death Frank had become virtually the moving force in all the higher musical enterprises of Denver. It seemed to me that the time had come to urge him to return to New York and together with me continue the work my father had begun. He was promptly engaged as chorus master at the Metropolitan Opera House, and also became more and more active in pedagogic work, for which he had a special enthusiasm which has never waned.

His activities extended in many directions. He founded the Young People's Concerts at Carnegie Hall, and became supervisor of music in the public schools of New York, completely reforming the teaching of music. The good effects of this are felt to this day. He also founded the People's Choral Union, in which working men and women were taught singing and the rudiments of music and then promoted into a chorus of twelve hundred voices which studied and performed the old oratorios of Handel and Haydn.

He officiated as conductor of the Oratorio Society from 1898 until 1912, and during this period conducted first performances in New York of Edward Elgar's "The Dream of Gerontius" and "The Apostles," Anton Dvořák's "Stabat Mater," Gabriel Pierné's "Children's Crusade," Johannes Brahms's "Song of Fate," and Wolf-Ferrari's "La Vita Nuova."

His interest in the pedagogy of music culminated in the founding of a music-school—the Institute of Musical Art —which was liberally endowed by James Loeb and others, and which has developed into one of the few great music-schools of this country and Europe. This school soon began to assume such proportions as to demand all of his time and vitality. He therefore retired from other public work, with the exception of the conductorship of the Society of Musical Art, a unique chorus of sixty-five professional singers, giving only two concerts during the season, representing the highest that can be attained in choral singing. For its programmes he drew upon the rich and partly unknown treasures of the *a capella* choruses of such masters as Palestrina, Orlando di Lasso, Cornelius, and Brahms; and as this chorus was composed of the very elect of New York's church and concert singers he obtained results ravishing in their beauty.

When we were boys together we quarrelled dreadfully and outrageously. Frank would try to assert his two years' seniority over me and I would resent this with both hands and feet. I remember my mother resolutely separating us and giving me a little room to myself, as that seemed the only way to achieve peace between us. But I am happy to say that since 1885, when Frank returned to New York, we have lived and worked together in absolute harmony and mutual helpfulness. In fact, the unity between us has been so complete that we are now inclined by contrast to consider each other as having been exceptionally devilish and nasty during those early boyhood years. I know, of course, that the blame was entirely his, as he was so overbearing and presuming because of the accident of his earlier birth, while he is equally convinced that I was altogether too cheeky for my age and it was absolutely necessary for my own good and future welfare to put me where I belonged.

In 1919 I was again asked to assume the direction of the Oratorio Society. Their affairs had not prospered after my brother had relinquished the conductorship. A huge debt threatened to engulf them, and, while I was overwhelmed with work in connection with the New York Symphony Orchestra, with which I gave over a hundred concerts every winter, I could not resist their appeal and promised to stay by them until they could find a permanent conductor to their liking.

I am glad to say that the man was found in Albert Stoessel. He had been a bandmaster in the A. E. F. during the war, had been chosen as teacher of conducting at the bandmaster's school in Chaumont, which I had founded for General Pershing, and had become my assistant conductor at the rehearsals of the Oratorio Society. The chorus were delighted with him, and he was elected as regular conductor of the society in 1920. He has already conducted two highly successful seasons, and I think that our beloved old society will have many years of life and success under his direction.

XIV

THE NEW YORK SYMPHONY ORCHESTRA

When my father died there were only three symphony orchestras in America, the New York Symphony, the New York Philharmonic (Thomas formed his travelling orchestra from this), and the Boston Symphony. The last of these was supported by Major Higginson, and was the only one whose members received weekly salaries for a season of thirty weeks, met every morning for rehearsal, and devoted themselves exclusively to the playing of symphonic music. It was the first so-called "permanent orchestra" founded in America. The New York orchestras at that time played only a very small number of symphony concerts, for each of which they had about three rehearsals. Their members added to their earnings by playing in odd concerts, opera, theatre, in fact, in almost anything that they could find.

To-day the New York Symphony is splendidly maintained as a permanent orchestra through the generosity of its president, Mr. Flagler. The Philharmonic is similarly supported by liberal contributions from various sources, and other orchestras in Philadelphia, Chicago, Detroit, Minneapolis, Cincinnati, St. Louis, San Francisco, and Los Angeles use from a hundred thousand dollars a year upward, donated by their respective citizens, over and above the receipts from the sale of tickets, in order to maintain themselves as permanent symphonic organizations. Without such subsidies these orchestras could not exist, as, even though the concerts are crowded, the expenditures are much greater than any possible receipts.

I wonder how many of the conductors of these orchestras, who all receive generous salaries and have no personal financial risk in the enterprise, realize what up-hill pioneer work we had to do in the early days to keep our orchestras alive and to lay the musical foundations on which they are now so solidly built.

After my father's death I was elected, at the age of twenty-three, conductor of the New York Symphony Society. We used to give six concerts and six public rehearsals during the winter, and for the seven years following my election this orchestra was also employed for the German opera at the Metropolitan. But when German opera was supplanted by Italian under Abbey, Schoeffel, and Grau, I was hard put to it to find sufficient work for my men to keep them together. The little subsidy which was at that time contributed by the directors of the Symphony Society was only large enough to give the six regular concerts of the winter season. I had learned the difficult art of accompanying soloists sympathetically with the orchestra, and the foreign artists who came to America, such as Sarasate, Ysaye, d'Albert, Joseffy, Paderewski, Kubelik, and many others, always chose my orchestra to accompany them. But these concerts were comparatively few, and I had to look for other ways of giving my men enough work to make it worth their while to stay with me instead of accepting travelling engagements with little opera companies, etc. Gradually I developed Sunday-afternoon symphony concerts, a complete innovation, as up to that time the only music given on Sundays was in the evening and of the more popular and trivial character. I argued that Sunday was the one day in the week when men were not immersed in business cares, and that on that day they and their families would be more susceptible to the appreciation of a higher and more serious class of music. I therefore boldly inaugurated a series of symphonic concerts for every Sunday afternoon during the winter; and my faith was justified, as not only were these concerts attended by huge audiences, but the percentage of men was greater than had ever been seen at symphony concerts before. For several years I enjoyed a monopoly of my idea, but then other orchestras and soloists perceived its value, and to-day I have to share Sunday afternoons with two or three other organizations who also give high-class concerts, all of which are generally well attended.

I also gradually developed long spring tours with fifty men, which in those days was considered a travelling orchestra of good size. On these tours I penetrated the South, the Middle West, and, later on, the Far West of California and Oregon.

Many of the communities that we visited had never heard a symphony orchestra before, and for them we did real pioneer work, as I maintained a high standard of music on my programmes. The classics were, of course, the foundation; but Wagner very soon became a great drawing power, and Wagner programmes were often the most asked for.

The general plan of my tours was to have the advance agent organize three-day festivals with a local chorus which would take part in some oratorio or concert excerpts from the operas of Wagner, Verdi, etc. I would also carry a quartet of solo singers, sometimes supplemented by a "star," for the average American public dearly loves a "name." Many of these stars make their greatest money long after their vocal powers have diminished, and they are compelled to make up this lack by adventitious means such as extraordinary costumes, perhaps more decolleté than local custom would sanction, but which are always considered as quite the right thing for so exotic a personage as the "prima donna."

During these three-day festivals we would generally give five concerts, and, as we often booked two festivals in one week, the ten concerts and necessary rehearsals often proved a great strain on my vitality. But it had to be done, as the local festival committees were compelled to crowd in as many concerts as possible to make their expenses. It has always been fascinating to me to do pioneer work, either by organizing something new, introducing a new composer, or penetrating into regions where symphonic music was not yet known. The gratitude of the people was often very touching, and if my profits at the end of an arduous tour were sometimes not so large as they should have been, I had at least kept my orchestra together for eight, ten, or even twelve weeks, and had enlarged the radius of musical activity by many hundreds—sometimes thousands—of miles. I marvel now at the courage with which I would start on a tour in which perhaps only half my concerts were guaranteed, and these guarantees, alas, not always paid up in full. But for years I was almost the only one travelling through the country with an orchestra, and as railroad fares were just half of what they are to-day I was generally able to end my tour with some profit.

I also began to tackle the question of how to utilize my orchestra during the summer months, and had the good luck to solve that problem for many years very effectively. As early as 1885 and 1886 I was invited by the

Southern Exposition of Louisville, Kentucky, to come there with my orchestra and play the entire summer, giving two concerts a day. I shall always look back on those two summers with delight and gratitude. I was very young and it was my first experience of a prolonged stay in a Southern city. Louisville at that time was a small community, but with an old civilization which manifested itself in a circle of charming people of established culture and social relations. They opened their doors and their hearts to my brother and me. The Pendennis Club, in its old-fashioned courtesy and hospitality, was like a page out of Thackeray or Dickens. Most of the people had never heard symphonic music, and as we played twice a day for about three months, I gave them almost the entire orchestral repertoire, ranging from the good popular music of Johann Strauss through the symphonies of Mozart, Beethoven, and the modern composers, to Wagner, who immediately became their "favorite composer." The members of my orchestra were also received with great cordiality, and several very tender and romantic love-affairs were the result. I too would gladly have fallen a victim to the charms of these Southern beauties, but, alas, I was such a hard-worked young man with my two concerts a day and rehearsals that I could not indulge myself much in romance.

One evening, during a terrific thunder-storm, the lightning crashed into the machinery furnishing the electric light of the music-hall, and plunged it in darkness. It was crowded with thousands of listeners and for a few minutes there was an awe-struck silence, broken only by the great crashes of thunder. Gradually hysterical cries from the women were heard here and there and a rush for the doors began. The darkness was intense, but I knew the orchestra could play the march from "Le Prophète" by heart, so I shouted to them to begin this number. I can still hear old Karl Deis, who had been trombone player under my father, beginning all alone with the opening theme, followed immediately by the rest of the orchestra. I was conducting like mad, although, owing to the darkness, not one of the players could see me, except when the flashes of lightning momentarily illuminated the hall; but the music immediately calmed the audience, who sat down and at the conclusion of the march applauded vociferously. We then started the "Beautiful Blue Danube," and in the second bar the electric lights of the hall blazed up again. The following evening the chief of the fire department and other city officials appeared, and with several bottles of champagne toasted the orchestra and its conductor for their "great life-saving act" of the evening before.

On Sundays there were no concerts, and they became blessed days of peace and rest. I usually spent them at the country place of a friend—a roomy, hospitable, Southern mansion, delicious noon dinner, and afterward a lazy, happy time on the lawn, watching the horses, beautiful, full-blooded, Kentucky bred, gambolling about without saddle or bridle, like young puppies, according to the old-established Sunday custom of the place. To the Kentuckian the love for his horses and pride in their qualities is part of the romance of his life; at least it was in those days, long before the automobile had made its appearance.

The many concerts at the Louisville Exposition, coming at the beginning of my career as an orchestral conductor, gave me enormous routine and acquaintance with the entire orchestral repertoire.

I found the South exceedingly receptive. New Orleans had, of course, been a supporter of French opera for years—its opera-house was one of the most charming I had ever seen—but I also established new centres for music, one of which developed very successfully in the little town of Spartanburg, South Carolina. The impulse here came from the Converse College for Women, which has a high reputation in the South. The young ladies of this institution formed the nucleus of a large and well-trained chorus of two hundred and fifty voices. I went there with my orchestra every spring for over ten years. We succeeded in building up a great love and appreciation for music there and in other near-by places, as it was the custom for the alumnæ of the college to return to Spartanburg for Music Festival week and then to carry back and spread their musical enthusiasm in their home towns.

Gradually I penetrated farther and farther West. In 1904 I made a tour as far as Oklahoma City with the orchestra and quite a large group of solo singers, with whom I gave excerpts from Wagner's "Parsifal," connecting the various numbers with a few explanatory remarks. The tour was highly successful, as the public had read much about the first performances of "Parsifal" at Bayreuth and New York, and were keen to hear the music. I recall an amusing incident in Oklahoma City. Our concert had been scheduled as part of a course of entertainments under a local manager. The theatre was crowded and I had just finished the Prelude to "Parsifal" and was ready to begin the excerpts from the first act, when suddenly the manager popped up on the stage and addressed the audience somewhat as follows: "Ladies and gentlemen: I am proud to see so many of you here to-night and take this opportunity of announcing to you that I have already made arrangements for next season for a course which will be in every respect finer than the one I am giving you this year! I also would like to announce that Stewart's Oyster Saloon will be open after the concert for lunch." (Sic.) This was, however, our only interruption, and the rest of the music was listened to with evident interest and enthusiastic approval.

After the concert was over, as I left by the stage door to return to my hotel, I was met by the crowd of people descending from the top gallery. A young man who had been lounging against the stage entrance went up to one of the men who was coming out of the theatre and said: "Well, how was it, Jim?" and Jim answered: "This show ain't worth thirty cents." The woes of *Amfortas* and the lilting measures of the *Flower Maidens* had evidently not appealed to this young Oklahoman!

In contrast to this experience I should like to relate what happened another time when we were giving a symphony concert, perhaps the first ever heard there, at Fargo, North Dakota. Efrem Zimbalist, delightful man and artist, was our soloist on this tour, and after the concert, when we met for supper, he related with shouts of laughter that while I was playing the "Lenore" Symphony, by Raff, he was sitting behind the scenes of the "opera-house"—every Western city has a "grand opera-house"— listening to the music, when a cowboy, young, handsome, in flannel shirt, high boots, slouch hat, etc., came on the stage and sat down amicably next to him. The cowboy was perhaps a little "mellow," as this was before the days of national prohibition, but he evidently had a musical ear, although he had never before in his life heard a symphony orchestra. Every time that the music developed into a kind of joyous climax, he would grab Zimbalist's knee in convulsive delight and shout: "God damn it, but I like that music!" Then he would sit in rapt silence until the next outburst, when he would again grab Zimbalist and shout: "They can go to hell, but they know how to play!" We all envied this man, because, no matter how much we may appreciate music, we have heard so much that we can never again experience the thrill of hearing a symphony orchestra for the first time in our lives.

The story, of course, went the rounds of the orchestra, and for weeks afterward, if we were seated in the dining-car of our train, the voice of one of the musicians might be heard above the roar of the cars and the din of the clattering knives and forks shouting in joyous accents: "God damn it, but I like this omelet!"

Speaking of dining-cars, on one of our Western tours during the first years of the war we had heard much about the sad conditions of the Belgians, whose territory had been so ruthlessly overrun by the German armies. Our entire orchestra had just responded unanimously and generously in contributing toward the Belgian Relief Fund, and in the dining-car at the table opposite mine were seated our second flute player, a Belgian, together with his son, who was one of our talented violoncellists. Their plates were heaped with turkey, cranberry sauce, and potatoes, and there was an apple-pie in the offing. I said: "I thought the Belgians were starving!" "Oh," said Barrère, the ever ready and ever witty, "ils mangent pour les autres."

How much we have owed on these tours to George Barrère! He has always been for me a model member of an orchestra. He is a great artist—perhaps the greatest on the flute that I have ever heard—but no rehearsal is too long for him, and the inevitable contretemps of travel are accepted by him with imperturbable good nature. I have described elsewhere with what difficulty I was enabled to import him from France seventeen years ago, owing to the opposition made by the New York Musical Union, but he has more than justified his claims to American citizenship since then, not only by his artistic work, but by the group of American pupils whom he has gathered around him, who are devoted to him and have received and made their own much of his artistry. He is a delightful mixture of Gallic wit and American humor. He was asked once: "If you were not a musician, Monsieur Barrère, what would you like to be?" and he promptly answered: "An orchestral conductor!" A wicked remark, but as he has since then become the conductor of Barrère's Little Symphony Orchestra I can give him tit for tat.

When the war broke out I found that as we had thirteen nationalities in the orchestra, including all the nations at war, relations might often become strained, especially on our long tours when the men are forced, in the sleeping-cars and at the concerts, into constant and close companionship. I therefore gave them a little talk in which I explained that as they were gaining their living in this country and as they were artists—for otherwise they would not be in the New York Symphony —their first duties were toward their art, toward me, and toward their families whom they were supporting in honorable fashion, and that therefore for the time being it was for the good of all to sink their political differences and their various attitudes toward the war, and to live in harmony with each other. This talk had good results, as during the entire four years of war I cannot recall any serious difference or quarrel between them.

There were, of course, serious discussions and sometimes good-natured raillery. At that time Rudolf Rissland was the leader of my second violins and had charge of the orchestra during the long tours. He has been with me a great many years and I value him highly as a man of character and loyalty. He is of German birth, and, although he had become a patriotic American, he always wore his blond moustache combed upward in German fashion. We had been informed before our Canadian tour that no players of German birth would be admitted into Canada, but, thanks to the British ambassador, Sir Cecil Spring-Rice, an old friend of my wife's family, we received a special permission for the few German-born who had not yet received their second citizen papers, to enter Canada, as I gladly made myself responsible for them. We were the only orchestra that gave concerts in Toronto and Montreal during the war. On this particular trip, after our train had left Toronto, the orchestra began to twit Rissland unmercifully, accusing him of having in most cowardly fashion combed his moustache downward before coming on the stage for the concert. At first he denied this absolutely, but finally confessed that he had combed down the side turned toward the audience, but had kept the other side defiantly turned upward!

The idea of venting their feelings against a nation by maltreating the music of its composers at rehearsals or concerts never entered the minds of our players. Our Frenchmen would play a symphony of Beethoven or an excerpt from a Wagner music-drama with the same care

and enthusiasm as a work by one of their own composers.
The same was true vice versa of our German-born members.
To the good musician art is international, although
each nation has its own standards and traditions of interpretation, and it is interesting to note how sharply opposed these sometimes are. There is often a curious
racial antagonism between the French and Italian musicians. The Frenchman will insist that the phrasing of
the Italian is sloppy and hypersentimental, while the
Italian will retort that the Frenchman's is academic and
rigid. Every nation has its excellent qualities, and the
finest orchestra in the world is one composed of the best
of the different nationalities moulded into one harmonious whole by a master conductor without racial musical
prejudice.

Our visits to California were perhaps enjoyed the most
of all. These began long before the earthquake and fire
had destroyed the old San Francisco, and when the city
had all the romance of earlier days and Chinatown was
still an exotic and fascinating region of mystery. The
society of San Francisco was different from that of any
other city in the United States. It was composed largely
of restless pioneers from the East and from other countries who, having "worked their way" across the continent, had finally stopped and settled in San Francisco
because the Pacific Ocean prevented them from going
still farther, and also because in California nature opened
both arms wide in welcome, and gave of her bounty so freely
that life and the necessity of supporting it became an easy
matter. Many of the well-to-do sent their sons and
daughters, not to New York and Boston, but to Paris
and London, for their education. Society was international in that it comprised Americans, Germans, French,

and Italians. They all loved music instinctively, and gave it enthusiastic acclaim, much as in a city of Italy or the Midi of France.

Few trained symphony orchestras had penetrated so far West, and my orchestra was a revelation to many of our hearers.

For me there were also pleasant visits to San Mateo and other beautiful places near by, where one could see a good game of polo or tennis and have one's gastronomic needs delightfully ministered to by Chinese cooks and Japanese butlers. In those days Los Angeles was but a small city and no one then dreamed of the unique and lightning-like development which has made it in a few years one of the most important cities in America.

In continuing our tour farther north we came under the management of two very remarkable women, under the firm name of "Steers and Coman," who virtually control the musical field from Oregon and Washington as far east as Denver. Miss Lois Steers and Miss Wynne Coman live in Portland, Oregon. By dint of their organizing genius and enthusiasm for music, and an absolute integrity in all business dealings, they have not only won the highest respect and confidence of the communities to which they minister but have built up a very effective organization. Under their auspices every great artist who has ever visited this country has appeared not only in the larger cities of the States which they control, but in many of the smaller university towns and farming communities in which the Misses Steers and Coman have been able to develop an interest in music. They are not only business women of superior qualities, but ladies of such fine sympathies and breeding that I have always felt particularly honored by their friendship.

On our tours, Miss Steers usually attended to the local needs of the cities we visited—the music committees, the hall managers, and the newspapers—while Miss Coman travelled with us as general railroad manager, baggage despatcher, and "committee of one," to smooth out all difficulties, adjust any disputes and, in general, to "oil the wheels." As soon as we came into their territory everything moved like clockwork. I remember one agonizing day, however, when we had to make Salt Lake City from the West and terrible floods had disarranged all railroad schedules. The final jolt came when, at some station on the way, John Drew's two cars containing his dramatic company and scenery were added to our already overheavy train because the floods had compelled him also to change his route. All hope of reaching Salt Lake City in time for our concert seemed gone. Miss Coman hopped onto the engine and sat down next to the engineer and stoker. I did not know whether she used a woman's wiles or brute force or a combination of both, but we arrived in Salt Lake City at nine P. M. on a lovely summer evening. An audience of two thousand had been notified that we would be late and were calmly promenading up and down in front of the theatre. Trucks were in waiting at the station to rush our baggage to the auditorium, our men had put on their evening dress in the baggage-car, and I began the opening overture with all the instruments properly tuned at ten minutes before ten. Symphony concerts were so few and far between in Salt Lake City that the audience did not mind this long wait one little bit.

Of course all these difficulties could not have been so happily solved had I not always had devoted and efficient heads of the different departments of our organization.

George Engles is the most careful of business managers; Rissland, the orchestra manager, has always been tireless in his efforts to keep the men in good discipline and spirits and to look after their welfare; and Hans Goettich, who has been my baggage-master and librarian for over twenty-five years, is a perfect marvel. I remember seeing him flag an entire train because he had suddenly noticed that our baggage-car, containing all our music and musical instruments, had been hooked on to it by mistake. As this train was going to New Orleans, while we were headed for Chicago, we would have had to stop giving concerts for several days until that baggage-car had been traced and sent back to us! On Goettich devolves the entire responsibility for the library, which is packed in dozens of boxes and kept according to a system of his own. On these long tours our programmes are changed more or less every day, partly to avoid the monotony of repetition for us and partly because each community has its own needs according to its stage of musical development, which I try to gauge very thoroughly when making up my programmes. This means incessant work for the librarian and mistakes might easily occur, but during all these years I cannot recall a single concert when, through fault of Goettich's, an orchestral part has been lost or misplaced. This is a remarkable record.

I remember giving a symphony concert in William J. Bryan's town of Lincoln, Nebraska. I found a typical Middle Western community, living in nice houses with green lawns, with neatly bricked streets and concrete sidewalks, and roomy large-windowed schools. The theatre in which we played was thoroughly modern, clean, and well lighted, and the audience well dressed and appreciative. One of my double-bass players told me that he had played there thirty years before with Theodore Thomas. In those days Lincoln was but a frontier town and the theatre and the public who had come to hear the Thomas Orchestra were of a more or less primitive character. My double-bass player told me that with a colleague, whose head was devoid of hair, he had stood directly below a proscenium box in which a group of cowboys were seated. While the orchestra was playing Beethoven's "Fifth Symphony," one of these cowboys, who was chewing tobacco violently, amused himself by spitting frequently and always aiming for the bald head of the bass player, who had to keep one agitated eye on the conductor and the other on this horribly resourceful listener, in order to avoid his only too-well-directed shots.

Our orchestra always enjoyed the long spring tours, although now and then uncomfortable happenings would mar their pleasure. Nothing makes a musician so ill-natured as to be deprived of a good square meal, and sometimes our dining-car would not connect properly or we would be so delayed as to arrive in a town only just in time to rush to the theatre and give our concert. Then I would have to exert all my powers as an orator to induce them to go directly to the theatre instead of "loitering by the wayside," and I would quickly order large quantities of ham and swiss-cheese sandwiches to be distributed behind the scenes just before the concert.

At present our players while on tour receive so much per day above their salaries for meals and beds, but in the early days I used to pay their hotel expenses, my manager engaging rooms and arranging the rates "on the American plan" before we arrived in the city in which we were to play. This system, however, never worked well because there was always intense jealousy among the musicians as to the quality or conveniences of their respective rooms; and if the first oboe found that his room did not front on as agreeable a locality as that of the first horn, he would perhaps sulk and consider that he had been unfairly treated. The newer arrangement proved much better, as it enabled some to save from the money allowed them and permitted others to "splurge" by spending more.

I remember that once in those early days we had to fill in a date in a small New York State town on our way to Canada. The principal hotel had room for only about twenty, and the other members of the orchestra were quartered in four other hotels. Naturally the unfortunate five who were put into the last of these had a terrible story to tell of their sufferings when we met the following morning at the station. To be sure, the manager of the hotel had charged only a dollar for each person, and this included his supper, bed, and breakfast, but their rooms had been dismal and the beds hard. The climax was reached in the morning, when, as a frowsy waitress began to serve them their breakfast in the fly-specked dining-room on a table covered with the inevitable dirty red and white checked cloth, the manager, putting his head in at the door, shouted: "Lizzie, no eggs for the band!" This phrase became a catchword in the orchestra, and whenever my manager or I refused anything to our men, the cry immediately resounded: "Of course, no eggs for the band!"

Orchestra players through experience become remarkably routined travellers. They know the good hotels and restaurants in every city of the Union, and during the long railroad jumps, especially west of the Mississippi, where distances between important cities become greater and greater, they know how to amuse themselves, each one according to his fashion. There are, of course, a few groups who play poker violently from morning till night. Others are equally constant to pinochle or bridge, while a few are perfect sharks at chess. The Frenchmen, as well as the Russian Jews, are great readers of serious literature, and books on history, philosophy, and music are in great demand among them. Whenever the train stops, even for a few minutes, a dozen jump off to play ball. As a rule, during the day we have two cars, one of which is given up to the smokers, where indeed the air becomes so thick that one could cut it with a knife. At night three or four sleepers are necessary to take care of us comfortably. The old days, when I travelled with fifty men, have gone long ago, and now we should not think of touring with an orchestra of less than eighty-five.

The time for spring tours seems to be passing, however, as the Western cities are beginning to minister to the needs of their respective communities with their own excellent orchestras.

For many years I accepted long summer engagements with two concerts every day, first at Willow Grove near Philadelphia, and then at Ravinia Park, on the North Shore near Chicago. The former became a great educational factor, as Philadelphia at that time had no orchestra of its own. Willow Grove Park is situated seventeen miles from that city and was built by the Rapid Transit Company in order to stimulate travel on their trolley lines. The first season, for which a military band had been engaged, had not proven a success, and I was invited the following year in the hope that a symphonic organization might do better. I began by giving them popular programmes of good music with a regular symphony night every Monday and a Wagner programme every Friday evening, with excellent results. Our audiences usually numbered from fifteen to twenty thousand. The Rapid Transit Company, realizing the importance of the concerts, promptly built a huge open-air auditorium after my own design, consisting of only a roof on pillars connecting with the shell in which the orchestra was placed. The acoustics proved exceedingly good and the out-of-doors atmosphere was preserved.

I continued these concerts for seven seasons, thereby developing an audience for symphonic music which eventually and inevitably demanded a resident orchestra of its own. To-day the Philadelphia orchestra, under the leadership of Leopold Stokowski, ranks as one of the foremost of our country. Its concerts are crowded to the doors and I like to think that our seven years of pioneer work in Willow Grove have helped to lay its foundations.

I also conducted a series of concerts at Ravinia Park, organized by the Chicago and Milwaukee Electric Railway to serve a similar commercial purpose. Chicago had, of course, enjoyed for years the splendid winter concerts of the Chicago Orchestra, first under Theodore Thomas and then under his successor, Frederick Stock, but this was the first time that symphonic concerts were given during the summer amid such charming surroundings on the borders of Lake Michigan. These concerts proved exceedingly popular, the audiences consisting not only of the North Shore residents but of thousands who came out from Chicago on trains and trolleys.

After several years of this work, however, the incessant

daily concerts, coming after an arduous winter season, began to pall on my musical nerves. I ran a real danger, if I continued, of becoming nothing but a musical routinier, with an inevitable loss of the enthusiasm and freshness which is an absolute necessity for the interpreter. I therefore gave up all conducting during the summer months.

I founded the Damrosch Opera Company in 1895, and the harassing question of how to maintain my orchestra seemed solved, for, during the first year, my opera season lasted thirteen weeks and during the following three years, from twenty to thirty weeks each. This not only enabled me to maintain a beautifully trained orchestra for the Wagner operas, but also gave to my symphony performances a greater finish. The orchestra was now under my exclusive control and could rehearse as often as the endowed orchestra of Major Higginson. But as it was the opera that enabled me to give my men such a long engagement, its needs had to control all other arrangements, and gradually the regular sequence of my winter concerts in New York began to suffer. I could not keep my opera company in New York except for a limited period each year, and therefore had to fill in much of my time in Philadelphia, Boston, and the larger cities of the South and Middle West. In 1899 I was therefore finally compelled to give up the regular subscription series of our New York concerts and the New York Symphony Orchestra became a part of my travelling operatic organization.

I made this sacrifice with a heavy heart, but at that time it was the only solution. An orchestra devoted only to concerts could not be maintained without an endowment, and that I did not have at the time, while the length of my Wagner opera season enabled me not only to give my men a good engagement but to have the pick of the best musicians in New York.

From then on until 1903 most of our playing of symphonic music was only on our spring concert tours and at irregular intervals in New York.

In 1900 Maurice Grau asked me to conduct the Wagner operas at the Metropolitan, and in the spring of 1902, at the close of my second season with him, I received an invitation from the New York Philharmonic Society to become its conductor. This invitation was a great surprise to me, as the Philharmonic had been, ever since my father's day, the rival orchestra. In many ways it seemed a flattering proposition, as it was the oldest organization of its kind in America and had had an honorable history. Under the leadership of Theodore Thomas and later on of Anton Seidl, the audiences had been large and its affairs had prospered. It had always been a co-operative association, composed of the members of the orchestra, who had complete control of its affairs, receiving no salaries, but dividing the profits equally among themselves at the end of each season. I accepted the conductorship, but found very soon that my acceptance was a blunder. The society had come upon evil days, and under its last conductor attendance had dwindled to less than one-half. Of the membership of the orchestra only the skeleton remained, and I found to my amazement that of the hundred players at the concerts, less than fifty were actual members of the organization, the rest being engaged from outside, and often changed from one concert to another. Some of the members were old men who should no longer have played in the orchestra at all; but they were devoted to the concerts of the society, and as the orchestra was regulated by their votes, they naturally would not vote themselves out of it. Many of them had been excellent musicians and were personally upright men, but age, alas, is no respecter of technic, and the fingers of the left hand and the muscles of the bow arm gradually stiffen with advancing years. Most of the wind instruments were outsiders and therefore could not be properly controlled regarding their attendance at rehearsals and concerts, while, on the contrary, nearly all of the first violins were old members, several of whom were no longer fit to play first violin.

The fact was that Major Higginson, of Boston, with his permanent orchestra composed of young men, many of them the best of their kind, with their daily rehearsals and at least seventy-five symphony concerts a season, had set a new standard of orchestral technic which the old Philharmonic, under its archaic conditions, could not hope to equal.

The only solution seemed to me to lie in gathering together a fund large enough to produce the same conditions and results as Higginson had achieved in the Boston Orchestra, and, above all, to put the management of the Philharmonic into the hands of a committee which should not be composed of members of the orchestra, but of music lovers and guarantors of the fund.

I discussed this idea with several of my friends and some old subscribers and friends of the Philharmonic at a meeting held on January 5, 1903, and it was resolved to obtain a fund of fifty thousand dollars a year for four years, to be administered for the benefit of the Philharmonic Society as a permanent orchestra fund by a board of fifteen or more trustees, but it was not to be subject to the control of the Philharmonic Society.

This fund was to be the beginning of an endowment for a permanent orchestra, of which the Philharmonic Society was to be the nucleus. The terms of the deed of trust under which the fund was to be held were to be determined by a committee of three, consisting of Mr. Samuel Untermyer, Mr. John Notman, and Mr. E. Francis Hyde.

The members of the Philharmonic Orchestra were not unfavorably disposed toward our scheme. The idea of being guaranteed a yearly salary instead of sharing problematic yearly profits, naturally appealed to them; but when our committee explained to them that, under the terms of such an endowment, several of the playing members would have to resign their places because in the opinion of the committee they had passed the age of usefulness, they rebelled. Nor did they feel inclined to give up the absolute management of their concerts.

Among the most respected members of the Philharmonic Orchestra were two old violinists. The one, Richard Arnold, vice-president of the society, had been concert master under my father twenty-five years before and still officiated in that position in the Philharmonic. The other, August Roebbelin, who had played as first violinist in the orchestra for nearly forty years, had also acted as manager of the society and unselfishly given his best energies to its affairs. As a violinist, however, he had passed his time of usefulness. Our committee, perhaps rather bluntly, informed the Philharmonic committee that under the reorganization the selection of the orchestra must be left in the hands of the conductor and that Mr. Arnold would have to content himself with a second position at the first stand, so that a younger artist could become concert master, and that several of the first violinists, among them Mr. Roebbelin, would have to be retired altogether.

I had made it particularly clear that my selection as conductor for the following year was not in any way a necessary part of the reorganization scheme, as it seemed to me that the only way to achieve a real permanent orchestra for New York was to unite the conflicting factions and to let the choice of conductor be made after the organization had been properly placed upon a sound and comprehensive basis.

After lengthy negotiations the Philharmonic, in a letter of February 28, 1903, definitely refused the offer of the reorganization committee because, as their secretary expressed it, the amendments required by our committee "would so change the nature of the society as to seriously interfere with the control of its affairs by its members, which has always been its vital principle, and that the future prosperity of the society would thereby be impaired."

As I had no desire to continue another year with the orchestra on the basis of existing conditions, I wrote to Mr. Arnold and requested that my name be not proposed as a candidate for the following year. I had been in a very delicate position during all this time, as I had grown quite fond personally of some of the very men whom, for artistic reasons, it was necessary to retire. It was not in human nature that they should have seen themselves as others saw them, or heard themselves as others heard them, and at our rehearsals and concerts they all certainly gave the best that was in them. The changes which I had proposed were necessary, however, if the society expected to continue its existence as an orchestral body.

For a few years they staved off the inevitable by engaging for each season a number of European guest conductors. This served as a stop-gap, as it diverted the attention of the audience from the deficiencies in the orchestra to the different and interesting personalities and musical specialties of the conductors. But then a reorganization plan, exactly on the lines originally proposed by me, completely eliminating the power of the orchestral players to manage the concerts or to select the players in the orchestra, was accepted by them, and to-day the orchestra of the Philharmonic Society is organized and successfully working on exactly the same basis as the New York Symphony Society and the Boston Orchestra.

For me the rejection of our reorganization plan was at the time naturally a great disappointment, but not for long, as my efforts had made new friends for me and in a new direction, which eventually proved a turning-point in my life.

On March 19, 1903, I received a letter which read as follows:

I have been instructed by the members of the Permanent Orchestra Fund Committee to express to you their appreciation of the spirit of unselfishness and of loyalty to the highest artistic interests which has characterized your attitude during the negotiations which have been in progress between our Committee and the Philharmonic Society. We regret that a consolidation of our interests has proved impossible, but we relinquish the plan we had in view with the greatest respect and admiration for your broad attitude of mind in regard to the undertaking, for your musicianship, and for your devotion to the cause of music in which we are all working.

HARRY HARKNESS FLAGLER,
Secretary Permanent Orchestra Fund.

Years before I had met Mr. Flagler through his friend, Max Alvary, when the latter was a member of the Damrosch Opera Company, but the meeting was quite casual and I had not seen him again until the meetings of the Philharmonic Orchestra Fund Committee, of which he had become a member. I had been singularly attracted by him and his gentle and quiet, almost diffident manner. He had been a great lover of music all his life and had found in his wife Anne an enthusiastic companion in his love for the art. As the reorganization scheme of the Philharmonic Orchestra gradually unfolded itself, he became more and more interested in it as the right solution of the problem of developing a symphony orchestra in New York which should be the equal of the Boston Symphony or the Chicago Orchestra, and he was ready to help such a scheme to the fulness of his financial ability. Very quickly after the failure of this project, many of the forces concerned recruited themselves anew, and a large proportion of the would-be guarantors turned to me with the suggestion to reorganize the New York Symphony Orchestra, and by subsidizing all the first players and thereby binding them to the orchestra, make a new beginning in the right direction. During the interregnum of three years the orchestra had maintained itself fairly well through the earnings of our long spring tours and summer engagements, but I joyfully hailed this opportunity to renew the New York winter concerts. A reorganization of the Symphony Society of New York was quickly effected by the re-election of most of the old directors and of many new ones. My old and loyal friend, Daniel Frohman, at whose theatre I had given many a Wagner lecture in the years past, accepted the presidency pro tem and was of great assistance in procuring outside work for the members of the orchestra. He was succeeded by Mr. Samuel Sanford, a man of real musical ability, who had founded the musical department at Yale University and had contributed liberally to many musical enterprises. He immediately became one of the largest guarantors of our orchestra fund.

We accordingly resumed our New York concerts under the best possible auspices with an enthusiastic directorate and a large subscription list. I was, however, not satisfied with the wood-wind players at that time available in New York. The Musical Union, which controlled all orchestral players, had made the influx of good musicians from Europe almost an impossibility by insisting that a player must have lived at least six months in this country before he could join the union, and that until he became a member no other member of the union would be allowed to play with him. As all orchestral engagements in opera, concert, or theatre were in the hands of union men, this meant that the newcomer would have to starve for six months before he could begin to earn a dollar toward his maintenance. This law was not enforced by the union men for patriotic reasons, as most of them had been born in Europe, but because they feared the possible competition for the positions they monopolized. The best wood-wind players at that time—and, generally speaking, this applies to-day—were French or Belgian. The Conservatoire of Paris has for years produced very superior artists on these instruments. The Boston Orchestra, which is non-union, had several among its members, and their exquisite tone and beautiful phrasing always particularly enraged me because, owing to the union restrictions, I could not have players of equal merit.

I determined therefore to throw down the gantlet to the union by deliberately going to France to engage the five best artists I could find in flute, oboe, clarinet, bassoon, and trumpet, demonstrate their superior excellence to anything we could obtain in New York at that time, and through the pressure of public opinion—and, above all, the necessity of artistic competition with the Boston Symphony—force the union to accept these men as members. When the Frenchmen arrived, the rage among the members of the New York union knew no bounds. I had a summer engagement for the orchestra on one of the roof gardens, but the union refused to let them play with us except as "soloists," and I determined to take the matter higher up to the annual convention of the National Federation of Musicians, which was held in Detroit in the summer of 1905.

I found the national delegates much more amenable to reason than my New York colleagues. There were more real Americans among them and many of them listened to my pleadings with interest and sympathy. The president of the federation, Joseph N. Weber, is a man of real intellectual ability; and while he and I have had some violent quarrels and disagreements during these many years, and while I have sometimes denounced him to his face as a fanatic and he has given me tit for tat, I must acknowledge that he not only has had the ability to build up a remarkable organization of great power, but has often acted with great fairness in disputes that have come up between the directors of the New York Musical Union and myself.

The National Federation decided in my favor and gave me the permission to incorporate these five Frenchmen in my orchestra and to enroll them as members of the New York union, but as I had "sinned against the laws of the federation in bringing them over from a foreign country," I was fined one thousand dollars. It was,

however, intimated to me privately that if I would return
to the next convention of the federation, which was to be
held in Boston the following summer, I would in all
probability receive a remission of the greater part of this
fine. It is needless for me to say that I never saw any
part of that one thousand dollars again.

I returned to New York jubilant and my French
players proved themselves such superior artists that, together with our other excellent members, many of whom
had been with me for years, the orchestra quickly took
rank among the best in the country.

The leader of my first violins was Mr. David Mannes.
I had discovered him a few years before at one of the
New York theatres, where he was a member of the little
orchestra and where I heard him play a solo charmingly
between the first and second acts. The beautiful quality
of his tone, and a fine sensitiveness to the melos of the
work he was playing, attracted me and I engaged him
for the last stand of the first violins. From there he was
quickly promoted until he occupied the position at the
first stand of concert master. He married my sister Clara,
a pianist of fine accomplishment. Their sonata recitals
have become models of intimate unity in chamber-music
playing, and several years ago they founded the David
Mannes Music School. This encroached so much upon
his time and energy as to compel him to resign his position in the New York Symphony Orchestra, which he had
held so honorably for many years.

Each year the guarantee fund for the maintenance of
the orchestra was increased by the supporters of the New
York Symphony Society, and more and more men were
engaged on regular weekly salaries. At last my dream was
realized, and New York had an orchestra organized on the

same lines as the Boston and Chicago Orchestras, devoted exclusively to symphonic music and assembling daily for rehearsal.

The fund at this time reached over fifty thousand dollars a year, mainly subscribed by the directors of our organization. Several of these had been supporters from my father's time, among them Isaac N. Seligman, who, with his family, had been interested in music in New York for many years. Others had come into the organization when I became its conductor and had remained loyal supporters and close friends from that time on. Among them were: Richard Welling, a director since 1886, a well-known lawyer and reformer in municipal politics, and who as a member of the Naval Reserves promptly enlisted as an ensign when we entered the Great War, although he was then well over fifty years of age; Miss Mary R. Callender and Miss Caroline de Forest who had been directors since 1885. Miss Callender further signalized her affection for the orchestra by leaving fifty thousand dollars to the pension and sick fund after her death in 1919. The complete list of the subscribers to the fund at the time was as follows:

Mrs. H. A. Alexander
Mr. C. B. Alexander
Miss Kora F. Barnes
Mrs. William H. Bliss
Miss Mary R. Callender
Mr. Robert J. Collier
Mrs. Paul D. Cravath
Mr. Paul D. Cravath
Miss Caroline de Forest
Mr. Charles H. Ditson
Mrs. S. Edgar
Miss A. C. Flagler

Mr. Harry Harkness Flagler
Mr. Edward S. Flagler
Mrs. Frances Hellman
Mr. Otto H. Kahn
Mr. A. W. Krech
Mrs. Daniel Lamont
Mr. Albert Lewisohn
Mr. Frank A. Munsey
Mr. Emerson McMillin
Mme. Nordica
Mr. Stephen S. Palmer
Mrs. Trenor L. Park

Mr. Amos Pinchot
Mrs. Joseph Pulitzer
Mr. Thomas F. Ryan
Mr. Charles E. Sampson
Mr. Samuel S. Sanford
Mr. R. E. Schirmer
Mr. Henry Seligman
Mrs. Henry Seligman
Mr. Isaac N. Seligman

Mr. Jefferson Seligman
Mrs. Jesse Seligman
Mr. Frank H. Simmons
Miss Clara B. Spence
Mrs. F. T. Van Beuren
Mr. Richard Welling
Mrs. J. A. Zimmerman
Mr. Paul Warburg

The ideal conditions under which I now worked gave me the opportunity to carry out several artistic plans which I had had for a long time. The first of these was a Beethoven cycle, in which I gave not only all the nine symphonies in chronological order, but other compositions of Beethoven, some of which had not yet appeared on the concert programmes of New York. Accordingly, in the winter of 1909, I prepared six programmes composed of Beethoven's works, and at the last concert gave a double performance of his "Ninth Symphony." This was a real *tour de force*, but not original with me. During the summer of 1887, which I had spent with von Bülow in study of the Beethoven symphonies, he had told me of having given such a double performance in Berlin and that the results had been very remarkable, inasmuch as at the second hearing, the audience had been able the more perfectly to grasp many of the intricacies of this "Hamlet" among symphonic dramas. Our double performance caused a good deal of comment, most of which was very favorable. Between the two performances the orchestra and chorus were refreshed with hot coffee and sandwiches, and as the work takes about an hour and ten minutes to perform, the repetition, together with a half-hour of rest between, brought the final tumultuous outburst of the choral "Ode to Joy" to eleven o'clock. Not-withstanding the lateness of the hour, the audience began a great demonstration of approval, applauding and shouting for many minutes; but while I and my performers took some of this as ours by right, I have always felt that the audience intended a good part of it as directed toward themselves for having so nobly endured the great strain which I had put upon them.

This was the first Beethoven Festival ever given in New York, and a few years later I organized a Brahms Festival on similar lines. I directed his four symphonies, the ingratiating Zimbalist playing the "Violin Concerto," Wilhelm Backhaus the great "B-Flat Piano Concerto," and my brother with the chorus of the Oratorio Society conducting a very beautiful performance of the "Requiem."

Such festivals devoted exclusively to the work of one composer are a great lesson to the serious music lover, and I think that as Beethoven represents almost the alpha and certainly the omega of symphonic music, there should be repetitions of Beethoven cycles every few years. I have never been able to understand why it should not be similarly possible to give Shakesperian cycles in spring, in which all of our best actors could combine to make up ideal casts. We should certainly make American children as familiar with Shakespeare's great tragedies as, for instance, the children of Germany, to whom Shakespeare is much more of a household word than he is to those of this country or England. If music can find Flaglers and Higginsons to endow it as an educational necessity, why cannot similar men be found to do the same for the drama and thus help to lift it as an educational factor from its painfully weak position to which the necessities of making it a paying institution have driven it.

During all these years my relations with Mr. and Mrs. Flagler became more and more intimate. I had never met such people in my entire life. Their devotion to and interest in the orchestra increased constantly, and Mr. Flagler's contributions to the fund became greater and greater as the needs of the orchestra increased. But his help was offered with a shyness, as if it had been the orchestra that conferred the benefit upon him. He also took over a work which I had always detested more than anything else, and that is the collection of funds. As the expenses of the orchestra increased with the years, it became necessary to collect money from outside sources beyond the large sums already contributed by the directors of the society. With constant good humor, patience, and infinite tact Mr. Flagler, whose own donations to the fund were greater in proportion to his income than those of many others, would write letters or call personally on well-to-do musical patrons to collect perhaps a few hundred dollars toward the fund, and he would be inordinately proud of his success as a financier and collector.

Finally even his infinite patience wore out under this yearly strain and this manifested itself in a very remarkable way.

In the spring of 1914 he quietly informed me that he had decided to assume the entire financial responsibility of the orchestra himself and to contribute all necessary funds for its proper maintenance. This amount was double what would have been considered necessary ten years before, but salaries of orchestral players and other expenses in connection with the giving of concerts had increased enormously and it was Mr. Flagler's desire that, while there should be no waste, the affairs of the orchestra should be managed in such liberal fashion that the artistic needs could first be considered in shaping its policy.

This magnificent and unique act naturally created a great excitement in the musical circles of New York, and Mr. Flagler was universally acclaimed as its foremost musical citizen.

I have a characteristic letter of his, dated August 31, 1914, in which he says:

Indeed I am not overmodest about my gift to the Symphony Society. It is not that, but what I am doing is so little in comparison with what the *real* makers of music, creators and interpreters like yourself do for the betterment of the world through their art, that it doesn't deserve to be thought of. I *am* proud and happy in the thought that I may be the means of helping you to put before the world your ideas in regard to the interpretations of the masters and to bring the God-given art of music to many who would not otherwise have its uplifting and consoling power, and that is what we are doing together. You shall be free as never before to work out your own ideas unfettered by thoughts of the financial necessities. . . .

Since then the society has pursued the even tenor of its way and, freed from all financial worries, has contributed much to the cause of music. The orchestra plays over a hundred symphony concerts during the winter, in New York and elsewhere. These include a series of Sunday-afternoon concerts at Æolian Hall, Thursday-afternoon and Friday-evening concerts at Carnegie Hall, and a series of young people's concerts and another of children's concerts. There are also subscription concerts in Brooklyn, Philadelphia, Baltimore, Washington, and Rochester, and several tours every winter to Canada and the Middle West. During the war Mr. Flagler often gave the services of the orchestra for charities connected with the war, and several times donated the gross receipts of our regular concerts to such organizations as the American Friends of Musicians in France, in which he and his wife became very much interested. But perhaps the climax in the history of the orchestra was reached in its great European tour in the spring of 1920. To this I shall devote a separate chapter following one on my experiences in France during the Great War.

XV

THE GREAT WAR

When America finally entered the Great War I was, like most of my fellow citizens, anxious to do something to help, and therefore shared the restlessness and discontent which most men of maturer years felt because they were not "too proud" but too old to fight.

A number of music lovers had formed an organization, "American Friends of Musicians in France," the object of which was to collect money with which to help the families of musicians in France who were suffering or destitute because of the war. Through my French colleagues we had heard of many such cases—some of the most famous musicians were at the front, in the trenches, and in the hospitals, doing their share just as did the men in all the other professions and callings. Several organizations had been formed in France to help toward maintaining their families, but much remained to be done, and through our society, which aroused immediate response in America, we were raising considerable sums and expected to continue this work until the end of the war.

I had been elected president, and while discussing with our committee the best ways and means of helping the older French musicians, it was brought out that many of them were too proud to accept alms. What they really wanted was opportunity to work in their profession, as the constant air raids and bombardments of Paris had almost entirely stopped the giving of lessons and concerts. During our discussion Henri Casadesus, a French musician who was then on a concert tour in America with his Society of Ancient Instruments, and who had given us much valuable information regarding conditions in France, suggested that an orchestra could be formed of such musicians as were still in Paris, which might be used to travel around the country to the various camps in which our huge army was forming and drilling, and to give our soldiers good popular music during their hours of rest and recreation.

It was suggested that a French conductor be engaged to lead this orchestra, but Casadesus asked whether it would not be possible for me to go over and take charge personally. He thought that the French Government would look on this idea very favorably, and through the Ministère des Beaux Arts would give us every assistance possible toward the forming of the orchestra and its transportation through the country. Needless to say, my heart leaped with joy at this suggestion. One step led to another, and Mr. Harry Harkness Flagler immediately and with characteristic generosity donated a check large enough to pay the entire expenses and salaries of a French orchestra of fifty men for six weeks.

The plan was outlined to the National War Work Council of the Young Men's Christian Association, who accepted it with enthusiasm, and to the French High Commission in Washington, of which Mr. Tardieu was at that time the chief. He sent one of his staff, the Marquis de Polignac, to New York to discuss and arrange details, and immediately cabled to Paris to obtain for me the necessary authority to enter France and to proceed with the plan. The acting director of the Ministère des Beaux Arts was at that time M. Alfred Cortot, the distinguished pianist, and within a week he cabled us that he could place at my disposal the Pasdeloup Orchestra of fifty men who would be ready on my arrival to travel throughout our recreation centres, camps, and hospitals.

As no civilian who was not in government employ could sail for France except under the auspices of one of the welfare organizations, I was to sail as a war worker for the Y. M. C. A., whose entertainment division was under the direction of Mr. Thomas McLane, an earnest, patriotic citizen of New York who gave his entire time enthusiastically to this arduous work. A few weeks before sailing, however, the war situation became so serious that the possibility of carrying out our scheme seemed very doubtful, but Mr. McLane and his chief, Mr. William Sloane, felt strongly that I should go over anyhow, look over the field, and make myself useful in one way or another.

The regulations of the Y. M. C. A. demanded that each one of their workers should submit an indorsement by three well-known American citizens, and as I had the honor of many years' acquaintance with Theodore Roosevelt, I gave his name as one who might be willing to testify to my Americanism. The letter which he wrote is so characteristic that I am vain enough to reprint it here.

DEAR MR. McLANE: Sagamore Hill, May 4th, 1918.

Mr. Walter Damrosch is one of the very best Americans and citizens in this entire land. In character, ability, loyalty, and fervid Americanism he, and his, stand second to none in the land. I have known him thirty years; I vouch for him as if he were my brother.

Faithfully
(*Signed*) THEODORE ROOSEVELT.

The assurance of a safe-conduct from the Ministère des Etrangères was a rather important item as I had been born in Germany, even though only the first nine years of my life had been spent there. My father emigrated to America in 1871, and as I had received my education here, had lived in America ever since, and had married an American, I had never felt myself anything but an American and of the most enthusiastic variety. When the Germans invaded Belgium, when they sank the *Lusitania*, and when they seemed to have broken all laws of international relations, I expressed myself, both personally and in newspaper interviews, so strongly that long before we entered the war several Berlin newspapers violently took me to task and honored me by calling me a renegade and a traitor to the country of my birth.

There was an understanding between our country and France that no American civilian of German birth should be permitted to enter France except by special permission of either M. Clemenceau or M. Pichon, then Minister of Foreign Affairs. The French high commissioner cabled to the latter and in most cordial terms recommended that I be permitted to enter France, both because of my office as president of the Society of American Friends of Musicians in France, and because of a life-long admiration for French music, which I had demonstrated for thirty-three years by producing in our country nearly every important symphonic work that French composers had written before and within that time.

M. Pichon promptly cabled the necessary visé and with all proper credentials I set sail on June 15, 1918, on the French steamship *La Lorraine*.

The ship's passengers were almost entirely soldiers and war workers. There were two hundred and fifty Belgian soldiers with their officers returning to France after three years spent in Russia, and who, when the revolution broke out, had after incredible hardships reached Vladivostok, sailing from there to California. There were Polish soldiers on their way to join the Foreign Legion of the French army and there were dozens of Red Cross, Y. M. C. A., K. of C., and S. A. workers. There were not more than a dozen civilians, among them my friend, Melville Stone, director of the Associated Press, and M. Sulzer, the Swiss minister then accredited to our country. It was strange to be on a transatlantic steamer without any idle rich, tourists, or commercial travellers; and the large guns mounted fore and aft with a gun crew watching, ready day and night, gave one a grim foretaste of the war raging on the other side.

On the first day out Stone told me that M. Sulzer would like to meet me. I expressed my pleasure and laughingly said: "I will promise not to ask him any questions regarding the Swiss citizenship of Doctor Karl Muck." Stone must have repeated this to Sulzer, for immediately after our introduction he said: "I want to tell you that Doctor Muck had no more claim to Swiss citizenship than you have. The facts are as follows: After the Franco-Prussian war, Muck's father—a Bavarian living in Munich—was afraid that Bavaria would become completely Prussianized, and, as he had no liking for that country, he preferred to emigrate to Switzerland, where he acquired citizenship which at that time was very easy, as Switzerland was glad to receive the intelligentsia of other countries. His son Karl left Switzerland as a boy to be educated in Germany, and never returned. He went to a German university, studied music, became an orchestral conductor, and as such officiated in various German opera-houses, until he became conductor and Generalmusikdirektor at the Royal Opera in Berlin.

There he remained for many years and when the war broke out offered his services to the German Ministry of War in a clerical capacity. The Swiss Government does not recognize him as a citizen and refuses him the protection which such citizenship would afford him."

Our journey was uneventful. We saw no submarines and, what was still more important, no submarines saw us. When we reached the "danger zone" some hundred miles from the coast of France, I was solemnly appointed a committee of one to inform M. Sulzer that as he was the Swiss minister and as such the representative of German interests in the United States during the war, we intended to bind him to the foremast and play a searchlight on him and on a large Swiss flag hanging over his head, during the two or three nights before we dropped anchor in the Gironde. He smilingly expressed himself as so willing to act in this capacity as our guardian angel, that we refrained and trusted to luck, which indeed never failed us.

We dropped anchor at the mouth of the Gironde to take on the usual officials, among them the secret-service men who were to look over the passengers while we waited the turn of the tide before proceeding up-stream to Bordeaux.

It was a beautiful sunlit evening, and as I was standing at the rail watching the tide, which ran out to sea like a mill-race, suddenly there was a splash and we saw one of the Belgian soldiers lying on the water, his face downward and his arms and legs outstretched and motionless. He was being carried out to sea with incredible speed by the tide, and it was evident that he was trying to commit suicide, as he made no effort to struggle. The sailors were all busy elsewhere getting out the mail-bags and trunks, and for a few minutes nothing seemed to be done. Suddenly there was another splash as, from the deck above, a man dove after the Belgian. It was Lieutenant Shirk, an aviator in our marines, who had not even taken the time to throw off his coat or leather puttees. A life-saving belt had been thrown just previously and floated with the tide several yards ahead of the Belgian soldier, but both were carried along so swiftly that it was some time before Lieutenant Shirk could reach him. As he approached, the Belgian promptly kicked at him, and it took several moments before he was overpowered and dragged toward the life-belt. In the meantime a boat had been lowered, but so swift is the tide in these waters that when the boat reached the two men, they seemed like two small black spots in the distance. The excitement and enthusiasm when they were brought back to the ship may easily be imagined.

Lieutenant Shirk proved to be a well-to-do young business man from Indianapolis, who when the war broke out had immediately enlisted, leaving a wife and children and large important business interests to give himself whole-heartedly to the service of his country.

If you "tell this story to the marines" they will refuse to acknowledge that it is anything extraordinary, and they will also tell you that that is just a way they have of dealing with any emergency on land or sea.

The sad part of this heroic rescue is that a few days afterward, meeting one of the Belgian officers in Paris, he told me that the soldier, soon after landing, had succeeded in his effort at self-destruction, and had shot himself in a fit of despondency. He had been away from Belgium for four years, and during all that time had had no news of his wife or children; his little farm was in the hands of the Germans, and there was neither hope nor desire to live left in him.

We all had to assemble in the saloon of the ship to present our passports, and when it came to my turn I was politely told to go to my cabin with two secret-service men, that they might question me further regarding my mission. One of these men was silent, but the other a very voluble, polite Frenchman. But even the visé by the Minister of Foreign Affairs and the French High Commission did not seem quite to satisfy him. The fact that I had been born in Germany evidently impressed him unfavorably. He asked me finally: "Do you intend to take any money out of France?" "On the contrary," I replied, "here is a letter of credit, every cent of which is to be used on French orchestra musicians." In corroboration I showed him the cable from the Ministère des Beaux Arts offering me the use of the Pasdeloup Orchestra, the conductor of which was M. Rhene Baton. The face of my secret-service man suddenly became wreathed in smiles. "Ah!" he said, "M. Baton! Why, before the war I used to play third horn in his orchestra in Bordeaux. Everything is all right." With a bow he handed me back my passport, and at this point his silent companion suddenly gave me a most genial wink, the nationality of which could not be mistaken. I said: "You are American." "Sure!" he answered, and thus I was enabled to land at last in France with colors flying.

The next morning saw me in Paris at the little hotel "France et Choiseul," to which I had always gone on my visits to Paris during twenty-five years preceding. I found the same courteous, smiling directeur, M. Mantel, to receive me. Even the old canary-bird, hanging in the courtyard, was still living, but either corpulence or old age had stopped his musical demonstrations.

It would take a man of much greater eloquence than I

can claim, to give an adequate picture of Paris at that time. It seemed to me more beautiful and more noble than I had ever seen it during my many visits in times of peace. The streets were almost empty, there were no tourists, no pleasure-seekers, no idlers, and therefore that part of Parisian life which usually stands out so prominently and which, alas, is generally the only part that the average visitor sees, was entirely absent. One saw only the French people going about their daily tasks and the soldiers of France and her allies. The Champs-Élysées, the Tuileries, and, above all, the Jardin de Luxembourg seemed more charming than ever, but the tragic note was that the lovely children who in former times crowded these gardens were all gone. Constant air raids and the frequent bombardments by the "Big Bertha" had driven them away. It was said that a million and a half people had left Paris, and that, owing to the nearness of the German armies, the entire evacuation of the civilian population was imminent. Rumors had it, furthermore, that all the banks had sent their securities to Orleans and that the embassies and various relief organizations were ready to leave Paris at a few hours' notice. There was not the least sign of panic, but an indescribable sadness brooded over the city.

During the long twilight, which is the most beautiful time to see Paris, when the sky and the clouds seem to hover most intimately and caressingly over its wonderful vistas, I used to take long walks along the banks of the Seine. Even the complete darkness at night, the absence of all electric lights or signs, with only an occasional half-hidden blue lamp here and there, made the city more picturesque and wonderful. It was almost as if the centuries of civilization and modern inventions had been

swept away and we were back again in the time of the
Grand Monarque, when Paris was only dimly lighted by
faintly flickering oil lamps.

Of course, I soon made the acquaintance of the noc-
turnal air raids, and when the sirens placed at various
high buildings of the city sounded their horrible warning
that the German Gothas were approaching, every inhabi-
tant was supposed to seek shelter in the cellars. I did
this dutifully for two or three nights, but as it meant
leaving one's bed at about 11.30 or 12 and returning at
about 1.30 or 2 A. M., I gradually realized that my own
pet cowardice was more the fear of not getting enough
sleep, as I was completely knocked out during the daytime by the lack of it. After weighing the alternatives
carefully I decided to take the small risk of remaining in
my bed and getting a good night's rest in consequence;
and having solved this question to my complete satisfaction, I used to wake up on hearing the warning of the
sirens, stretch myself comfortably, and immediately go
to sleep again.

The gatherings in the *abri* of our hotel were, however,
quite amusing. The guests used to assemble in the wine-
cellar, which was protected by walls several feet thick,
and in which we could further fortify ourselves by sam-
pling a bottle or two of the excellent claret and burgundy
which it contained. If one of our little number was an
army officer we would make him tell us his experiences
at the front, and listen with awe and eager interest until
the bugles of the fire department outside sounded the
"all-clear" signal. Then the old portier, whom we used
to call "Papa Joffre," would come down and, with the
sweetest smile on his dear old face, assure us that all was
safe and we could creep back again to our beds.

In the meantime I began to investigate the conditions under which to carry out our plan of giving orchestral concerts for our soldiers at their rest camps and in the hospitals, and soon discovered that the recent developments at the front would make it exceedingly difficult, if not impossible. Paris was in a state of great depression. The enemy were threatening the city, our rest camps were empty, and our soldiers were being drilled furiously in order to put them as soon as possible either in the line or behind the line as reserves. Every available inch of space on the railroads had to be used for military purposes, for the transportation of men and material, and to have intruded an orchestra of fifty men with cumbersome luggage, musical instruments, etc., would have been a nuisance instead of a service.

The French Government, through its various departments with which I came into contact, especially the Ministry of Fine Arts and the French High Commission, received me with the greatest courtesy and kindness. M. Cortot, at the Beaux Arts, had taken steps to procure an orchestra for me and I was already getting the full benefit of the friendliness for everything American which, after the first entry of our troops into the fighting-line at Seicheprey, Belleau Wood, and Château-Thierry developed into an enthusiasm, the like of which cannot be imagined. I saw the change from deepest despondency to greatest optimism come over the city like a wave, and especially after the heroic stand of our men at Château-Thierry there was nothing which an American could possibly want that a Frenchman was not willing to give to him with both hands.

For the morning of the Fourth of July a Franco-American demonstration had been arranged which was to culminate in a parade of French and American troops from the Arc de Triomphe down the Champs Élysées to the Place de la Concorde. I was naturally among the crowds of eager spectators who lined the avenue to greet our troops, which included a company of our marines who had fought at the front but a few days before. This was literally the first time that I had seen a crowd of people in Paris, and it marked in significant fashion the change from the gloom that had hovered over the city when I first arrived.

Paris had been decorated as only the French know how, and the noble vistas of the city looked their best under a glorious sky of blue slightly flecked with white clouds. In the waiting crowd there were no young men, not even middle-aged, for all these had been at the front for four years, but there were old men, boys, and women of all ages down to a charming little girl of twelve, evidently of the poorer class, who was standing by my side on tiptoe with excitement. She could speak a few words of English and every now and then, with the sweetest and shyest glance at me, she would demonstrate her knowledge of our tongue, and then supplement it with more voluble French, as she pointed out to me the various wonders of the day.

Overhead some of the most expert of the French airmen were flying backward and forward, looping the loop, dipping the dip, and executing marvellous manœuvres as they swooped down, sometimes almost brushing the trees on either side of the magnificent avenue, all to the great delight of the crowds awaiting the coming of our soldiers. As the mounted police of Paris, a splendid body of men, came down the avenue, the excitement became intense, and when our khaki-clad boys swept into view the enthusiasm exceeded all bounds. Young girls, with their arms literally banked with flowers, ran across the empty spaces cleared by the police, and began to distribute them among our soldiers who, looking straight ahead, awkwardly grabbed the flowers, stuck them into the tunics, or held them in the hand not occupied with the rifle, all the time keeping their alignment with the most rigid discipline, just as if they were ignorant of the sweetest tribute that one nation could offer another. The whole scene was so indescribably touching that every one in the crowd, including myself, stood there with the tears rolling down his cheeks.

On my other side stood an American bandmaster who recognized me, and while we were waiting for the parade he implored me to do something for the bandsmen in the American army in France. He told me that he had drilled his little band of twenty-eight men for six months before being sent overseas, that they had continued to work faithfully during their stay in France, and that they had achieved a good standard of efficiency. But, according to old American army custom, they had been sent into the firing-line at Seicheprey as stretcher-bearers, and in consequence so many had been either killed, wounded, or shell-shocked that his band had become completely disorganized. His regiment was in consequence without music, and he had been detached and sent to Paris as general purchasing agent for musical instruments. He said: "It takes at least six months to train a good bandsman, while a stretcher-bearer can be trained in as many hours. We serve a real purpose, while the men are in camp, in taking their minds away from the drudgery and monotony of army life. Our music cheers them; a silent camp is almost unendurable. Can't you persuade General

Pershing to change this custom, just as the British and other nations have done?" I told him that I sympathized with his views, that it seemed to me wrong to use the band for any other purpose than music, except in case of absolute military necessity, but that I was without any official connection with the army and so did not think that I could be of much service to him.

When the parade was ended and the crowds dispersed, the little French girl on my right said "Good-by" to me in English, ever so prettily, and then very shyly pressed into my hand as a parting token a tiny little American flag that she herself had painted on a bit of cotton, the stars and stripes on one side and the French tricolor on the other. Needless to say I still possess this charming symbol as a *porte-bonheur*.

I had arranged to conduct two concerts in Paris, one on July 13 at the Théâtre des Champs-Élysées, exclusively for our soldiers and Red Cross nurses stationed in and near Paris, and the other on the following afternoon, Sunday, July 14 (the Fête Nationale of the French), the entire proceeds of which were to be given to the Croix Rouge Française. For the latter concert the French Government immediately offered their historic *Salle du Conservatoire*, a courtesy that had never been extended to a foreign conductor before. This was to be a symphonic concert, entirely devoted in honor of the day to works of the great French composers, but at the first rehearsal it looked as if the concert would have to be cancelled because it seemed impossible to collect a first-class orchestra of eighty men. The four years of war had called almost every male citizen of France into military service, and the recent evacuation of Paris had drawn with it many of the musicians who had until then remained in the city. At my first rehearsal only forty-three men appeared, and these were divided in most abnormal fashion. There were five first violins, ten seconds, two violas, one violoncello, and three double basses. There was no oboe or English horn; only two French horns, one trumpet, etc. Of the forty-three men assembled seven were members of the *Garde Républicaine*, the famous Paris military band, but which unfortunately for me had to attend an official celebration of the Fête Nationale at the Trocadéro on the Sunday afternoon. The President of the republic was to be present with various other dignitaries and a chorus of three thousand school children.

I was in despair, and finally made an appeal to the orchestra in very voluble but ungrammatical French, the gist of which was that America had gladly sent one million soldiers to France and was getting ready to send two millions more; all I asked in return was an orchestra of eighty men! Could they not help me to supplement their thin ranks with a sufficient number of trained musicians to complete the orchestra? My little speech was received with an agitated enthusiasm. They immediately began to gather in excited groups and swore to me that the orchestra could and would be obtained. One assured me of a fine oboe, another of a trumpeter, another of a first violin, and so on. M. Cortot also got busy. He sent for Captain Ballay, the conductor of the *Garde Républicaine*, and represented to him in what seemed to me an eloquent oration worthy of the *Chambre des Députés*, that after Seicheprey and Château-Thierry France could not and would not refuse an American anything he asked for. Captain Ballay enthusiastically agreed, and promised to send the seven members of his band whom I needed for my concert—in the swiftest taxi-cabs he could procure—

from the Trocadéro, where the governmental celebration was to begin at three o'clock, immediately after they had played his opening overture, to the *Salle du Conservatoire* at which my concert was scheduled for four. He thought that the President of the republic was not musical enough to notice the absence of these seven men, and that he would manage to get along without them for the rest of his programme.

At the same time, noted French soloists who ordinarily did not play in orchestras, offered their services— Captain Pollain, famous violoncellist from Nancy and M. Hewitt (whose great-grandfather had been an American but whose family had lived in France for three generations), solo violinist of the Instruments Anciens. And at the second rehearsal, whom should I see, but dear old Longy, for thirty years celebrated oboe player of the Boston Symphony, who said to me most touchingly: "I see you have no second oboe. I have no instrument in France as I left mine in Boston, but I will borrow one and play for you if you need me."

At my second rehearsal an excellent orchestra of seventy-seven men assembled, and at the third the orchestra was complete, including many French soldiers in uniform, four or five distinguished virtuosi who played in orchestra only for this occasion, and even one of my own first violinists from the New York Symphony Orchestra, Reber Johnson, who, having been rejected for the army as physically not fit, had immediately volunteered in the American Red Cross, and turned up at the rehearsal in his uniform in the most natural way, as if this had been one of the regular daily rehearsals of the New York Symphony.

My first trumpeter was a young French soldier who

had played clarinet before the war. His arm had been shot off only a year before, and as soon as he left the hospital he studied the trumpet and with his one arm not only held but fingered it with remarkable facility.

I do not think that in all my long career I have ever conducted concerts or rehearsals in which both conductor and players were enveloped in such an atmosphere of emotional excitement. Our young, handsome boys in khaki seemed like demigods to these tired and worn people who had fought with such incredible tenacity for four terrible years. The members of the orchestra received every criticism which I made during the rehearsals with a quick nod or an engaging smile, and every now and then some remark of mine regarding the proper interpretation would be followed by a murmur of approval, which would spread through the orchestra and sometimes even vent itself in applause. I hope that my criticisms, as well as my interpretations, pleased them, but I know that even if they had not, it would have made no difference. I was an American and that was enough.

At the Saturday-night concert, which was more popular in character, I gave our American soldier audience Victor Herbert's clever medley on American airs, and those Frenchmen played as if they had known them all their lives. The huge audience in khaki fairly seethed with patriotic excitement, which of course found its climax when we turned into "Dixie." All jumped to their feet and cheered and cheered, so that for ten bars or so literally nothing of the music could be heard, and cnly by the waving of my stick and the motions of the players could one tell that the music was going on.

The following afternoon the programme was one of real symphonic proportions, and included Saint-Saëns's great

"Symphony No. 3" for orchestra, organ, and piano, Debussy's "L'Après-midi d'un Faune," and the "Symphonic Variations" for piano with orchestra, by César Franck.

The organ part in the symphony was played by Mlle. Nadia Boulanger, without doubt the greatest woman musician I have ever known, and the Franck "Variations" were superbly interpreted by Alfred Cortot. M. Casadesus played an exquisite concerto for the viola d'amour by Laurenziti.

The little *Salle du Conservatoire*, its quaint architecture dating from the time of Louis XVI, with its tiny boxes and balconies, was jammed to the doors—the janitor told me that it was the largest audience he had ever seen there. Every available space was filled twice over and the walls literally bulged outward. The audience was a very interesting one. The French Government, with its usual politeness, had sent official representatives from the *Ministère des Etrangères*, the *Ministère des Beaux Arts*, and the French High Commission—many of them in uniform. There were also many French musicians of distinction, among them dear Maître Charles Widor, the *Secretaire Perpetuel de l'Institut de France*, and, of course, many French, British, and American soldiers. A New York fire commissioner would have gasped at the way in which all precautions were disregarded, and the excitement in the audience, when at the end of the concert we played the "Marseillaise" and the "Star-Spangled Banner," can be imagined.

To add to my pleasure my daughter Alice, who was doing war work away down in Brest, had received permission to come up to Paris for the great occasion. My old friend, Paul Cravath, vice-president of the New York Symphony Society, who was at that time at the head of our Finance Commission in London, had flown over in an English airplane, and smiled upon me from a centre box in all his splendor of six feet four as I turned around to make my bow to the cheering audience.

I think we gave them an exceedingly good concert. The orchestra were delightful in their keen desire to carry out my intentions; but I think if we had played less well the enthusiasm would have been just as great, for while we were playing, the names of Seicheprey and Château-Thierry were vibrating in the hearts of all listeners, and their enthusiasm was poured out upon me as if I, single-handed, demonstrated the valor of our American troops.

At the end of the concert, the president of the Musical Orchestral Union of Paris presented me with a large bouquet of roses tied with the American colors, and in a very eloquent speech voiced the gratitude of the French musicians for the assistance which had been given them by our Society of American Friends of Musicians in France. I was able to supplement my words of thanks with a further substantial check, which had been sent by Mr. Flagler and which was to be devoted to the families of orchestral musicians serving at the front.

The week had been fully occupied with the preparations for these two concerts, but notwithstanding the attendant excitements and elations I had periods of great despondency. The possibility of continuing my mission in France seemed less and less capable of fulfilment, partly owing to the tense military situation and partly because I did not seem to get the proper assistance from the Y. M. C. A. Mr. McLane and Mr. Sloane, at the head of affairs in New York, had given me their enthusiastic support, and I had sailed at their urgent request. They had cabled and written full instructions to the

"Y" in France, and on my arrival Mr. Ernest Carter, the head worker, whom I liked exceedingly, had promised me the fullest co-operation. But he was evidently harassed and overworked and did not get the efficient help which he should have had in the running of so large an organization in war time. Many of the heads of departments were ex-clergymen or church and Sunday-school workers who were evidently inexperienced in the management of practical affairs. I am told that later on this condition was much improved and that the men who were subsequently sent out from America were chosen more for their business ability, but at the time I mention, the confusion at the headquarters in the Rue d'Agesseau was often great and there seemed to be insufficient co-operation between the different departments. In order to be able to travel around France unmolested I had to have a *carte rouge*, and this card it seemed impossible to obtain for me, notwithstanding all my proper and complete credentials as an American, as a musician well known all over our country, and, above all, as a *persona grata* with the French Government.

A few days before my first concert I was informed that it was impossible to procure this card for me, and that therefore I could not be permitted to leave Paris. When I asked for an explanation, it was refused by a rather sanctimonious person who put his arm around me, called me brother, but expressed his regret at the unfortunate fact of my having been born in Germany. I swallowed my rage as best I could, but my chagrin was all the greater because in the meantime M. Casadesus and four other distinguished French artists had offered me their services to travel around with me in a motor-car and give concerts in our camps and hospitals. I finally obtained the information from a very nice young man who was in charge of the entertainment division of the "Y" that he understood that the objections came from the Intelligence Department of the A. E. F. I immediately called on Major Cabot Ward, the head of the Intelligence Division in Paris whom I had known in New York for twenty-five years. I showed him my various credentials, and he assured me that: "As far as the United States army is concerned, you are as free as air." I returned with this information to the Rue d'Agesseau and was met by the same impenetrable wall of ignorance or ill-will; and, as my friends at the French High Commission had already assured me that as far as they were concerned all France was open to me, I seemed to be at my wit's end how to unravel this riddle.

I finally called on my friend, Robert Bliss, counsellor of our embassy in Paris. I can never forget his kindness and helpfulness during this period. He and his charming wife had made their apartment the very centre of American life during those trying times. Mrs. Bliss had resolutely refused to leave Paris, and dispensed a generous hospitality at their apartment in the Rue Henri Moissan. When I told him of my troubles and that I, who had lived in America forty-seven years, should now be thus treated, he smiled and said: "We can do nothing for you at present, as you are still a part of the organization of the Y. M. C. A., but as soon as you get that uniform off, you will find every road open to you."

That wretched uniform! It had annoyed me from the first moment I had put it on because the tailor to whom the "Y" had sent me had made a miserable job of it. It was too narrow between the shoulders, which is fatal for an orchestral conductor, and the trousers were a tragedy.

But there was no time before sailing to order a better-fitting uniform, and as I had been told that I could not move an inch in France without it I had literally taken no civilian clothes with me! I had ordered some new clothes in Paris, but there was a tailors' strike on and I was therefore, for decency's sake, compelled to hold on to that uniform, much as I longed to divest myself of the symbol of the sacred triangle. However, I began to see daylight, and as I hoped by the following Monday or Tuesday to get my new civilian clothes, I decided to conduct the two concerts on Saturday and Sunday and then magnificently hand in my resignation. But I was not spared a last drop of bitterness, for on Saturday morning I received a visit from a very stupid and exasperating *officier de liaison* of the Y. M. C. A., who proceeded to inform me that as I had been "born in Germany" and therefore could not obtain my *carte rouge*, the committee of the "Y" thought that I should not conduct the two concerts in their uniform. Again that accursed uniform! I was so enraged that I said I would either conduct in it or in my underclothes, that my resignation had already been written and would be presented on Monday, and that I insisted on an interview with Mr. Carter and his executive committee, as I wished them to know how I had been treated. I knew that Mr. Carter, poor man, had no knowledge of the entire affair, as he had been zigzagging around France all this time to the various posts and supply centres of the "Y," trying to bring some kind of order out of chaos. He immediately accorded me a meeting, and when I told my story, made me an apology so ample and generous that I left him with none but the kindliest feelings and really regretted that he, a man of high ideals and spiritual power, should through the exigencies of war have been so overburdened with practical affairs. For a few of his aids I have nothing but absolute contempt, but there were many among the men workers and certainly the majority of the women who gave wonderful service and gladly suffered all kinds of annoyances and deprivations in order to help the soldiers, who were not all angels by any means.

But my real triumph was to come on the very Sunday morning of my concert when General Charles Dawes, of the American army, called on me at my hotel and, to my amazement, asked me whether I could come to the general headquarters of the A. E. F. at Chaumont, and confer with General Pershing regarding the possible improvement of our army bands. I could not believe my ears that so suddenly after my bitter experiences with the "Y," the commander-in-chief of the American army in France had personally sent for me.

General Dawes was at that time at the head of the army supplies, with headquarters in Paris. A great lover of music, he had contributed largely to its cultivation in his own city of Chicago. He was an old and valued friend of General Pershing and I think that it was he who had suggested my name to him. I can never thank General Dawes enough for giving me, a musician and over fifty years of age, this wonderful opportunity to touch even the outer hem of the robes of the war goddess.

Needless to say, my despondent mood immediately changed to one of elation. I accepted the invitation with alacrity and arranged with General Dawes to go to Chaumont on the following Wednesday, July 17.

In the meantime the air had been full of rumors regarding the "Big Bertha" who had been conveniently silent ever since my arrival in Paris. It was persistently said that on Monday morning seventeen of these ladies bearing the same name would again begin a bombardment of Paris, and I confess that it gave me something of a shock, when, on the Monday morning after my concert while I was still luxuriating in bed—thinking with pleasure of the triumphs of the day before and with eager anticipation of my approaching trip to Chaumont—I suddenly heard a curious reverberation, different from the explosions of the Gothas or of the answering air-guns. It was the first greeting of Madame Bertha, and this greeting was repeated punctiliously every fifteen minutes throughout the day, the shells striking in Paris in different quarters.

It was interesting to watch the French people. After every shot, crowds of them would run into the streets, talking, gesticulating, and speculating where that particular shell had fallen. This would go on for thirteen or fourteen minutes and then all would scoot back into their shops and houses as they knew that the next shell was about due.

That evening I had been invited to dine at Mrs. Edith Wharton's, at her lovely apartment in the Rue de Varennes. Just as I got to her door a Frenchman stopped and said to me that he had been at the concert on the preceding day. He then added: "I see that you are making the acquaintance of 'La Grosse Berthe.'" Thinking that he referred to the return of the bombardment, I smiled assent, and then proceeded to Mrs. Wharton's apartment. I found our great novelist with two other ladies, an American officer, and an American composer, my dear friend Blair Fairchild, who had been living in Paris for several years and was acting most ably as distributing agent for the money which our "Society of American Friends of Musicians in France" was sending over. The dinner proceeded as if we lived in times of deepest peace. It was served with punctilious efficiency, the flowers were charming, and the conversation delightful, and it was only when dinner was half over that I found out, quite casually, that what my French gentleman at the door had referred to was, that only two minutes before my arrival the last shell of the Big Bertha had fallen on the roof of the house opposite, demolishing it and parts of the upper story.

On the following Wednesday, July 17, I took the morning train for Chaumont, again comfortably clad in civilian clothes. I was met at the station by a young officer, Lieutenant Wendell, nephew of my old friend Evart Wendell, who took me to general headquarters and introduced me to Lieutenant-Colonel Collins, secretary of the General Staff, who explained to me in detail various points on which General Pershing desired information and assistance. I was then most comfortably put up at the guest-house, formerly a large private residence in the town, which had been taken over by General Pershing to accommodate his visitors. I was to dine at his château that evening, and spent a great part of the afternoon walking through the quaint old hill town situated on a high cliff overlooking the valley of the Marne. It was during this walk that I saw the only drunken American private during my three months' stay in France. I was following a picturesque road leading out of the town into the country, when a colored boy in khaki reeled toward me and said: " 'Scuse me, sah. Are you a Frenchman?" I said "No," and he replied: "Then foh Gawd sake, will you please tell me whar ah can get a drink?" I answered: "No. You have evidently had enough already." He tried to follow me and I, seeing two white soldiers approaching, turned to them and said: "I think you had better take care of this boy. He has had too much to drink." They briskly answered: "Certainly, sir." But as they went up to him he kept peering at me and said: "I want to talk to that gen'leman. That's Mr. Damrosch!" I laughed out loud, for here I was, over three thousand miles from home, and this boy, who perhaps had musical inclinations and had heard me conduct in some concert, recognized me even through the alcoholic vapors which surrounded him so thickly that one could have cut them with a knife.

One of the other visitors at the guest-house was General Omar Bundy, who commanded the first division and had come to Chaumont to receive the congratulations of the commander-in-chief on the splendid work of his division. He proved a delightful gentleman, and we chatted together very amicably as a motor-car took us that evening about five miles beyond Chaumont through most lovely country to the château surrounded by exquisite gardens and woods which General Pershing had taken for his personal residence. A scene of greater peace and tranquillity could not be imagined, and literally the only sign and symbol of war was the solitary sentry pacing up and down before the entrance, with bayonet fixed.

As this happened to be the first day of General Foch's great attack in which he pushed the Germans back six miles, General Pershing, who had been at the front all day, had not yet returned, and General Bundy and I walked through the grounds in the lovely evening twilight for perhaps half an hour, when a motor-car drove up and our great commander-in-chief, accompanied by his aide, immediately came over to us and made us welcome in hearty and simple fashion. He reminded me that we had met at the Presidio in San Francisco during the great exhibition of 1915, and indeed I remembered it well, for shortly afterward he had been sent to the Mexican border in command of the troops, and while there had been overwhelmed by the terrible tragedy of the death of his wife and children, who were suffocated in a fire at night which destroyed their home at the Presidio.

So much has been written regarding the wonderful impression which General Pershing made in Europe on all who came in contact with him that it is not necessary for me to more than echo the general chorus of praise— soldierly, dignified, courteous, and simple in his bearing, wearing a uniform as only a man can who has been a soldier all his life.

We entered the house and shortly after sat down to dinner. The party consisted of the commander-in-chief, General Bundy, and a most delightful staff of eight officers—I being the only civilian. As such I expected and half hoped that the talk would be all about the wonderful success of the first day's push by Foch, of which I had already heard enthusiastic rumors in the town, or of great military secrets, affairs of strategy, monster guns, thousands of airplanes, and new, mysterious machines of destruction. But, to my surprise, the conversation during almost the entire dinner was of music, of its influence in raising the spirits of the soldier, in giving him the right kind of recreation and the necessary relief from the monotony of camp work or the horrors of battle. General Pershing told me that after hearing some of the crack military bands of France and England he had been so overwhelmed by the consciousness of our inferiority that he was eager to know if something could not be done to improve the general standard of our army bands, and, more particularly, whether it might not be possible at least to take out the best players from among the bands then in France and to form a headquarters band of superior excellence, led by the best bandmaster among them, and in this way form a model which the others could endeavor to copy. This suggestion seemed to me excellent, and I asked how many bandmasters there were at present in France, as I would like to examine them as to their fitness. General Pershing said, with a smile, that there were over two hundred, but this did not phase me and I agreed to examine them all, provided that proper arrangements could be made for a fitting test of their qualifications. Various plans for such an examination were discussed and General Pershing finally decided to send them all to Paris in batches of fifty every week, together with a military band which should be stationed there for the following four or five weeks, thus giving me abundant opportunity to test their efficiency in conducting as well as in harmony and orchestration. It seemed to me at the time remarkable that, in the midst of war and with all its many immediate necessities weighing upon him, General Pershing should have had the acumen to perceive the value of music in war time and to interest himself in its improvement.

As I sat there, the memory of the hollow-cheeked Bandmaster Tyler who had stood next to me at the Fourth of July parade in Paris suddenly came back. I thought to myself that here I was, the only civilian at the table, and that therefore I might say anything I pleased without being put up against a wall at sunrise and shot, for at the worst they could only consider me as very ignorant of army customs. Therefore I watched for my opportunity and suddenly plunged in and spoke of my conversation with Bandmaster Tyler while we were waiting for our marines to march down the Champs-Élysées. I said that in my humble opinion it was a great mistake to use musicians as stretcher-bearers in battle, not that their lives as soldiers were any more valuable than those of any others in the army, but that a stretcher-bearer could be trained in a very short time while it took many months to train a bandsman; that the Canadian regiments had followed the same custom during the first months of the war, but the results had been so dire in destroying the bands and their usefulness, that the soldiers themselves had implored their commanding officers not to let their bandsmen be sacrificed in this way, as there was nothing so terrible as coming back after battle to a silent and therefore desolate camp. After I had finished my rather impassioned peroration, General Bundy and others heartily agreed with me, but General Pershing said nothing at all, and I felt that I had perhaps talked too much and *mal à propos*. But the following morning, as I was seated with Colonel Collins at general headquarters arranging the details of my examinations, he smilingly handed me an order from the commander-in-chief which had just arrived and which was to be sent to the division commanders, to the effect that "from now on bandsmen are not to be used any longer as stretcher-bearers except in cases of extreme military urgency."

One of General Pershing's remarks during the dinner is so characteristic that I repeat it here. He said: "When peace is declared and our bands march up Fifth Avenue I should like them to play so well that it will be another proof of the advantage of military training." Subsequent developments and meetings with this interesting man further deepened the impression which he made upon me.

I returned to Paris and proceeded to make all necessary arrangements for the examinations of the two hundred bandmasters. Our army had leased a large hotel near the Bastille on the banks of the Seine, and a large room on the ground floor served admirably for my purpose. The band of the 329th infantry soon arrived and was quartered in this hotel, and every morning at 9.30 the examinations began and continued from Monday to Thursday at the rate of about fifty bandmasters a week, who arrived from all quarters of France—from the seaport towns, from the training camps, and some even from the very front line of the trenches. Fridays I would usually return to headquarters and report on my findings and begin recommendations, which gradually assumed greater and greater proportions as the magnitude of the work developed.

To assist me in this prodigious work, I engaged the services of M. Francis Casadesus, brother of Henri and a splendid musician. He examined the men as to their qualifications in instrumentating and in their general knowledge of the various instruments, while I examined them in the actual process of conducting and drilling a band. I would first let them bite their teeth into an overture like the "Oberon" of Weber, or a movement from a classical symphony, and then would let them conduct a composition of their own choice. I found very soon that while most of these young bandmasters were musically talented and ambitious, they had had no or but little opportunity for acquiring what we may call the technic of the baton. They had had no intensive disciplinary training such as our young officers from civilian life had received at Plattsburg and similar camps. Many of them did not know how to beat time properly, much less train a band in phrasing or rhythmic accuracy; and I soon saw that unless some opportunity was given them to learn at least the rudiments of their calling, the effort toward improving our bands would be useless. It therefore seemed to me that the quick formation of a band-masters' school was the only solution of the problem, and as our army had had the help of French military and aviation officers as instructors, loaned to us by the *Ministère de la Guerre*, I thought that a similar arrangement could be made, under which we might obtain the necessary musical instructors also from the French army, as nearly all the musicians of France were at that time in uniform.

I also discovered that some of the most important musical instruments which give mellowness and nobility to the tone of a band were almost utterly lacking. We had hardly any oboes, bassoons, French horns, or flügel-horns. I knew that some of the greatest masters of these instruments, first prizes of the Conservatoire of Paris, were serving in the French army, and immediately, through the *Ministère des Beaux Arts*, obtained their names and the regiments to which they belonged. On the following visit to Chaumont I proposed to General Pershing that we form a music-school at which fifty band-masters could get the most intensive musical training and discipline for eight weeks, to be succeeded by a new batch of fifty, etc., and at the same time forty pupils each in oboe, bassoon, French horn, and flügelhorn could get a similar training of twelve weeks on their respective instruments.

General Pershing and his staff were delighted with the plan and I offered to procure the necessary instructors from the French army, promising General Pershing that the school would be in complete running order by October 1, provided a proper building could be obtained. The general asked me where I wished to place the school and offered me Longres, where several schools on the strategy of war were already in progress, but I claimed that the surroundings for my music-school should be of a more "peaceful and even academic character," and suggested Chaumont. General Pershing smiled, but insisted that it was already overcrowded and that I would not be able to find a building large enough to house so great a number of instructors and pupils. He gave me full power, however, to see what could be done, and I set forth immediately with a French liaison officer—member of the French Military Commission at Chaumont, and in G-5, general headquarters, under which department the proposed music-school would come—who proved a most remarkable and valuable assistant in my work. He was Lieutenant Michel Weill, nephew of the owner of the well-known White House in San Francisco, and an enthusiastic musical amateur who, through his long residence in America, had acquired a knowledge of English and a sympathy for America only second to that for his own native land. He belonged to a delightful French officers' mess at Chaumont, and they immediately made me a kind of honorary member and in most hospitable fashion invited me to their Lucullan repasts. As they were all enthusiastic lovers of music, I endeavored to repay them by pounding out Wagner, their supreme favorite, to their hearts' content on an old upright piano placed in a little sitting-room next to their *salle à manger*.

Lieutenant Weill and I first paid a *visite de cérémonie* to the *Maire* of Chaumont and explained to him our desire. The idea of what he called "*un petit conservatoire de musique pour les Américains*" in Chaumont appealed to his fancy immensely, and he immediately picked up his telephone and called up an old friend of his, a fellow citizen and mill owner. He explained to him the great honor that was about to befall their town if a proper building could be found, and exhorted him to show himself as a really patriotic citizen of France and friend of the Americans by giving the mill which he owned just outside the city and only a few minutes' walk from our headquarters for this noble purpose. We motored to this building and met there an elderly, dignified, and courteous Frenchman who told us that anything he had was at the disposal of "les Américains." We found a huge mill with walls two feet thick, the machinery in disuse, and with large empty spaces that our army engineers could easily turn into sleeping-quarters, practising-rooms, and other needs for a music-school. In one large wing we found a few women and many children playing about. I said: "Of course, we shall need this wing also." "Then I regret," answered the owner, "but this wing you cannot have, because I have given it to forty-eight refugees from Verdun with the promise that they shall occupy it until the end of the war." Naturally Lieutenant Weill and I reconsidered, and concluded that a large tent could be put up in the meadow as an eating-place, and that we could get along without the extra wing. I then asked the owner what rental he would demand. "Oh," he said, "anything that the American army wishes to pay." But when Lieutenant Weill informed him that he should fix a fair price, he asked timidly: "Would the American army consider five hundred francs a month reasonable?" I tell this to offset the tales of those people who keep harping on the commercial greed of the French in anything that concerned the needs of the American soldier.

We returned to general headquarters jubilant, and, after a satisfactory interview with the officer in charge of building operations, it was decided to place the school in Chaumont, and I returned to Paris to complete my plans.

My brother Frank had recognized the lack of good schooling for our army bands and bandmasters many years before the war, and had very patriotically placed the entire machinery of his Institute of Musical Art at the disposal of the secretary of war. An arrangement had accordingly been made by which a bandmaster's school at Governor's Island, New York, was placed under my brother's control, and for several years before the war a small number of bandmasters were graduated from it who ranked well on a par with those of other countries. But when we entered the war and our army was organized on a scale of millions these were but a drop in the bucket, and heroic measures were necessary to bring some semblance of order into this musical chaos of hundreds of uneducated bandmasters and thousands of still less educated bandsmen.

During these five weeks in Paris and Chaumont I worked very hard and, while my life has been crowded with affairs of all kinds relating to my profession, I cannot recall any time when the work was so constant day and night or when I was more jubilantly happy in the doing of it. During the forenoons Casadesus and I would examine the bandmasters, discover what they could and could not do, give them, so to speak, "first aid to the wounded" by pointing out their worst failings or their greatest weaknesses. In the afternoons Lieutenant Weill and I would run around to the various French government departments on the track of this or that musician whom we wished to corral as professor for our school. At night I would sit propped up in bed and work out the entire tuition plan of the school, down to the minutest details.

My general recommendations to general headquarters, all of which were subsequently carried out, included classes for the bandmasters' instruction in the technic of conducting, in harmony, and in orchestration. These classes were put in charge of M. Francis Casadesus and M. André Caplet. The latter was later on succeeded by Lieutenant Albert Stoessel, a highly talented bandmaster in our army, who has returned to civilian life and has now become my successor as conductor of the New York Oratorio Society.

Captain Ellacott, of the A. E. F., became the military head of the school to which he gave most sympathetic assistance.

There were two professors each for oboe, bassoon, French horn, and flügelhorn, all of whom were graduates and first prizes of the famous Paris Conservatoire. I also recommended that the beautiful B-flat bugles of the French army be adopted by us and that a French drum-major, proficient on this instrument, be appointed as instructor to drill successive classes of fifty for one month each, the graduates to become first buglers of our regiments, in order that they might, in turn, instruct other buglers in their respective drum and bugle corps.

At the examinations I also asked the bandmasters certain questions regarding their position in their respective regiments, the attitude of their colonel toward music, their general treatment, and the hours allowed them for musical practice, and here I came on all kinds of conditions. Some of the commanding officers had no sympathy with music or with the bandsmen, and instead of making them practise their six hours a day, they were put to work as kitchen police and on other fatigue duties. I therefore urged that the commanding officers be impressed with the fact that the primary object of the band is not to fight, but to cheer the fighters, and the better their music, the greater its beneficial effects upon the spirit of the soldiers, and that therefore all bandsmen should be compelled to devote at least five or six hours every day to the practice of their instruments and to rehearsals, and that other duties should be made subsidiary to their musical work and should not be of a character to unfit them for a proper performance on their respective instruments.

I also discovered that there was a terrible wastage as regards musical instruments and that in several instances, preparatory to going into action, the instruments had been thrown away or simply left behind, nevermore to be recovered, and that therefore it might be wise to appoint a travelling inspector of musical instruments whose duties should be to attend to the speedy replacement of missing parts, the repairing of instruments, and the supplying of new music.

A really excellent headquarters band was formed at Chaumont, which became a source of much gratification to the commander-in-chief and his staff, accompanying him on many of his ceremonial visits and functions.

One of my most important recommendations for the school was that every week at least one concert should be given by the professors and such of the bandsmen as were really competent musicians. The programmes should be made up only of the great master composers, in order that the students—many of whom had come from isolated communities in our country and had had but little opportunity to hear good music—should become sensitive to the finer and more spiritual qualities of music as an art. This was carried out in most remarkable fashion during the entire existence of the school, and the programmes and their performance were worthy of a place in any highly cultivated musical community.

When I returned to Chaumont on a visit of inspection the following year, I heard one of these concerts, which included a quintet of Mozart for oboe and strings and a sonata for violin and piano by César Franck. I sat in delighted amazement as I saw the happy faces of over a hundred students in khaki who were listening to this divine music in rapt silence. What a pity that such a school cannot be founded in every State in America now that the war is over and our soldiers have returned home! This would speedily result in an excellent band for every town and lay a real foundation for the musical development of the people at large.

During these weeks in Paris I also saw a great deal of some of my French musician colleagues, all of whom had refused to leave Paris in spite of the Gothas and Berthas.

When I first called on Charles Marie Widor, the famous old organist of Saint Sulpice, I found him installed, by virtue of his office as *Secrétaire Perpétuel* of the *Institut de France*, in a charming Louis XVI suite of rooms in that building. He showed me a hole in the window of his workroom and told me that a few days before he had just stooped down to pick up a musical score from the floor when a shell from the Big Bertha burst in front of his apartment and a piece of it hurtled through his window, missing him only because he was in a stooping position.

His Gallic wit and versatility make him a delightful companion, and I am grateful for the opportunity the war gave me for more intimate acquaintance and friendship with him. Indeed, this applies to all the friends made during that eventful summer. The war brought us more quickly and closely together than would have been possible otherwise, and as I was an American I reaped the full advantage of all the intense gratitude which the French felt for us, some of which was hardly deserved, as our government certainly had shilly-shallied and waited until it was almost too late before they threw our great weight of men and treasure into the balance.

I have already spoken of Mlle. Nadia Boulanger, who played the organ for me at the performance of Saint-Saëns's "Third Symphony" on July 14. Among women I have never met her equal in musicianship, and indeed there are very few men who can compare with her. She is one of the finest organists of France, an excellent pianist, and the best reader of orchestral scores that I have ever known. Again and again I have seen her take up a manuscript orchestral score, sit down with it at the piano, and brilliantly read it at sight, transcribing it for the piano as she played along. When we first met, she and her dear mother were in the greatest grief. A younger sister, Lili, had died only a month before at twenty-four years of age. Beautiful, exquisite, and marvellously talented, she had won the much-coveted *Prix de Rome* three years before—the first woman to have gained it. A mortal illness had slowly sapped her strength, and as she had been the idol of her mother and sister, her loss was to them a tragedy almost beyond endurance. Nadia, besides keeping up her professional duties—she was substitute organist at the Madeleine during the war—hurled herself into war work and more especially the care of the students of the Conservatoire who were at the front. She knew all their names and the numbers of their organizations and founded a kind of musical gazette, mimeographed copies of which were sent out every month to the students. All kinds of musical news and musical questions were published in it, so that these boys, in the midst of their military duties or while convalescing from their wounds in the hospitals, could have something to think about more immediately connected with their own profession. It is interesting to note that, in answer to the question, "Should German composers like Brahms and Wagner be played at our concerts during the war?" out of fifty-eight, forty-seven answered unequivocally "Yes" for Wagner and Brahms, three "Yes" for Beethoven and the classics, two were undecided, and six said "No." These answers were accompanied in many cases by highly interesting essays on art and nationality of art, and, altogether, the judgments thus expressed reflected the high intellectual standard of these young French artists at the front.

I saw many instances of how keenly the French separate their artistic from their political convictions. One night my friends of the French Military Commission at Chaumont had come to Paris and one of them, Captain Guegnier, invited me to dinner at his apartment. His wife and the wife of one of his colleagues had come to Paris from the country especially for the occasion. We sat down, a very jolly party of six, to a most delicious dinner such as only the French can devise and properly execute. As all the party were musical we naturally had a good deal of music after dinner. The ladies sang charmingly and I had to play excerpts from their beloved Wagner—"Tristan," "Meistersinger," "Parsifal," and the "Trilogy." My hostess sang songs of Fauré, Chausson, and Debussy, and just then the sirens boomed out their disagreeable message that the Gothas were taking advantage of the moonlit night to make one of their raids over Paris. At the same moment the taxi-cab man, who had come to take me back to my hotel, announced that he had arrived. Would he like to come up-stairs? Oh, no, he would just sit inside the cab and wait till I got ready. "Then let us have some more music," said my hostess, and simply drew the curtain over the windows. And, while the Gothas were scattering their shells over Paris, she turned to me and said: "Now let me sing for you this lovely song of Schubert." There was my French hostess singing German songs, and it was not until about one o'clock in the morning that Lieutenant Weill and I turned homeward.

The vast difference in attitude between the French and certain of my compatriots regarding the proper stand to be taken in time of war toward the art of an enemy nation was very striking. I had myself decided that the New York Symphony Orchestra should not play the works of living German composers, and that the German language should not be sung at our concerts during the war. There seemed to me good and valid reasons for such a course. But Beethoven, Mozart, and Wagner I considered as classics, belonging to us just as much as to Germany, and their divine message had naught to do with the political and military leaders of Germany who had plunged the world into this horrible bath of blood.

There was, however, in New York a small but noisy group led by a few women who sought to demonstrate their "patriotism" by hysterical outbursts and newspaper protests against the performance of all music composed by Germans, no matter how many years ago. Some of these women, through the curious psychosis of war, really thought that they were serving their country by their protests. In the winter of 1918 the orchestra of the Paris Conservatoire made a tour through America under their conductor, André Messager. When I called on him the day after his arrival he showed me a letter he had just received from one of these women protesting against his performing a Beethoven Symphony during his stay in America. He was white with anger, and when I asked him how he would answer it, he said: "I will answer it as a French artist should." I said: "The best way to answer would be to put Beethoven's 'Eroica' Symphony on your first programme." "I will," he said; and he did.

The opposition to Wagner was based on very amusing premises. Because some of his heroes were wont to appear on the stage in very blond wigs and beards, these lady sleuth-hounds seemed to perceive some evil and subtle connection between *Siegfried* in the "Nibelungen Trilogy" and Nietzsche's "blond beast," which, according to his prophecy, was eventually to control the earth. Their studies of Wagner were too shallow to enable them to realize that the whole philosophy of life as expressed by Wagner in the "Nibelungen Trilogy" was in direct contrast to the desire of the modern militaristic German to rule and control the world by force. Wagner depicts a prehistoric world in which the gods of greed, lust, and power rule, carrying, however, the seed of their own destruction within them because of the materialistic quality of their desires. As their power wanes and the old gods perish, a new religion is born, the religion of self-sacrifice through love, as symbolized by *Brunhilde* in her self-immolation on the funeral pyre of *Siegfried*.

But all this is already ancient history, and I for one confidently believe that the racial spirit which created the Germany of Bach, Beethoven, Goethe, Kant, and Wagner will soon return again to brighten and ennoble the world.

In five weeks all necessary arrangements for the school were completed and notices were sent by the General Staff to the bandmasters of the entire A. E. F. who had not come up to the necessary qualifications during the examination which I had given them, to report to the Chaumont School in batches of fifty every eight weeks, beginning on October 1, and to start their studies. Students for oboe, bassoon, French horn, and flügelhorn were also selected from the hundreds of applicants. At first we had great difficulty in finding the necessary instruments for them. France is famous for its wood-wind instruments, but the various factories had long since ceased operations, as all the workmen were in the army. The ever-ready and ingenious Lieutenant Weill, however, succeeded in scraping together enough oboes and bassoons to start the classes, and I cannot say enough for the willing assistance which was accorded me by every United States army officer with whom I came in contact. From the commander-in-chief down to Lieutenant Kelley, who sat in the anteroom of General Dawes's office in the Champs-Élysées, and whose principal duty seemed to be to ward off disagreeable or tiresome callers who wished to rob General Dawes of his valuable time, all made me feel as if the improvement of the army bands was the one thing necessary to win the war. It was high time for me to leave France and "get back to earth," as I no longer walked on anything but air and with my head projecting far above the clouds.

During my last visit to Chaumont I motored down to Domrémy, the birthplace of Jeanne d'Arc, and found the little village in just about the same state it must have been when she was born in the little house next to the church, both of which have been carefully preserved for the worshippers of to-day. The open space in front of her house, the trees surrounding it, and the monument in the centre seemed to me to form a natural stage on which a peace pageant could well be enacted, and as I sat there and the bell began to toll from the little church in which Jeanne had whispered her prayers, I began to dream of a possible peace celebration in which a company of American soldiers, a company of French soldiers, an American and a French military band, singers from the Opéra Comique, and a children's chorus should take part; the climax to be the joyous meeting of the military forces around the monument and the awakening of Jeanne from her sleep of centuries, opening the door of her little house and standing there looking with astonishment at the unwonted sight of American soldiers in khaki as brothers of her beloved countrymen.

On my return to Chaumont I outlined this idea to several officers of the Staff and of the French Commission, who received it with enthusiasm and promised every assistance, but, alas, nothing ever came of it. When I returned to France the following spring the armistice had been arranged and the Versailles Conference was dragging its weary and dreary deliberations toward an unsatisfactory conclusion. There did not seem to be enough illusion or enthusiasm left to celebrate anything international connected with the war.

On my last visit to Chaumont I gave a little dinner to Colonel Collins, secretary of the Staff, whose constant interest had been invaluable and whose mind seemed to be capable at a moment's notice of turning from the consideration of some intricate military problem to the great advantages to be derived from the introduction of the French B-flat bugle into our army. Over a very good magnum of champagne I rose and made him, Colonel Boyd, and Lieutenant Weill solemnly swear that for the rest of the war and as long thereafter as necessary the bandmaster's school at Chaumont should be to them as the apple of their eye, and this oath they faithfully kept. The school flourished from October, 1918, until June, 1919, when it was discontinued owing to the return of our army to America. The relations between the French professors and our boys, all living together like a happy family, became so sympathetic and intimate that the results may truly be said to have been remarkable. The soldiers realized that they were receiving an education in music equal to that of the foremost schools of France or America, and the French professors entered into their duties with an enthusiasm which was touching. Casadesus told me that many of his pupils worked at their musical problems twelve hours a day and I urged him, in some way or other, to continue these pleasant and important international musical relations by founding a summer school somewhere in France, preferably near Paris, to which American men and women, already sufficiently advanced in their study of music, could repair for three months every summer in order to acquaint themselves with French art and French methods of teaching. Until the war began, hundreds of American students had gone to Germany every year, and it seemed a pity that, owing to the Frenchman's lack of propaganda for what his country could offer to our students, some of this stream could not be diverted to France. Our talks eventually led to the founding of the *Conservatoire Américain* at Fontainebleau, of which details are told in another chapter.

By the courtesy of General Pershing I received permission to leave for home on the army transport *America*. This ship sailed from Brest, and I was anxious to go there in order to see my daughter, Alice Pennington, once more. She and her friend, Miss Letty McKim, had been there for a year and had founded the naval Y. M. C. A., to the great satisfaction of Admiral Wilson and our navy stationed there. My daugther's enthusiasm and vitality, together with that of her equally able friend, had created an atmosphere which our sailors greatly relished, and I was keen to see some of her work.

My train was to leave Paris in the evening, and my faithful friend and companion of the last five weeks, Lieutenant Weill, came to the station to bid me good-by. There were no regular sleeping-cars on this train but only what the French call "couchettes"—four bunks in each compartment, two on each side. The names of the occupants were carefully written on a slip of paper and pasted on the outside of each door, and Lieutenant Weill informed me that a French general occupied the lower bunk opposite mine. Sure enough, a handsome, youngish-looking general presently appeared and, politely touching his cap, entered our compartment and seated himself in his bunk. Weill, in French fashion, kissed me good-by on both cheeks, and as I had still ten minutes to spare, I stood outside and saw an American naval commander coming toward me with rather unsteady steps. He told me that he had had thirty-six hours' leave and that he and his two aides had decided to spend it by going to Paris. As the train took twelve hours each way this gave them only twelve hours in the city of delights and he had evidently taken full advantage of every minute of it. He told me that his two aides had not yet turned up, that they had all the tickets and all his money; he also confided to me that one of them was so rich that he could have bought the entire train. I finally found his name on the list of our coupé, his bunk being directly over the French general's, and as it was getting late, I advised him to enter. Just at that moment two handsome young naval lieutenants rushed up, and he received them with enthusiasm, for they had his railroad tickets. I helped him into our compartment, where he presently sat down right next to the general, who wrapped his cloak about him and cuddled up into his own corner. I said to my compatriot: "I think you are in the French general's bunk. Yours is the one above." Whereupon he said: "The French general can go to hell!" I was frightened out of my wits, as I expected an immediate international encounter which might have the most serious consequences. Luckily the general understood no English, and I finally induced my new naval friend to climb up into his own bunk, but I made a solemn vow that I would never again try to interfere where the army and navy of two different countries were concerned.

I turned into my own bunk and slept well until next morning, when I found the commander also awake and possessed of a thirst which knew no bounds. There was, of course, no drinking-water on the train, but I rushed him to the restaurant of the next station where we stopped, and he seized a carafe of water and put it to his lips with such avidity that you could almost hear the water sizzle as it passed down his throat. He turned out to be a delightful fellow. He was commander of a destroyer and had spent dreary and terrible weeks in his little craft watching for submarines. The monotony and discomfort of such a life cannot be imagined, as these ships are so small that their motion is incessant and they have to go out in the dirtiest of weather. There is hardly ever a chance to cook meals, and those on board must eat what and how they can. For weeks and weeks nothing happens, but my commander had had the good luck on his last trip to get a sub, and had received his thirty-six hours' leave in consequence. Small wonder that he and his colleagues sought some relief in honor of the great event!

At the next station my French general and I got a cup of coffee. Sugar was at that time taboo, and as, thanks to my army friends, I had my pockets full of this precious stuff, I offered him some in place of the awful saccharine, which he accepted gratefully and then told me that he was going on his first vacation in two years to spend with his family in a little watering resort this side of Brest. Sure enough at the next station, as he got out, a charming boy and girl, browned by the sun, rushed up to him and fairly smothered him with kisses. It looked for all the world like a scene at a Long Island station in August, when the various New York fathers commute on a Friday afternoon to spend Saturday and Sunday with their families by the sea.

I found my daughter Alice waiting for me at the station in Brest, and on the way to the little apartment which she and Miss McKim occupied together, she told

me that Admiral Wilson wanted to meet me before my
departure on the transport the same evening. She
begged me to support her if he denounced jazz music,
against which he had a particular hatred, for she had
always insisted to him that the sailors loved it and that
in time of war they certainly should have anything they
wanted.

In the afternoon the admiral's band gave a concert in
the public square, and I, of course, attended it and met
the bandmaster and his players, who did very good work,
several of them having been members of the Boston Symphony Orchestra. They begged me to conduct them in
one of the numbers, and I took up the stick and solemnly
played through the "William Tell Overture" with them.
At the end I saw Admiral Wilson on the balcony of his
apartment applauding vociferously, and he presently
came running, bareheaded, across the square to greet
me. Almost the first thing he said was: "Doctor, don't
you think jazz music is horrible? It destroys all taste
for real music." "Indeed I heartily agree with you," I
answered. Whereupon my daughter Alice turned on me
and said, "Coward!" implying that as the admiral was the
autocrat of Brest I did not wish to brave his wrath even
in order to please my daughter. But indeed I was thoroughly in accord with him; and I wish that either some
popular substitute could be found for the interminable
jazz that is ravaging not only our country but all Europe, or that a genius would come along who would pour
into this very low form of art some real emotion which,
welling from the very heart of man, might give life to
what is at present but a nervous excitement.

That evening I went on board the transport *America*,
and sailed for home. I found the voyage exceedingly in-

teresting. The ship had been a Hamburg passenger liner, the *Amerika*, taken over after her internment by our navy; the "k" having been carefully removed and an American "c" substituted. Various German signs had been scratched out, but the table and bed linen, as well as the knives and forks, still bore the mystic initials, *H. A. P. A. G.—Hamburg Amerika Paketfahrt Actien Gesellschaft.*

I was the proud occupant of a cabin and bathroom of the so-called "Roosevelt" suite, which the ex-President had occupied during his trip around the world, and the faucets over the bathtub still bore the signs "Kalt," "Warm," and "Gemischt." The various luxurious furnishings of the ship showed the wear and tear of army-transport usage. The marble was cracked and the electric bells did not ring.

The first-class cabins were occupied by several hundred officers, a curious mixture of men, some returning on leave or to become instructors in the officers' camps, or being mustered out of service, either for ill health, drunkenness, or incompetence. For days I was pursued, even into my cabin, by a man from a Western city who had enlisted as a dentist. He was evidently out of his mind and was to be mustered out of the service on his return home. He had conceived the mysterious idea that I could influence the powers that be to have him reinstated, and I finally found the glitter in his eye so ominous that I reported him to the colonel in command and he promptly had him put under medical observation. Two days later his companions in the hospital ward, whom he had already annoyed and frightened by suddenly grabbing their legs at night, found him in the bathroom with his throat partly cut by his razor; and I confess that

I was glad when I heard that he had been put into a cabin by himself, with a soldier guarding the door.

We were, of course, under army regulations and in many respects life was much stricter than on the passenger liners. We were compelled to wear life-preservers almost the entire voyage and no lights were permitted after sundown. We were not told at which American port we were to land, and I was much astonished one morning to find our ship anchored in Boston Harbor alongside the old 1812 frigate *Constitution*, whose broadside-guns looked delightfully picturesque and inefficient compared with the modern monsters I had seen in France.

During the following winter my wife and I often received visits from navy officers and sailors bearing greetings from our daughter Alice in Brest, and I remember one red-cheeked youngster who made so agreeable an impression on my wife that she invited him to return the following day, which was Sunday, for luncheon. On that morning the telephone rang. It was our old friend, Admiral William Rodgers, who asked whether he could come to luncheon. My wife said we would be delighted, but my youngest daughter Anita, who was well versed in the etiquette of the navy, called out: "Oh, we can't have the admiral lunching with us to-day. An admiral can't sit down at the same table with a gob!" My wife repeated this to the admiral, who insisted that it made no difference and that in war time everything was possible; that he certainly wanted to come and would be very glad to meet the "gob" who had brought greetings from Alice, of whom he was very fond. The sailor boy arrived first, and when we told him that our other guest was to be an admiral he grew pale as death, but when Rodgers arrived he was so kind to the boy that luncheon passed off fairly well, except that the boy became rigid at attention whenever the admiral spoke to him. During the luncheon Admiral Rodgers said to him: "You have just seen Mrs. Pennington in Brest?" "Yes, sir." "And what was she doing when you saw her?" "She was selling postage-stamps, sir," was the answer. And I have no doubt this was true, as Alice in her capacity of naval "Y" worker not only took the sailors out to picnics with swimming contests, arranged vaudeville entertainments and concerts, but in between times sold them chocolate, cigarettes, postage-stamps, picture postal-cards, lemon-drops, and ginger ale.

After luncheon my daughters discreetly took the young sailor into the front parlor in order to relieve the tension a little, and Rodgers asked me about an orchestration of the "Star-Spangled Banner" which I had made at the beginning of the war and which had aroused some attention. I had always felt that this good old English tune had a fine ring to it, provided it was played in the proper tempo, and I had given it an orchestration which developed into quite a climax on the last two lines of each verse. I sat down at the piano and played it for him, explaining the difference between this version and the old one which had been generally used before the war. He was much interested and wanted to introduce it in the navy.

The sailor boy finally took his departure, and my daughters came smiling into the music-room and told us that while they were sitting talking with the sailor, he suddenly jumped up from his chair and stood at rigid attention. He had heard the strains of the national anthem coming from our room and, remembering the admiral, knew his duty! Who shall, after that, deny the power of music in peace or in war?

XVI

THE EUROPEAN TOUR

In the spring of 1919 I received a letter from M. La-fere, then *Ministre des Beaux Arts* in France, which interested the directors of the New York Symphony Society and myself exceedingly. In this letter he referred to the services of the New York Symphony Orchestra and myself to French art in America and invited us to make a professional visit to France the following year. He promised every assistance from the French Government and assured us of a warm welcome.

Mr. Flagler immediately decided that this invitation must be accepted inasmuch as it was the first time a foreign government had extended such a courtesy to an American musical organization. He also thought that our visit coming so soon after the war and including possibly the countries of the other allies in the war, such as Belgium, Italy, and England, would not only make a good impression but would help to establish musical relations with Europe on a more equal basis. Up till then the current had been all the other way. European singers and instrumentalists had been coming to America in a steady stream for many years, but in the meantime America had developed several orchestras of her own which could compare favorably with those of Europe; and he was very proud that the organization of which he was president and supporter should have been singled out for so great an honor and opportunity.

I sailed for Europe in the spring of 1919 to confer with the Beaux Arts about arrangements for our visit to Paris and other cities in France, and at the same time I also received invitations from the governments of Belgium and Italy to visit their countries with the orchestra. In London Augustus Littleton, the publisher, head of the old house of Novello & Co., also received me very cordially and insisted that our visit to Europe would not be complete if we did not include London. As England, like our country, has no Ministry of Fine Arts and can therefore take no official cognizance of musical affairs, he immediately and energetically set to work to form a committee of invitation, headed by King George and composed of all the foremost composers and conductors of Great Britain.

Affairs began to shape themselves very favorably, and our manager, Mr. George Engels, began to map out a tour of seven weeks, during which we were to visit five countries and play, in all, twenty-seven concerts. But in the meantime foreign exchange sank lower and lower and reports of transportation conditions in Europe were so gloomy that I began to be seriously doubtful of the possibility of the proposed tour in the spring of 1920. I finally decided in January to send our manager to Europe personally to look over the ground, and at the same time I expressed my fears to Mr. Flagler.

I told him that we would have to pay enormous sums for travelling expenses, the item of steamer passage alone amounting to fifty thousand dollars, and that while we would have to pay our orchestra salaries in American dollars, our receipts in Europe would be in francs, lire, etc. The dollar was then selling for seventeen francs in France and for twenty-three lire in Italy. I suggested to him to postpone the tour until a time when war-torn Europe would be economically in a better condition and when her transportation system would again be more nearly on a pre-war basis.

Mr. Flagler listened to me and said: "I do not see how we can possibly postpone the acceptance of these official invitations from four countries to a later period. Now is the psychological moment to do it. How much do you think the tour will cost?"

I had made a kind of general calculation and mentioned the amount, which seemed to me large.

"Isn't that curious?" he answered. "That is exactly what I thought it would cost. Go right ahead with your preparations."

I was naturally delighted at his decision. I knew that American orchestras had achieved a perfection of ensemble which but few, if any, European orchestras could equal. I was proud of our organization and anxious to demonstrate it as a standard of American musical culture.

The members of the orchestra were wild with excitement at the marvellous news. Many of them had been born in America and had never seen Europe. It was the wonderland of their imagination. Others had been there as soldiers during the war, and still others had left Europe years before to found their fortunes and families in the New World and had not been back since. They immediately appointed a committee to agree upon a minimum salary schedule which, while giving them a fair recompense for their time, would yet make that part of it not too difficult for us. To this sum, however, Mr. Flagler later added ten dollars a week more for each player, as he thought that their hotel expenses might be greater than we had calculated.

The managerial work of constructing the tour was beset with many difficulties, as the war had disorganized many of the regular concert organizations in Europe under whose auspices we would have played under normal conditions. The railroads, also, made much slower time than formerly. But gradually the tour began to assume shape and the first concert was scheduled to be given on May 6 at the Grand Opera in Paris, which the *Ministère des Beaux Arts* had offered to us, and the last concert at the Royal Albert Hall in London on June 20. In order that this tour might be representative in every way of the best in American music, Mr. Flagler suggested that we take along two young American-born soloists of distinction—Albert Spalding, violinist, and John Powell, composer-pianist. I immediately set to work to prepare a series of appropriate programmes which should serve the double purpose of demonstrating the fine qualities of our orchestra and soloists, and also pay proper tribute to the great composers of the countries we proposed to visit.

We were to open with three concerts in Paris, and as I was conversant with all the details in connection with Paris especially, I preceded the orchestra and arrived there April 22. At my hotel, the "France et Choiseul," I found a letter from my old friend, Robert Underwood Johnson, who had just left Paris to go to Rome as American ambassador to Italy. He said:

DEAR WALTER:
   It is pleasant to think that, within a few days, you will be occupying the "ambassadorial suite" in which I am writing these lines (Davis of London had it also). We leave day after tomorrow and shall be very happy to see you all when you come to Rome. We are looking forward with pride and agreeable anticipation to the invasion of

Italy by the Symphony and its director and the assisting artists.
We have no Embassy, alas! being "all dressed up (or nearly so) with
no place to go to" and so we shall slum it at the Grand Hotel until the
money seems to be giving out.

Don't let any of your party perish by stumbling over the torn
carpet at the entrance to this apartment. I have tried to have it
mended, but my failure shows that I am no diplomat—yet.

                                    Au revoir. Bientôt à Rome.

My first act was to have that carpet mended, and I
immediately sent a telegram to the American Embassy
in Rome announcing the important news. And then the
affairs of the tour began to engulf me to such an extent
that until Mr. Engles arrived and relieved me with able
hands of a great deal of that burden, I thought that I was
back again in the old days of the Damrosch Opera Company, when I was owner, director, orchestral conductor,
stage-manager, and prima donna pacificator all in one.

To add to my worries, a railroad strike was announced
for May 1, the day on which the orchestra were to arrive
at Le Havre, and not content with that, the dock workers of Le Havre intended also to lay down their "tools,"
whatever they may be, and stop working on that date.
When I thought of the musical instruments and trunks
of my orchestra in the hold of the steamer *Rochambeau*,
which was to arrive on or about May 1, my heart stopped
beating. However, I had been in too many close shaves
on my great Western orchestral tours to be altogether
dismayed, for even if the railroad stopped running there
would always be motor-trucks and airplanes. We had
made arrangements with Thomas Cook and Sons to take
care of all transportation matters from the day the orchestra arrived in France until their sailing for home from
England, and they assured me that, if necessary, they

would have camions, such as were used during the war, to carry my whole orchestra, together with their baggage and musical instruments, from Le Havre to Paris.

Luckily the ship docked several hours before the dock workers' strike began, and double basses, kettle-drums, and innumerable music boxes were safely landed from the hold of the ship. I had intended to go to Le Havre to meet the orchestra, but the strike conditions were too uncertain and I thought it better to remain in Paris and direct operations from there.

The government was moving several trains, and the telegram that the orchestra had started for Paris cheered me up considerably. I was at the station at 3.30 that afternoon, to be met with the news that the train was delayed and would be in at six. At six there was no sign of it, and, as is usual at French stations, there was absolutely no one who had any idea when it might arrive. I stayed there till eight o'clock—no train. Finally there was a whistle. Every one dashed out. It was a freight-train, but, like the dove from Noah's Ark, I saw the "man from Cook's," a little man, attired then and during the entire tour in a very small derby hat and an exceedingly long double-breasted frock coat, sitting on top of one of the cars. He was tired, dirty, but triumphant, for all our musical instruments and music boxes were in these cars. He had passed the orchestra half-way at Rouen, where they were held up by a hot box. This sounded like home to me, as I had heard those magic words only too often when our train, coming through Idaho or Arizona on our way to or from California, would be held up for hours and we would wonder whether we could "make" the concert that evening.

The orchestra had rehearsed our repertoire with me so

thoroughly before we sailed that but little more was necessary. I gave them three rehearsals, however, before our first concert, the first two at the *Salle du Conservatoire*, to shake them together again after their long voyage, and the last on the afternoon of the concert, May 6, at the Opera House in order to accustom them to its acoustics. The orchestra played so superbly at the two first rehearsals that I was jubilant and proud of them. The ensemble was perfect and each man played as if the success of the concert depended on him—which it certainly did. But when we began rehearsing at the Opera House the tone of the orchestra suddenly seemed so thin and lifeless that I was nearly beside myself with anxiety. The orchestra was placed on the stage, but the local management had not seen fit to provide us with any proper scenic setting or roof, so that the sound of our large and noble orchestra was completely dissipated in the flies. When I remonstrated, I was told that they had a roof for the stage but that it was in the storehouse, situated beyond the fortifications of Paris, and that this was the first time in many years the Opera House had been used for a concert. They finally agreed to have at least half a roof up for our concert and to set a smaller scene, which would contain the sound and throw it into the audience-room in more compact fashion. After twenty minutes or so of rehearsing, I threw down my stick and told the men to call it a day. I went back to my hotel very depressed, as so much depended on the first impression which our orchestra would make that evening. The programme was as follows:

1. Overture, "Benvenuto Cellini".......................Berlioz
2. Symphony No. 3, "Eroica".......................Beethoven
3. "Istar," Variations symphoniques.....................d'Indy
4. "Daphnis et Chloe" (Fragments symphoniques)........Ravel

The reader will notice that we placed on it two works by living French composers, both of whom were to be at the concert. The house was completely sold out, and greeted me in very friendly fashion when I came on the stage.

From the very first chords of the "Eroica" Symphony, I noticed that the slight improvements in our scenic surroundings, and above all the fact that the house was filled with people, had acted like magic on the acoustics. The tone of the orchestra had become full, clear, and incisive. My spirits rose and I forgot everything except the orchestra before me and Beethoven's score. After each movement the applause was deafening, and at the end of the symphony there was joyous shouting from the galleries. We seemed to have played our way into their hearts, and after the first part there was a steady stream of French musicians to my dressing-room to congratulate me on our marvellous orchestra and its ensemble, and to express their delight that we had come over on such a friendly mission. Among them were: Vincent d'Indy, Gabriel Fauré, André Messager, Gabriel Pierné, Theodore Dubois, Paul Vidal, Nadia Boulanger, and many others.

As we turned into the French part of our programme the enthusiasm became still greater, and at the conclusion of "Istar" some of my first violins discovered the composer, d'Indy, in the audience and, pointing toward him, stood up to applaud. In a minute not only the whole orchestra but the audience were on their feet and with loud cries of "Auteur!" "d'Indy!" the house was in an uproar until d'Indy, his face as red as a beet, was compelled to rise and acknowledge this tribute.

The programme finished with the marvellous "Daphnis

et Chloe," by Ravel, in which the luscious tone of the orchestra and its virtuosity demonstrated themselves so successfully that not only did the concert come to a tumultuous climax, but several of the French papers announced afterward that this work had never had such a vivid and perfect rendering before.

My interpretation of the Beethoven "Eroica" Symphony puzzled some of the newspaper critics, as it did not conform to their French traditions. These do not permit such slight occasional modifications of tempo as modern conductors brought up in the German traditions of Beethoven believe essential to a proper interpretation of this master. But I was much pleased and honored to receive a complete approval of my interpretation, not only verbally from several of my French colleagues, but also from M. d'Indy in an article which he wrote on our concert and in which he said:

Leaving aside everything that Walter Damrosch has done for our country and the French musicians, generous acts for which our gratitude has often been expressed, I wish mainly to pay my tribute to the extremely expressive interpretation at the concerts he has given lately at the Opera. Whether it is classical, romantic, or modern music, Damrosch first of all endeavors to set off and illustrate what we call the "melos," the element of expression, the voice that must rise above all the other voices of the orchestra. He knows how to distribute the agogic action, the dynamic power, and he is not afraid —even in Beethoven's works and in spite of the surprise this caused to our public—to accelerate or slacken the movement when the necessities of expression demand it.

The French are a courteous people, and at the end of the concert there was an even greater crowd of musicians and friends behind the scenes to express their pleasure at our success.

The programmes of the other two concerts were as follows:

MAY 8

1. Overture, "Le Roi d'Ys" .... Lalo
2. Symphony, "From the New World" .... Dvořák
3. Concerto for Violin and Orchestra in B Minor ...... Saint-Saëns
MR. SPALDING
4. a. "Pélléas et Mélisande" (Fileuse) .... Fauré
   b. Ma Mère L'Oye (Les Pagodes) .... Ravel
5. Prelude to "Die Meistersinger" .... Wagner

MAY 9

1. Symphony in C (Jupiter) .... Mozart
2. Poems (d'après Verlaine) .... Loeffler
3. Symphony in D Minor .... Franck
4. Negro Rhapsody for Piano and Orchestra .... Powell
JOHN POWELL

The two young American artists, Albert Spalding and John Powell, made a splendid impression, and of the orchestral works the Prelude to the "Meistersingers" of Wagner and the Mozart and Franck Symphonies received special acclaim.

It was delightful to hear the half-suppressed "Ah's" and "Bravos!" so characteristic of the French audience after the Andante of the Mozart Symphony. I confess that the more spontaneous approval which European audiences give in drama, opera, or concert is exceedingly gratifying and stimulates the artist to the very best that is in him. Every artist who is worth his salt will always approach an audience with the feeling that they are as strangers whom through his art he must win over as friends. This feeling exists whether he makes his first bow as a beginner or appears for the three thousandth time after twenty years of public work. It is a wonderful moment for him when, after having done his best and given all there is in him, his audience show by the intensity of their approval that the "song which he breathed into the air" has found its home "in the heart of a friend."

On Sunday morning, May 9, at eleven, the orchestra of the Conservatoire gave a great party in our honor as a return courtesy for one that we had given to the French Orchestra on their arrival in America in 1918. We all met at the *Salle du Conservatoire* where M. Leon, representing the Ministry of Fine Arts, was waiting to receive me. With the Conservatoire Orchestra were various French masters, including the venerable Gabriel Fauré, and Messager, the conductor.

After various speeches of welcome, I was presented with a beautiful engraving of Beethoven and made an honorary member of the Conservatoire Orchestra. We then marched to the *Taverne du Nègre*, where luncheon was served. There were so many different kinds of wineglasses before each plate that I asked permission to make a short speech in English to my orchestra. It consisted of the following:

"Gentlemen, remember we have a concert this afternoon, so please mix your wine with much water."

Needless to say, in all the speeches the theme of the war was constantly played upon by the French orators —how much France owed to our intervention and to the bravery of our soldiers.

It would have been very pleasant to stay on in Paris, where our orchestra were beginning to feel very much at home, and rest upon our young laurels, but our tour had only begun and we had to carry on!

In the meantime Mr. Engles and our treasurer, Roger Townsend, had to smooth out all kinds of new difficulties and complications, among which the passport nuisance was the greatest. War conditions still prevailed and passports had to be carefully viséd by the ambassadors of every country we visited. All our orchestra were practically Americans, but technically they belonged to America, France, Belgium, Italy, England, Russia, Germany, Austria, and Czecho-Slovakia. Many of them had had only their first American papers when the war broke out, and according to war regulations could not yet obtain their American citizens' papers. They were therefore compelled to travel on foreign passports and some of their visés were exceedingly difficult to obtain, as new countries like Czecho-Slovakia, for instance, had not yet a properly organized diplomatic service. Others, like Russia, were not recognized at all and our Russians had to travel on Kerensky passports issued for them by the Kerensky ambassador who was still "holding the fort" in Washington. Through the kindly help of Mr. Grew, councillor at our embassy in Paris, and other friends in high places, we finally obtained our hundred visés and left Paris for Bordeaux on May 11, and—in spite of the railroad strike—with the passage of our train assured as far as Bordeaux.

The only fly in the ointment was a little revolution before we left the station. Some of the members of the orchestra had brought their wives and even a few small children to Europe with them. They very naturally desired to give their families a good time and wanted to have them with them and in the orchestra cars on the entire trip. As railroad space was exceedingly limited and the bachelor and straw-widower members of the orchestra strenuously objected to this addition, I had to veto the plan, and painted the difficulties of travel, hotels, passports, etc., in such lurid fashion that I succeeded in preventing their departure from Paris with us. The husbands promised to leave their families in Paris until our return, about three weeks later, but as all the wives and children came to the station to see their respective husbands and fathers off, I was nervous until the last doors of the car were slammed to and the whistle of the French locomotive, which always sounds like the shrill wail of the damned, announced that we were really off.

The orchestra were in a very gay mood and insisted on getting out every time the train stopped even a second, and then having to be pulled back as the train started again without any warning. A passport picture of one unfortunate little second violinist was sent through all the cars, pasted on a piece of paper with the inscription: "Wanted for bigamy. Member of the New York Symphony Orchestra. Reward of three francs if returned dead or alive to George Engles, Manager." This had been perpetrated by Willem Willeke, who was not only a master violoncellist but the master mind behind almost every practical joke indulged in during the tour.

We arrived in Bordeaux that evening and were welcomed at our hotel by a typical little hotel manager, with his head entirely bald on top but beautifully covered with the long hair combed forward from the back of his head. He also had a full beard neatly parted in the middle, and of course a long double-breasted frock coat. He rubbed his hands with the pleasure of welcoming us and assured us that all our rooms were properly reserved. Actually it took us three-quarters of an hour to get ourselves and our baggage straightened out in the proper rooms. Our party consisted of Albert and Mrs. Spalding,

John Powell, Mary Flagler, my daughter Gretchen, and myself, and the highly efficient manager had sent each one of us at first to the wrong rooms while our bags had still further gone astray. But a good bath and a delicious dinner at the famous *Chapon Fin* put us all in good humor.

The theatre at which we were to play the following evening was directly opposite to our hotel and its frontal façade is without doubt the most beautiful I have ever seen. Such examples of the finest architecture of the eighteenth century stand out in remarkable contrast to their more modern surroundings and it is difficult to understand how French architects, with such noble examples to follow and with a school in Paris which is still considered the best in the world, should have allowed their art to degenerate to such an extent within the last thirty years. One has but to compare the noble façade of the Place de la Concorde with such modern monstrosities as, for instance, the Hotel Mercedes or the Palais de Justice at Tours, to realize that in their endeavor to break away completely from their own noblest traditions they have deliberately courted anarchy, for their architecture rests upon no laws of beauty or symmetry. Many of our best American architects are graduates from the Ecole des Beaux Arts in Paris, but they have not become revolutionaries and have understood how to adapt their appreciation of the best French traditions to American needs. The results demonstrate an art of which every American can be proud.

Our concert, which was given under the auspices of the local symphony society, was received with great favor. The interior of the theatre is delightfully intimate, and the audience gave the impression of belonging to an old musical civilization. We were presented with huge bouquets of flowers tied with the American colors. Albert Spalding's performance made a splendid impression, and the "Meistersinger" Overture came in for special enthusiasm.

But what was my astonishment at suddenly beholding three of the "orchestra wives," who were supposed to have remained in Paris, seated in one of the boxes. I do not know to this day whether they rode on the bumpers or in one of the baggage-cars. However, they were charming ladies; and, as a married man, I could not be too angry with them or their indulgent husbands. We compromised in the matter by permitting them to continue with us for the rest of the tour, provided that they and their husbands occupied space elsewhere than that reserved for the orchestra, and that they looked out for their own passports whenever we approached the border.

As we returned to our hotel after the concert the smiling hotel manager stood in the lobby to receive us and to express his congratulations at the success of a *concert merveilleux*. As we entered the electric lift to go to our respective rooms, he himself shut the grating on us and pressed the button to send us slowly upward. (All French lifts move slowly.) Its almost celestial calmness irresistibly brought the Finale of Gounod's "Faust" to my mind, when *Marguerite* ascends heavenward. I began to sing the melody of the "*Anges radieux*," and just as we got up to the first floor we suddenly heard the voice of the hotel manager, a vibrant tenor, enthusiastically continuing the trio from below. I gazed downward and there he was, his face raised ecstatically toward us and his hand pressed to his double-breasted frock coat—perhaps a poor hotel manager but certainly an enthusiastic lover of music.

The newspapers of Bordeaux were full of praise about our concert, but one of them said: "The orchestra played with that dryness characteristic of all North Americans." Alack and alas! Had the Eighteenth Amendment, which went into effect the previous January, already made its dreadful influence felt?

Lyons was to be the next city on our itinerary, but unfortunately the railroad strike had completely isolated it and there was no way of reaching it from Bordeaux. We were therefore very reluctantly compelled to cancel the concert. Every seat had been sold long before, and as Lyons ranked next to Paris in musical importance the cancellation was a great disappointment to us.

The next morning Engles brought me a telegram which he had just received from our general manager in Paris, to the effect that at Marseilles the hall in which we were to play had been condemned by the fire department as unsafe, and that therefore the concert would have to be given at another theatre and under different management. Engles did not like the look of things and begged me, as he could not speak French, to go with him to Marseilles and look over the ground with him. We were to have played in Marseilles under the auspices and management of the local symphonic organization, which, however, turned out to be but a small and not very influential body of musicians, most of whom were amateurs. Their secretary, who was to attend to the details of management, was a newspaper man and an amateur double-bass player, of which instrument he was very proud. When we arrived, only two days before the concert, we found that absolutely nothing had been done to advertise it. There

were no posters, no advertisements, and the manager of
the theatre to which we had been transferred did not even
know before our arrival whether we were a jazz band of
colored people from America or perhaps a troupe of wan-
dering minstrels.

We were to give two concerts, and at first it seemed as
if, under such disheartening circumstances, it were better
to cancel them and proceed to Monte Carlo and Italy,
where already sold-out houses awaited us. The newspaper man, who was the real delinquent, was nowhere to
be found. He had gone to the country *"pour se reposer"*
and was not expected until the following day. Luckily
the theatre manager proved to be of the right sort.
When he saw what our organization really stood for he
would not hear of cancellation, and immediately went
around to all the newspaper offices with Engles. Posters, the principal method of advertising in Europe, appeared on the street corners as if by magic; and while it
was too late to attract a large audience for the first concert, he assured us that if this concert were the success
which he expected, the theatre, which held about twenty-
four hundred people, would be entirely sold out for the
second concert on Sunday afternoon. His prophecy
proved correct. There were not more than eight hundred
people at the first concert, but as they were real sons of
the *Midi* and as they had never heard a symphonic organization of such size and importance in their lives, they
went mad. They applauded with their hands, with both
feet, with their canes and umbrellas. They shouted in
eight-part harmonies and the rafters of the theatre
trembled in sympathy. After the concert they lined up
at the box-office in a great crowd while the theatre manager, grinning from ear to ear, said: "Did I not tell you?"

In the meantime the delinquent local secretary-manager turned up and I was fully prepared to annihilate him for his lack of proper preliminary advertising for our concert, but as he immediately called me "Cher maître" and expressed his delight in such eloquent French at the coming of so notable an organization as ours, he completely spiked my guns and I found myself unable to get in a word edgewise, much less tell him what I really thought of him.

I have told before that he was an amateur double-bass player in the local orchestra, and this was evidently the ruling passion of his life, although I never could understand why an amateur should choose this particular instrument for his delectation. After the second concert and while the hall was still ringing with the shouts of the fiery citizens of Marseilles, he came into my dressing-room as I thought to add his tribute of praise, but, alas, all he said was: "Cher maître, I could hardly hear your double-bass players during the entire concert." I presume that at the concerts of his orchestra he was so taken up with his own double-bass part that as he played he heard nothing of the other instruments around and about him. He became, so to speak, intoxicated with the resonance of his own instrument. At our concert, seated in the audience, he suddenly found, poor man, that the double bass was not the only pebble on the orchestral beach, and that occasionally the violins, the wood winds, or the brasses had also something of importance to enunciate. It must have been a sad revelation to him, and I do not wonder that he refused to accept it.

In the meantime the strike fever was spreading in every direction, and there was not a trolley running through the town of Marseilles nor a boat leaving the harbor. The effect was a very curious one, as the streets were filled with great crowds restlessly moving up and down, and seemingly without work or affairs of any kind to keep them busy. In several of the streets small bands were playing in roped-off circles while thirty couples or so were dancing madly around with hundreds of others outside the ropes watching them. The huge audience who arrived for our Sunday afternoon concert must have come on foot, as there was not a wheel turning anywhere.

After we got back to the hotel the great iron doors were suddenly closed and bolted, for quite a riot started in front of it. The trolley company was trying to run a car through the city, manned by young mechanicians from the School of Technology, and every once in a while a mob of strikers would rush at them, break the windows of the car, and pull off the young strike-breakers. But it was all done in rather an amiable fashion, while a crowd of men in light straw hats applauded with their hands and shouted "Bravo," all as if it were a performance gotten up for their pleasure. Then a couple of amiable gendarmes would come along and in the same placid fashion place the young men on the car again, which would then proceed for another few yards or so. Suddenly, however, this seeming comedy took a tragic turn. The mob made a vicious lunge; they were stopped by the police who suddenly acted with great energy, and soon there were several men seriously hurt. In the meantime the strike-breakers had again connected their car with the electric wire, and although the car with its broken windows looked a perfect wreck, it moved triumphantly along the tracks and the strike was broken. Next morning every car was running again.

Later that afternoon I received a visit from Morris

Tivin, the first double-bass player of our orchestra. He brought with him a boy of fifteen, a little Russian Jew, who had a most remarkable history. He had escaped from a prison in Russia and worked his way to Constantinople. As he was a violinist of exceptional ability, he had made a meagre living there playing in the cafés. Having read in some old Paris paper that we were to give a concert in Marseilles he had quickly made up his mind to get there and perhaps through our help reach the promised land of America. He arrived in Marseilles as a stowaway after incredible hardships, and when he introduced himself to some of his Russian compatriots in my orchestra, he was literally starving and without a cent in his pockets. Within a few hours our orchestra had subscribed enough money to send him to New York with several letters to their colleagues at the Musical Union, and within a week after his arrival he was engaged as second concert master at a large salary in one of our Western orchestras.

The generous spirit displayed by our men, which demonstrated itself in so quick and practical a fashion, is characteristic of the rank and file of our profession. I have never known a case of an orchestra musician or chorus singer in need that his colleagues were not immediately ready to help, and as their own earnings are comparatively small their generosity is much greater in proportion than that of many a rich man whose name figures largely among the subscribers to our charitable organizations.

Our next concert was to be in Monte Carlo, and I motored with my wife from Marseilles along the Riviera, reaching Monte Carlo on the evening of May 17. The orchestra had already arrived by train and were to be found all over the town photographing points of interest, especially the beautiful statue erected to Hector Berlioz, which we were all glad to honor. Every orchestra musician adores this great master, who in his scores has done more than any other to develop new tone combinations in the symphonic orchestra since Beethoven and before Wagner.

A great many of our men naturally went to the Casino to behold the world-famous gambling tables, but if I ever had any worries about their squandering their earnings they quite disappeared. Many only watched at the outer edge, or else bet one chip very timidly. An aged harpy, who looked as though she had played at Monte Carlo since the time of Napoleon III and who kept a note-book of her losses and winnings and never bet less than a hundred francs at a time, took it upon herself to teach one of our talented young flute players how to play with one white chip. She kept him in a state of the most panting thrills, while she placed his bets for him.

The next morning I found a note from Jean de Reszke telling me that he, his wife, and Amhurst Webber would motor over from Nice for the concert, and asking my wife and me to lunch with him at the Grand Hotel de Paris, where we were staying. It was such a joy to see him again. We had not met since 1902, when he had been at the Metropolitan at the height of his fame and I had conducted many a glorious "Tristan" performance with him in the title rôle. Amhurst Webber, a highly talented English musician, had then been with him as pianist and I had helped him a little with his studies in composition and instrumentation. Mme. de Reszke I had never had the pleasure of meeting before. A great tragedy had come upon her, as their only son had been killed in the first year of the war. It was heart-breaking to see her, as her face told the story of her irreparable loss.

The concert in the afternoon took place in the exquisite little theatre at the Casino. It seats only about four hundred people and of course every seat was occupied. Jean de Reszke was in the fifth row of the parquet, and as I came to the "Prize Song" in the "Meistersinger" Overture, which he had sung so often and so ravishingly in New York, I could not help but turn around to look at him. He gave me an immediate smile, but the tears were running down his face.

At the close of the concert I was solemnly informed by the very polite little intendant of the theatre that M. Blanc, the principal owner of the Casino, the opera, the gambling tables, the Hotel de Paris, in fact everything which draws the hundred-franc notes from the grateful tourist, had expressed a desire to meet me and to thank me for the "*concert exquis*." I was accordingly piloted to another part of the building, where, in an anteroom, five or six people were waiting as if in a doctor's outer office, while flunkies in livery were silently walking around or delivering whispered messages to this or that man. One of these approached my little intendant with a message, who turned to me and, with a face radiant with pride, said: "Think of it! He will see us first before all the others!"

We followed the flunky into an inner room where I found a tired-looking, gray-mustached little man whom I had noticed sleeping in one of the boxes during about half an hour of the concert. He congratulated me on the "splendid concert and the exquisite playing of the orchestra," and as I sat there I marvelled at it all. Here was a man whom we in America would call a gambling-house keeper, but he is certainly a king among them. He has provided his gambling tables with a setting so exquisite that words cannot describe it. Nature in her most charming mood, beautiful architecture, delightful music, exquisite cooking—all these so skilfully combined as to create an agreeable atmosphere for the thousands who come every year with full pockets and generally leave with empty ones. Incidentally he makes millions by thus cleverly pandering to the gambling instincts which are inherent in almost every man (and woman).

To me the most delightful feature of the concert, except of course the visit of Jean de Reszke, was a large audience of seventy-five who sat behind the scenes as there was no room for them in front. They were the orchestra of the Monte Carlo Opera, an excellent body of men who embraced us in true southern fashion between the parts and at the end of the concert.

The next morning I continued the trip by motor to Genoa. As there had been no strike of any kind in Monte Carlo I thought that our hoodoo had lifted, but, lo and behold, at Genoa we found only one old, gray-bearded portier at our hotel to greet us. All the waiters, porters, chambermaids, cooks, scullions, in fact everything that could strike in connection with a hotel, were on strike and the discomfort was considerable. We had looked forward with pleasurable anticipation to our first Italian dinner. We had dreamed of fritto misto, spaghetti, and of delicious Italian ices, but these dreams quickly vanished. There was not even a crust of bread to be obtained at the hotel. Finally we were furtively conducted through an alley into the back entrance of a little restaurant by way of the kitchen, and there we obtained some food, but of the simplest and poorest variety. The next morning a cup of wretched coffee and a piece of stale bread at the railroad station made our breakfast, but luckily for us a kind young American, Mr. Allan, called on us and whisked us off in his car to his house, where a delicious luncheon made us forget our deprivations of the night before.

I was again amazed at the cleverness with which the members of our orchestra adapted themselves to European travelling conditions. They had all found excellent restaurants and had really fared much better than we.

We gave our concert at the *Teatro Carlo Felice*, and our first Italian audience proved to be even more noisy in their demonstrations of pleasure than the *Midi*. I was very much touched to receive a large wreath tied with the stars and stripes, from the American Consul-General, who told me after the concert that he considered such a cultural mission as we were engaged in of as much importance for cordial relations between our country and Italy as any business enterprise. He said that music meant so much to the Italian that he was amazed and delighted to find that Americans did not only interest themselves in business but also cultivated the arts. As the Italians had been so bitterly disillusioned regarding President Wilson, after the phenomenally enthusiastic acclaim which they had given him on his visit to Rome only a year before, I was not surprised to have one old gentleman say to me after the concert: "We do not like your President, but we love the Americans."

We left next morning by train for Rome. The highly talented young composer, Signor Vincenzo Tommasini, had interested himself in our concerts there and had enlisted the sympathies of the Accademia Santa Cecilia, under whose auspices we were to play at the Augusteo. The Santa Cecilia, which is composed of musicians and music lovers, is perhaps the oldest musical organization in the world, as it was founded by Palestrina. Under the presidency of Count San Martino it maintains a symphony orchestra which gives a series of concerts during the winter under its own conductor, Maestro Molinari, and various guest conductors.

All these concerts are given at the Augusteo, so called because it was built by Augustus as a tomb for the Cæsars. It is a rotunda built of the old Roman bricks, but balconies, a stage, and an organ have been added to it in recent times to adapt it to modern concert needs. It very likely was an excellent tomb, but its acoustics are hardly suited for an orchestra. I do not know of any concert-hall built in circular shape that is satisfactory in that respect. The sound vibrations seem to travel around and around and great confusion of tones is the result, especially in such music where changing harmonies succeed each other rapidly. At our little preliminary rehearsal the hall was empty with the exception of half a dozen members of the Santa Cecilia, and as we began to play through a few bars of the symphony I thought I had suddenly become deaf, as the sound of the orchestra did not reach me where I stood. But I remembered our first experience at the Grand Opera House in Paris and trusted to better conditions when the hall was full. This hope was justified, as the tone of the orchestra was much clearer and better balanced at the concert.

After the first and second movements of the "Eroica" Symphony there were great applause and shouts of "Bravo!" from the boxes and parquet, but this was immediately followed by very disconcerting whistling from the top gallery, which seemed to develop into a kind of duel between the two factions. I was somewhat discon-concerted at this and thought that perhaps something in our playing had not pleased the galleries, but my friends of the Accademia Santa Cecilia assured me that this was nothing but a characteristic little demonstration which often occurred at their concerts. If the parquet and boxes approved of some particular composition or ren-dition the galleries felt it incumbent upon them to oppose it. I do not know how true this explanation is, but during the concert the whistling suddenly ceased and after the "Riccardo Wagner. Tristan e Isotta, Preludio e Morte di Isotta (Lipsia 1813—Venezia 1883)," as the Italian programme had it, the two factions seemed to have buried their hatchets completely and were in absolute harmony as far as their enthusiastic acclaim toward us was concerned.

During the two days following, the Romans over-whelmed us with hospitalities. The heat was terrific, but the entire orchestra responded to an invitation to be presented to the mayor and to visit the Capitoline Mu-seum, where they were offered a private view of its art treasures, followed by a luncheon given by the munici-pality in the adjoining ruins of the Tabolarium.

On the following morning Tommasini, Molinari, and a few others of my musician colleagues sauntered into my salon and suggested that we go to a concert given that morning at the Borghese Gardens by the famous Banda Communale di Roma. The heat was so overwhelming that I shuddered at the idea of standing under the blazing noonday sun listening to a concert, especially as I had to conduct our own second concert on that afternoon.

"Please come," said Tommasini.

"No, indeed," I said. "It is far too hot and I want to do good work this afternoon."

"But the concert is given in your honor."

"Good gracious! Why didn't you tell me that immediately? Come along!"

I grabbed my hat and we drove to the Borghese Gardens, where a crowd of several thousand people were gathered around the bandstand and where Maestro Vecella was conducting his band in a beautiful rendition of the Prelude to Wagner's "Parsifal." It was a wonderful performance. His clarinets played the opening unison phrase with a vibrant and singing quality that I have rarely heard equalled, and I was struck by the rapt silence with which the huge audience of Italians listened to it. I, unfortunately, arrived too late to hear the rendition of Beethoven's "Fifth Symphony," which Vecella himself had arranged for military band and which my musicians afterward told me had been beautifully performed. The concert came to a close with a selection of airs from one of the popular modern Italian operas. To my astonishment and delight, as the band began to play this or that air, evidently well known to the audience, groups of men around the band stand joined in singing it with the orchestra *mezza voce*, but with that perfect quality of tone which is inborn in the Italian race. And then, as the sounds of one group would die out, another from the other side would take it up, and this continued until the end of the number. It was a delightful demonstration of the innate musical genius of the Italian people.

I forgot temporarily that the sun was blazing down with a fierceness almost unendurable, but after I had thanked Maestro Vecella for this truly wonderful concert, I begged Molinari and Tommasini to take me back to my hotel.

"Stay a little while longer," said Tommasini.

"Impossible!" I answered. "I am melting away and there will be nothing left of me if I do not get to some shaded spot soon."

"Oh, but you will," he said. "The Banda Communale are now going to present you with the gold medal of the society, with a special inscription."

"Why in heaven's name did you not tell me this sooner?" I said to my friend, but he simply smiled his inscrutable Italian smile and lit another cigarette. With the resolve to do or die, I marched along with them to a private room in a restaurant adjoining the Gardens and there ices and vermuth were served to the members of the two musical organizations, and I was presented with the gold Roman medal, which I treasure very highly as coming from so remarkable a body of players as the Banda Communale di Roma.

For some years I have been interested in the new musical development that is going on in Italy. There had been a period when her church music led the world in the variety and beauty of its form. Later on, especially in the eighteenth century, she had produced many composers of distinction in instrumental music, but from then on and until very recent times, opera had almost completely monopolized her writers. The splendid opera-houses which are to be found in her smallest towns are eloquent testimony to the important place which that form of art occupies in the hearts of the Italian people. Every Italian can sing, and the critics and lovers of opera are to be found just as much among the poorer classes as among the aristocracy.

But all the testimony of older musicians with whom I have spoken and who have travelled through Italy is to the effect that her orchestras formerly were of a very poor quality. Their playing was slovenly and rehearsals few and insufficient. Many of the players in the opera-houses of even the larger cities followed some other calling in the daytime, and there was many a tailor or shoemaker who played his violin in the evening at the opera.

Within the last twenty-five years, however, a complete and almost miraculous change has come over musical conditions throughout Italy. Its conservatories in Rome, Milan, Bologna, and Naples turn out excellent players, and several of her conductors rank with the best of other countries. Signor Mancinelli, for instance, who was my colleague during the years that I conducted at the Metropolitan for Maurice Grau, was a first-class musician and conductor, well versed in more than Italian music. He was a great lover of Mozart and gave beautiful performances of the "Magic Flute" at the Metropolitan. He envied me my job of conducting the Wagner operas and later on conducted many of them in Italy and Spain.

Toscanini is one of the greatest conductors living to-day. His range extends to the music of all countries, and I have heard him conduct Mozart's "Don Giovanni," Verdi's "Falstaff," and Wagner's "Meistersinger" in one week with equal penetration into their beauties and, incidentally, without an orchestral score in front of him. He has made a virtue of necessity, as he is almost blind and has therefore developed his power of memory to a greater extent than I have ever seen in any other musician, not even excepting Hans von Bülow.

The result of Italy's more serious attitude toward instrumental music shows itself not only in the quality of Italian orchestras, but in a group of highly talented young composers who devote their principal efforts to symphonic music, and who are creating works that rank with the best that other countries are now producing. Several years ago I produced an orchestral suite written by a boy of sixteen, Victor di Sabata, which showed remarkable talent and fine orchestral coloring. Such men as Resphghi, Sinigaglia, Tommasini, Casella, Pizzetti, and Malipiero have found frequent places on our programmes, and I expect still further contributions, constantly growing in importance, from this new development of the musical genius of Italy.

I was much touched by the interest which our ambassador, Mr. Johnson, constantly showed in our success and well-being. He had invited the Queen Mother and several of the young Princesses to our concerts, and at the many official and governmental functions which I had to attend he was a sympathetic companion and real brother artist. He always responded very felicitously when occasion demanded, and all my Italian musician friends loved him.

At a farewell supper which I gave on the last night John Powell, whose negro Fantasy had interested our Italian audiences greatly, and the composer, Malipiero, sat next to each other, but as John speaks English and Malipiero Italian and French, the silence between them for about ten minutes was deep and profound. Suddenly they broke into the most fluent conversation and the words burst forth in torrents. They had suddenly discovered to their mutual delight that the German language was a common meeting-ground.

I left Rome very reluctantly. Quite apart from the many personal friends that I had made there, its eternal beauty again enveloped me and bade me stay.

I cannot imagine any movement or institution better calculated to help young American artists to further develop and stimulate their creative abilities than the American Academy in Rome. It has quite recently added three music fellowships to those for painters, sculptors, architects, and archæologists, and, as it has done me the honor to elect me as one of the trustees and the still greater honor of giving my name to one of the music fellowships, I revisited Rome in the spring of 1922 especially to observe the workings of our academy. I was amazed and delighted beyond words. The academy is intended for young artists who have already acquired the technic of their profession. They are selected by competition and are given absolute freedom from bread worries for three years, the first two of which they spend at the home of the academy, the Villa Aurelia. During the third year they may travel or live anywhere in Europe where they think their artistic aims can be further advanced. Rome and its surroundings are so romantic and its art treasures so unique that the perception of beauty and its crystallization into works of art cannot fail to be further stimulated in those of our American boys who have the good fortune to achieve a fellowship.

It is, of course, impossible for any man-made institution to guarantee that every incumbent will develop into a great genius, but it is certain that as only the best are chosen, they will become still better through such happy three years, and if among every two hundred only one real genius is found and thus encouraged the academy will have justified its existence.

Two of our music fellows had already arrived at the academy, Leo Sowerby, of Chicago, and Howard Hanson, of San Jose, California, and had immediately, with characteristic American energy, made themselves part and parcel of Roman musical life. The Italian musicians had welcomed them with open arms, and our boys were constantly found at the concerts and rehearsals of the Santa Cecilia or having some of their Italian musician friends at the Villa Aurelia for chamber-music, and a cup of tea in the beautiful gardens surrounding the villa.

America owes a great debt of gratitude to Major Felix Lamond, through whose single-mindedness of purpose and energy the fund has been collected which has made the three music fellowships possible. He is now continuing the work by giving his life to the music department of the academy, and as its director acts as guide, counsellor, and friend to its young incumbents. I must confess that during my visit I had the constant yearning that I might be forty years younger and could spend three wonderful years in Rome under such ideal conditions.

The last night Major Lamond, his wife, and I dined on the roof of the Villa Aurelia with Director Stevens, who is in supreme charge of the entire academy. According to Roman custom dinner began after nine o'clock. Beneath us and stretching out toward the Campagna was the entire city of Rome with its electric lights appearing like magic in every direction. Beyond the Campagna rose the mountains, still visible in the faint twilight. Opposite to us rose the hill of the Pincio Gardens, and on the left, just visible over the tree tops, flamed the cross of Saint Peter's. The silence was profound until suddenly the bells of Rome began to vibrate from all directions, and finally, faint but clear, came the sound of a bugle from the military barracks, blowing the retreat. By this time I was sunk in a silent ecstasy, but a further climax was yet in store for me, for as the last notes of the bugle trembled into silence a nightingale from the bushes directly below us began to pour forth her song.

Florence came next on our orchestral tour and I looked forward with eagerness after our crowded days of official receptions and concerts to a day absolutely free from duties of any kind. We arrived on May 24, and I hoped to sleep deep and late, but at nine o'clock next morning there was a knock at my door, and without any further preliminary warning in walked a young gentleman, who introduced himself as the representative of the mayor of Florence, who "sends regrets that he cannot be here himself but wishes me to give Maestro Damrosch the speech of welcome." I begged him to excuse me for a few minutes and attired myself so that I could receive the mayor's kind welcome in a more fitting garb and room.

Our concert was at the splendid Politeama Theatre, a great amphitheatre with fine acoustics. Albert Spalding was our soloist, and as he had been virtually brought up in Florence and the people there had watched his career with eager interest, his appearance was a real homecoming and the greeting affectionate in the extreme.

At a charming reception given at the house of Albert's father after the concert, I met the historian Ferrero and a delightful acquaintance from previous visits, Mrs. Janet Ross. She is a daughter of the beautiful Lady Duff-Gordon, and when she was a child George Meredith had occupied a cottage on her father's estate in England. He had adored her and it was said that she had been his inspiration for Rose in "Evan Harrington." I had met her in Florence in 1913, when she already was well over seventy and a woman of remarkable intellectual power and physical activity. She lives in a delightful old villa with walls two feet thick on a hill below Fiesole. Boccaccio had written part of his "Decameron" there and the house was filled with interesting old Italian furniture. She made her own olive-oil and vermuth on her farm and sold large quantities of it to England. When I admired some exquisite dining-room chairs, she told me she had found them in Pisa and that they were good eighteenth-century models. She said: "I have a little Italian carpenter who carves wood very well and if you like I can have these copied for you and they will cost you very little." I have these chairs in my house to-day and value them doubly as having come to me through the good offices of this interesting lady.

She had also made a remarkable collection of old Italian *stornelli*, which she had heard through mingling with the Italian peasants and farmers in Tuscany and elsewhere and had noted down. As this collection numbers literally hundreds of folk-songs, many of them dating back centuries, it should prove valuable to the connoisseur.

In Parma, the following day, I visited the Teatro Farnese. It is the oldest theatre in Italy, and while it is in a somewhat dilapidated condition and, of course, no longer used for performances, it is fascinating as a relic, and one can well imagine what splendid pageants and dramatic cantatas must have been performed there before the great nobles of that day and their retinue. The Teatro Regio seemed to me the most beautiful that we had played in. It seated over two thousand people and we marvelled that so small a town as Parma should be the proud possessor of such a home for music.

The heat was again intense, but as the audience were in an extremely receptive and tumultuous mood, we did not mind it, and the orchestra played superbly. I was sorry therefore to have been compelled to nip in the bud a little plot which I luckily discovered that evening. Sixteen adventurous young members of the orchestra had very quietly decided that they would take a midnight train for Venice, spend a happy day there on its lagoons, with perhaps even a swim on the Lido, and then take another night train for Milan, arriving just in time for our concert there. Milan is an important musical centre, and I did not wish to play there with an orchestra partly tired out by two night trips, besides the strong possibility of delayed Italian trains, which operate on the principle of *chi va piano, va sano, ma non lontano.* I therefore had to forbid this little excursion, although I sympathized strongly with our men for wanting to carry it out.

I arrived in Milan two hours ahead of the orchestra and was met at the station by a committee consisting of Signor Finci, the president of the Milan Symphony Society, under whose auspices we were to play, Campanari, brother of my old friend the barytone, and honorary secretary of the Verdi Home for Aged Musicians, the prefect of the police, and several others. All had pale and anxious faces, and had come to tell me that there was not a room to be had in Milan, that several hotels had closed their doors as there was a restaurant and waiters' strike, and that they wanted to consult with me what had better be done. That mischievous strike devil evidently was to be a permanent member of our organization on the entire tour. I retired with the committee to the room of the prefect at the railroad station and discussed various plans, although in the back of my mind was the firm conviction that my men would find rooms, beds, and food if they were suddenly dumped in the middle of the desert of Sahara. I finally asked Campanari if there were any spare rooms in the Verdi Home for Aged Musicians, and he informed me that the entire home was empty, as they had not been able to operate it at all during the war, owing to lack of funds. There were plenty of beds, blankets, and sheets, but no servants of any kind. This was at least something, and I thought that my young men would not at all mind sleeping in beds that were intended for aged musicians and doing their own chamber work. The prefect also suggested several empty beds in the city hospital, but this did not look to me so inviting. However, I finally arranged with them to meet again at the station on the arrival of the orchestra and I would put the matter before them, and then let them go forth and fare for themselves. Any one who had not found a bed should return to the station and report at the office of the prefect, who would then see that some kind of accommodation was found. This plan was carried out and my manager reported to me that at the final hour only two of our orchestra reported at the station, the one to say that he had found no room and the other that he had two. These two men went off arm in arm therefore, and my faith in the orchestra was again abundantly justified, although the hotel strike here was even worse than in Genoa. I was quartered with my family at the Continental Hotel and, with the exception of a few toothless old hags, who made a pretense of taking care of the rooms, there was no service of any kind. The principal cause of the strike seems to have been a realization on the part of hotel employees that it was undignified for them to accept tips, especially as the tipping system produced such unequal results, the chambermaid on the first floor of a hotel receiving often ten times as much in tips as the one who officiated on the fourth floor. They therefore demanded that a tax of ten to fifteen per cent be added to the bills of travellers, this amount then to be distributed among the employees according to a certain schedule. In the meantime we sizzled in the heat and suffered. To add to our discomfort, there was a great scarcity in the city supply of water, and if one wanted a bath it could only be obtained at six o'clock in the morning or after ten at night.

But again the discipline of the men and the determination to demonstrate themselves as an artistic organization manifested itself in a remarkable way, and both of our concerts were superbly played and enthusiastically received. We considered Milan one of the most important cities of our tour. Its opera at the famous La Scala is world-renowned, and of recent years, especially through the efforts of Maestro Toscanini, a highly cultivated audience for symphonic music has developed.

Toscanini, whom I had known and often admired in America, was rehearsing and conducting in Padua. To my surprise and delight he took a night train from there in order to be present at our Sunday afternoon concert and to give me a brotherly greeting. After the concert he accompanied me to the railroad station where he was to take the night train back to Padua. As we arrived my orchestra, who were already in their respective sleeping-cars, recognized him and with a great roar of welcome gave him three American cheers.

Our three days in Milan had been very busy ones. On Friday afternoon the Ricordi Music Publishing Company gave us a reception, showing the orchestra through their enormous printing works. The first concert was given that evening. On Saturday the mayor and commune of Milan gave us a reception with a visit to the City Museum at the Castello Sforzesco. This was followed by a concert given for us by the excellent municipal band in the courtyard, and a "tea" which consisted of all manner of sandwiches, ices, cakes, and, above all, innumerable bottles of champagne. We were all glad that there was no concert that evening.

After the Sunday concert a number of motor-buses took the orchestra and musical instruments quickly to the station, while our Italian friends stood around and marvelled at what they called "American efficiency," and we rolled out of Milan and Italy on our way to Strassbourg, exceedingly tired, but with a feeling that we had brought Italy and America many steps nearer to each other by our visit. We had been simply overwhelmed with demonstrations of affection from the moment we arrived in Italy, and there is something in the almost childlike manner in which the Italians demonstrate their feelings that endeared them very quickly to us. They are seething with vitality, and the very intensity of their emotions, which to the cooler North American temperament sometimes seems exaggerated, is a force to be reckoned with in the future of the world. While their civilization is the oldest in Europe they seem to be the youngest people of to-day, and in my profession and the kindred arts I expect great things from the Italian people as soon as the dreadful aftermath of the World War shall have been cleared away.

I was much interested in Strassbourg and Metz in the curious mixture of German and French civilization. In Strassbourg we were very cordially received by the new director of the Conservatory, M. Ropartz, of Nancy, one of France's most distinguished musicians.

At Metz the mayor made a speech of welcome and with

a group of citizens gave us a "vin d'honneur" after the concert. Both cities gave us audiences evidently accustomed to concerts of symphonic music and with a fine appreciation of what we would offer them.

On the public square in Strassbourg I noticed a group of citizens excitedly pointing toward a steeple on the opposite side and, lo and behold, I saw a stork, the first one to get back from his winter sojourn in Africa to spend the summer in his native haunts. The reader will wonder that I have not something more exciting to relate, but I confess that the complete freedom from the official and social engagements after our hectic weeks in Italy came like a heavenly balm, not to mention the agreeable change of living again in a hotel with real waiters, chambermaids, and cooks to minister to one's comfort.

I looked at that stork and suddenly an old doggerel jumped into my head that I had sung with other children over fifty years before, and which begins:

"Storch, Storch, Steiner, mit de langen Beiner"—

and here was perhaps a descendant of the very bird whom we had greeted so long ago. I was inclined to become sentimental over this interesting possibility, but the stork flew away without showing any reciprocal interest and my mood did not last long.

We returned to Paris the following day, and on the morning of June 4 started in a special train to Fontainebleau, where the entire orchestra were to be guests of the mayor and municipality for the day.

The suggestions which I had made to Francis Casadesus in Paris and Chaumont during our long talks in 1918, while he and I were examining the two hundred bandmasters of the A. E. F., had borne quick fruits.

Casadesus had communicated my suggestion of a summer school for American musicians to his very musical friend, M. Fragnaud, the sous-préfet of Fontainebleau. He in turn had interested M. Bonnet, the mayor, and in consequence a quick decision had been reached that the summer school should be placed at Fontainebleau and housed in an entire wing of the historic Palais de Fontainebleau, which would be donated for this purpose by the French Government. I was delighted at this happy outcome, and, as the people concerned evidently wished to signalize it by some special fête, I gladly accepted their invitation to give a concert there with our orchestra and make this, so to speak, the beginning of relations which will, I hope, help materially to bring France and America musically closer together for many years to come.

Many French musicians and dignitaries were on the train to take part in the day's celebration. There were M. Paul Leon, representing the Ministère des Beaux Arts; Alfred Cortot, distinguished pianist; Mangeot, editor of the *Monde Musicale* and founder of the École Normale de Musique in Paris; Francis and Henri Casadesus, Mlle. Boulanger, Albert Bruneau, composer of the opera "Le Rêve"; M. Dumesnil, deputy for Fontainebleau, and many others.

The whole town had been declared "en fête." Every shop was closed and French and American flags, gaily intertwined, festooned all the principal streets. The street leading to the Mairie was lined on both sides by French troops, and we all tried to look as if we were delegates to the Versailles Conference as we marched to the reception of the mayor, and looked at this martial array.

The luncheon which followed was one of those typical French affairs in which the gay was charmingly mingled with the more serious and ceremonial. M. Dumesnil proved himself one of the greatest orators I have ever heard and played upon every emotion of the human heart, evoking tears and laughter with the voice and diction of a virtuoso.

He was succeeded by M. Bruneau arising and suddenly addressing me, and at the close pinning the Legion d'Honneur on my coat, after which, to the huge delight of my orchestra, he, in true French fashion, kissed me on both cheeks. It is very agreeable to have one's orchestra present while such honors are conferred, as their approval demonstrates itself in most noisy fashion, and my boys know that this particular decoration is as much theirs as mine.

As there was no theatre in Fontainebleau large enough to hold the huge audience, the concert was given in the Ménage d'Artillerie, which had been hastily converted into a concert hall. It proved excellent for this purpose, except that as soon as we began playing, hundreds of birds, which had had undisturbed possession of the rafters and of the musical privileges of this building for years, were evidently disturbed and angered by our intrusion. They suddenly flew out from their nests and burst into shrill songs of protest, which mingled, not without interesting results, with the harmonies of the "New World Symphony," played by special request of the sous-préfet, M. Fragnaud, who is himself an excellent amateur oboe-player.

In the front rows of the audience were hundreds of school-children who had been dressed "en Américaine," with enormous bows and sashes composed of the American stars and stripes. That there were several hundred of these I can testify, as I had to shake hands with every one of them after the concert.

The following day, before leaving for Belgium, I received the welcome news that a rather disagreeable matter concerning our three concerts at the Paris Opéra had been most amicably settled. The Opera House, which is the property of the French Government, had been offered to us by the Ministère des Beaux Arts "free of rent," but we were to pay for the actual expenses of light, heat, and service incurred. When I first arrived in Paris our local manager informed us that the Director of the Opera, who holds a lease of the building, intended to charge us thirty thousand francs for his "expenses." This seemed to me excessive, and I remonstrated with M. Leon, the Director of the Beaux Arts. The Director of the Opera, who had lost millions of francs at the opera during the war, was a man of wealth to whom the opera was more or less of a personal toy, but he evidently wished to recoup somewhat on us, for he argued that, inasmuch as he might have given opera performances on the days and hours when we had our concerts, we should be charged with the pro-rata expense of his singers, orchestra, chorus, and ballet. This argument, however, did not seem valid to us, as since time immemorial there had never been any opera performances on those days of the week. I presented our case to M. Leon and told him that as I had never had any dealing or arrangement with the Director of the Opera but only with the Ministère des Beaux Arts, I was compelled to leave the matter entirely in their hands. We were their guests, and if they felt that we should pay thirty thousand francs for "expenses" we would most certainly do so. The results were most satisfactory, but not entirely unexpected by me, and the sum which we finally paid was a perfectly fair amount.

We went to Brussels on June 3 by motor, through a great

part of the devastated regions and all the horror and misery of destroyed villages, field after field pock-marked by shell explosions and dreary remains of a few stumps of trees where had been acres and acres of forest.

On our arrival we were welcomed with open arms by our ambassador, Brand Whitlock, and his wife. He told me that but two weeks before he had been suddenly informed that we could not play at the Théâtre Royal de la Monnaie because a socialist organization of Brussels claimed the right to it for an entertainment of their own. There had been a mix-up because the director of the opera, who had promised us the theatre, had died and the new incumbent claimed to have no knowledge of our coming. They intended to place us in a Flemish theatre, which of course did not have the dignity of the Royal Opera House, and Mr. Whitlock promptly told them that, as we were there by invitation of the Belgian Government and as our coming had an international significance, he could not permit us to be euchred out of our rightful possession of the Théâtre de la Monnaie, and if we could not have that he would telegraph to me urging us to cancel the concert. This evidently produced results. The socialist organization was appealed to, and immediately and courteously said that it would do anything for an American orchestra.

The same lack of what we would call proper management of concerts seemed to exist in Brussels as in many cities of France and Italy. Large advertisements, such as fill the amusement columns of American papers, are hardly ever used. Two lines inserted only once or twice are the rule. Reading notices, giving the programme or other information regarding the concert, are printed only if paid for at so much a line. Small posters, which are pasted on street corners for a week or two, are almost the only advertising indulged in.

Transfer companies—such as in our country meet a musical or theatrical organization at the station with a specified number of trucks to carry the musical baggage or scenery to the theatre—are not known. We had put this important part of our tour into the hands of Thomas Cook and Sons, and their representative, on the arrival of the train, would negotiate with this or that driver lounging around the station and lazily looking for jobs. In Italy the porters again and again simply refused to transport our stuff because the weather was too hot, and they would only begin at six or seven o'clock in the evening, when thirty little handcarts, pushed by as many men, would carry the musical instruments to the theatre. Luckily concerts in Italy begin at nine or nine-thirty, so we always managed in one way or another to get our instruments transported. Several times, however, even soldiers and military camions were bribed into service. This slovenliness, which is maddening to an American, is so universal in Europe, especially since the war, that one marvels how anything can be accomplished; and yet with the exception of places where strikes interfered we got along, even though we were sometimes wild with anxiety and foolishly furious at what we considered to be their national characteristics.

Everybody in Belgium, however, seems to read the posters, for the demand for seats in Brussels was so great that we could have filled the little opera-house twice over. Its acoustics are marvellous, and the strings vibrate like an old Cremona violin. They had specially requested that the concert should be purely symphonic and without any soloist. I therefore gave them the lovely Mozart

"Jupiter" Symphony and the César Franck D Minor. Franck had been born in Liège, and I wished to demonstrate to them our love and understanding of this noble musician. I do not think I have ever played before an audience more sensitive to the beauties of music. As a special compliment to Brussels we played an Adagio for strings by Lekeu, a modern, highly talented, young Belgian composer, who unfortunately had died at the age of twenty-four. The Adagio is a work of tender, melancholy beauty, and sounded so exquisite in this building that the players and I were intensely moved by it during the performance. This emotion was evidently communicated to the audience, so that at the close their applause could not be quieted, and I finally had to take the score of the composition from my desk and point to it in silent pantomime.

After the concert, as I was preparing to leave the theatre, two ladies came toward me with an old man who proved to be the father of Guillaume Lekeu. He tried to thank me for our playing of his son's composition, but broke down completely as the tears poured down his face.

The following day at Antwerp I saw again to my great delight the famous old tenor, Van Dyk, with whom I had given many a Wagner opera during our engagement at the Metropolitan with the Maurice Grau Opera Company. His villa, near Antwerp, had been occupied by a German general and his staff during the four years of the war. They had drunk up his entire wine-cellar, consisting of many hundred bottles of choice vintages, and had also removed every bit of copper from his door-knobs and kitchen. Otherwise they had left his house intact, and, with imperturbable good humor and courage, Van Dyk had taken up again the work of gaining an existence for his family. Twice a week he went to Brussels, where he had an interesting class in dramatic singing at the Royal Conservatory, and besides this he was busily engaged as a director of an insurance company.

In Antwerp, as well as in Liège and Ghent, we found the same discriminating and educated audiences as in Brussels.

Hardly anywhere did we see the ravages of war, and what little there were were being quickly repaired by the industrious inhabitants.

We left Belgium on June 10, to enter Holland, playing at The Hague that evening and in Amsterdam the day after.

In Holland our American diplomatic representative, William Phillips, Minister to The Hague, had been active in assuring us a welcome. He was an old friend and had invited not only the Queen Mother, who is the only musical member of the royal household, but a distinguished party of nearly one hundred, including all the diplomatic representatives and the highest officials of the court and governments, to be his guests at the concert.

After the first part he introduced me to the Queen Mother, who proved to be very charming and much interested in music, and who also possessed that delightful royal quality of putting you "at your ease." This consists in asking a question and then not waiting for you to answer, but answering it in all its possibilities and bearings herself. Conversation is thus made rather one-sided but agreeable, even though all the brilliant things one might have said remain unuttered.

After the concert the entire distinguished party assembled at the legation for a delicious supper, at which I met a great many charming Dutch ladies who, fortunately for me, spoke English or French.

The next day Mr. Phillips motored me to Amsterdam. There the members of the local orchestra immediately poured into the willing ears of my men dreadful stories of local jealousy of our coming, that several of the newspapers had been told to criticise us severely, and that all the adherents of the local orchestra had ostentatiously decided to absent themselves from our concert. Very little of this proved to be true. The huge hall in which we played, the Concertgebow, has a stage perched up so high that the people in the parquet literally have to strain their necks to see the performers, and the reverberation of sound is excessive. The hall seats three thousand people, and there were not more than fourteen hundred at our concert. However, they certainly made up in enthusiasm what they lacked in numbers. All previous notions of the phlegm of the Dutch people were completely dissipated. Not being a prima donna, I did not keep count of the many times I was recalled after the "Eroica" Symphony, but, as I had to march down and up a platform of about fifty steps each time, the exercise in connection with it was considerable. The newspapers next morning, in spite of all the dark rumors, were enthusiastic in our praise and generous in their comparison of our orchestra with their own splendid organization.

London marked the last lap of our musical race through Europe. We stayed a week and gave five concerts, four at Queens' Hall on June 14, 15, 16, and 19, and one on June 20 at the huge Royal Albert Hall. The lucky star which had accompanied us during the entire tour shone for us with steadfast light during this last week. The orchestra never played better and the newspapers heartily echoed the reception we received from the public.

I had not conducted in London since a concert mentioned elsewhere in these reminiscences, given at Princes' Hall by Ovide Musin in 1888, when I was but twenty-six years of age. Since then great changes have come over the musical life of England. At that time music was to a great extent in the hands of foreigners, and one has only to see the old pictures by DuMaurier in *Punch* to realize that the musician in English drawing-rooms was generally a long-haired German or Italian. Hans Richter was the great popular conductor in London and there were many foreigners in the British orchestras.

Since then the Anglicization of music had been going on rapidly, thanks principally to great music-schools such as the Royal College of Music, under Sir Charles Villiers Stanford and Sir Hugh Allen, and the Royal Academy of Music, under Sir Alexander MacKenzie. These schools educate great numbers of orchestral musicians, and to-day the personnel of British orchestras is composed almost entirely of native-born. Many of us consider Sir Edward Elgar the greatest symphonic composer since Brahms, and his education has been altogether British. A group of English conductors, of whom Sir Henry Wood is the dean and Albert Coates and Eugene Goosens among the most gifted, have made for themselves an international reputation. England has now the material for a strong national musical life. With such conductors as she possesses and her splendid orchestral material, her orchestras would soon rival those of America if her citizens would give them the same generous support which our organizations receive, but in this respect the condition of London is very much what it was in New York preceding and during the first half of my career.

Her orchestras are to a great extent co-operative. The

concerts are projected and given by the members of the orchestra and they divide the profits among themselves. These profits are exceedingly small and do not really pay them for the time given to the rehearsals and concerts. The London Symphony, for instance, gives only eight concerts during the winter, and rarely has more than three rehearsals to a concert. In consequence of this, while the players have developed a great facility in reading at sight and making the most of the limited rehearsal time, the results cannot be as finely worked out as is possible in the generously endowed orchestras of America, which assemble their players every morning for rehearsal and give more than one hundred symphonic concerts during a winter.

We lay great stress on unanimity of bowing, for proper phrasing can only be secured if the sixteen first violins, for instance, who have to play a phrase in unison, play as one. To the educated ear there is a great difference in the effect if one or two or more notes are played on the same bow or if a phrase is begun with an up or a down bow. Generally speaking, this unanimity in our playing impressed and delighted our London audiences and critics, but one of the latter was evidently annoyed by it as he began his analysis of our concert with the head-line: "Orchestra Too Perfect to be Good." His eye had evidently been accustomed to the more "free and easy" bowing at some of their own concerts, and he thought that a more emotionally inspired effect was produced if the individual member of the orchestra is not restricted by too much discipline. It must be acknowledged, however, that a good conductor must guard himself from the temptation to make a god out of technic, which should, after all, be merely a means to an end.

Because of our undoubted superiority in orchestras and opera we cannot, however, claim to be a more musical people than the British. Their love and cultivation of choral music is far greater than ours and they have a small group of composers whose work is more important and interesting than the aggregate we can as yet produce.

Augustus Littleton and his friends arranged many affairs for our pleasure, among them a ceremonial luncheon at the Mansion House by the Lord Mayor of London. This luncheon was attended also by the American ambassador, Mr. Davis, Viscount Bryce, and many of the foremost English musicians. My orchestra was hugely delighted and impressed with the quaint mediæval ceremonies, the gorgeous uniforms and liveries, and the prodigal hospitality displayed by our kind host. As a mark of special friendliness toward the New York Symphony Orchestra and its first visit to Great Britain I was made a member of the "Worshipfull Company of Musicians," founded by James I in 1604, and was presented with the silver medal of that ancient organization.

Our ambassador proved himself just as able to discourse eloquently on the importance of music as on any other theme which might tend to strengthen cultural bonds between the two nations. Both he and his wife had evidently endeared themselves to the English people, and many were the regrets when, with the change of party in Washington, he tendered his resignation.

Throughout the luncheon Lord Bryce beamed his approval of the proceedings, as he had given nearly all of his energies during the later years of his life toward a better understanding between the two English-speaking countries.

The orchestra sailed for America on the *Olympic* on

the Tuesday following our last concert, and I bade them good-by with my heart in my mouth; they had done such honor to our president, Mr. Flagler, to our country, and to their conductor. During the entire tour of seven weeks there had not been one lapse from perfect discipline, a discipline largely self-imposed. Each one had felt his responsibility and had acted accordingly. Their playing had been at high-water mark continually and they had borne the inevitable fatigues and annoyances of constant travel with unfailing good humor. On the other hand, their delights had been many. They had seen the great art treasures and scenic beauties of five countries, and with that quick perception which is one of the characteristics of American life, they had taken full advantage of their opportunities. If they gave of their best with both hands, Europe certainly returned with equal prodigality, and there is not one of my men who would not jump at the chance to repeat our experiences at the first opportunity, naturally still further extending the tour to include Germany, Austria, Poland, and Czecho-Slovakia. We are still somewhat shy of Russia, however, as the reports which my Russian musicians get from their former country are too dismal and uninviting.

XVII

WOMEN IN MUSICAL AFFAIRS

In Europe music sprang from the ground and it is the folk-songs and folk-dances of the peasant that have gradually—refined and developed in the hands of the great composers—worked their way upward and become the possession and delight of the cultured classes.

In this country we have no peasantry, and what slight remains of folk-songs and folk-dances we possess, apart from the music of the negro, have only recently been dug out of the isolated mountain fastnesses of Kentucky and Tennessee. These are generally of British origin and cannot be considered as having been part and parcel of our national life. As against the rich subsoil of the folk-songs of Germany, Bohemia, Russia, France, and Scotland we can show but the thinnest artificial layer of music, and this has been created and carefully nurtured by a small educated class.

The dreary social life of the early Puritan settlers and their frowning attitude toward the joys of life further retarded the growth of the arts among us.

I do not think there has ever been a country whose musical development has been fostered so almost exclusively by women as America.

Musical education began among the well-to-do classes who could afford to engage the European musicians who immigrated to America to teach their daughters—but not, alas, their sons. A strong feeling existed that music was essentially an effeminate art, and that its cultivation by a man took away that much from his manliness and, above all, made him unfit to worship at the most sacred shrine of business. I am speaking now of fifty years ago. Conditions have improved since that time, but not sufficiently as yet to produce normal and healthy conditions regarding the civilization of our people.

Women's musical clubs began to form in many a village, town, and city, and these clubs became the active and efficient nucleus of the entire musical life of the community, but, alas, again principally the feminine community. It is to these women's clubs that the managers turn for fat guarantees for appearances of their artists, and it is before audiences of whom seventy-five per cent are women that these artists disport themselves.

The result of this has been that the cultural life of American women has often been absolutely a thing apart from their relations with their men-folk. It has become accepted that of course men do not and need not share the women's interest in the arts; and while business does not perhaps monopolize the American man in quite as unhealthy a fashion as in former years, the principal change which has been brought about is the introduction of golf, at least an occupation in which men and women may share. What a pity that the elusive ball is not composed of a little Beethoven and Brahms instead of the mysterious mixture of concrete and gutta-percha, and that family life, which is the very fortress of civilization, cannot make use of the cultivation of music as one of the strongest ties to bind husband and wife, sons and daughters together!

Some of us are too prone to look upon modern plumbing, telephones, and motor-cars as evidences of high civilization or even culture, when they are really only more or less agreeable conveniences which minister to our comfort but not to our heart or head.

In Europe men and women share more equally in the love and cultivation of music, and the emotional and personal attitude of the women is offset by the more impersonal and mental attitude of the men. The result of this is shown in audiences in which neither sex predominates and, above all, in the cultivation of chamber-music at home in which professionals and amateurs, men and women, participate to their mutual pleasure and development. Nothing more charming can be imagined than such family evenings of music, during which the players indulge themselves in the string quartets and piano trios of Mozart, Beethoven, and Brahms, with perhaps a small audience of enthusiasts composed of other members of the family and half a dozen friends who afterward all join in a jolly supper of bread and cold meats, together with a good bottle of wine or beer.

My father carried this lovely custom into the New World, and I owe almost my entire education in chamber-music to the Sunday afternoons at his house, the tranquil and spiritual atmosphere of which is unforgetable.

A few years ago a meeting was held in the mayor's office at City Hall at which I had been asked to speak in behalf of good music for the people on Sunday afternoons and evenings. A clergyman from Brooklyn had made a tremendous appeal against any Sunday recreations and wanted the aldermen to revive the old blue laws of two hundred years ago. The room was crowded with people, and when I spoke of what the chamber-music on Sunday afternoons at my father's house had meant to me as a boy, this audience broke into such enthusiastic applause that there was no mistaking the general attitude, and my Sunday symphony concerts, which I was the first to inaugurate in New York, have only once been interfered with by municipal authorities.

Some American women have realized the false and one-sided condition of musical culture in our country and have sought to remedy it by encouraging their sons to take up the study of some musical instrument, but it has been up-hill work, as the general sentiment of the country has not yet been sufficiently awakened. Plato considered the study and appreciation of music an educational necessity for the young Athenian, but such schools as Groton, Saint Paul's, and Saint Mark's, for instance, have not yet admitted music to their regular curriculum, and in so far as it is studied there it is considered rather an outside privilege with which the school course has no official connection. Among the boys the necessity for excelling in football or baseball is so carefully and consistently insisted upon that almost the entire time left from school hours is devoted to these sports, and the boy who wants to continue the study of a musical instrument, which a fond mother has perhaps begun with him before he entered the school, is looked upon by the other boys as a sissy. The standard of personal conduct set in these schools is high, but the tendency seems to be to make the boys as like each other as possible. Many of them, if not discouraged, would develop decided artistic talent, but individuality and independence of thinking, which should be the end and aim of all teaching, is often frowned upon, and the results only contribute still further to the monotony of our social life, in which the courage to be one's self is submerged in the desire to be exactly like every one else.

The public schools of our country, however, show a

much more intelligent attitude than formerly; and, while the time allowed for singing and the study of the beginnings of music is still all too short, music is taught to the boys as well as to the girls. The singing of the children has greatly improved, and in many cities school orchestras have been formed, which the boys and girls enjoy immensely and in many of which music of good character is studied.

In Los Angeles and Berkeley, California, I heard some excellent school orchestras, and in Dayton, Ohio, Mrs. Talbot has interested herself personally in this movement with great enthusiasm and excellent results.

In New York, my brother Frank, while supervisor of music in the public schools, effected a complete reform in the teaching of the children and succeeded in interesting the authorities to give music a more important position. The singing improved immensely and since his retirement Mr. Gartlan, his successor, has continued the good work. I have several times used choruses of a thousand school children at the music festivals of the Oratorio Society in the production of such works as Pierné's exquisite "The Crusade of the Children" and "The Children of Bethlehem," and the children sang the three-part harmonies of their music with such purity and exquisite quality of tone as to bring happy tears to the eyes of the audience.

School orchestras have been formed all over the city, and once a year I take my entire orchestra to one of the large auditoriums of the public high schools and for two thousand little would-be orchestra musicians we play a programme composed of the music they have been studying during the winter. We never play before a more enthusiastic and delightful audience.

Thirty-one years ago I gave the first orchestral concert

for children, and twenty-five years ago my brother Frank founded the Young People's Symphony Concerts, which were designed to introduce the beauties of orchestral music to children, and in a short explanatory talk to unravel its mysteries of construction and demonstrate the tone colors of the different instruments of the orchestra. These concerts have proved an enormous success and of great importance for the education of the coming generation. When my brother retired from public work in order to devote himself exclusively to the direction of the Institute of Musical Art I took over these concerts, and have since added another course intended exclusively for little children from seven to twelve years of age. The audiences are truly remarkable. The faces of the children are aglow with interest and excitement, and when I sit down at the piano after playing an overture with the orchestra and, repeating some melodic phrase from it, ask them, "Which instrument played this melody?" their little voices ring out from all over the hall in high, shrill accents, like little pistol-shots, "The oboe! The oboe! The trumpet!" Then I let all those who think it was the oboe raise their hands, and if they are right great is their triumph, and if they are wrong equally great is their chagrin. Generally they are right!

On my orchestral tours I have several times given such children's concerts on the afternoon preceding the regular evening symphony, and while two such concerts in one day are a great exertion, the children's especially demanding a great output of vitality in order to keep their interest, I have felt more than repaid by the results; in many of the cities my work in this direction has been continued by the local orchestras or musical clubs (again the women!), and with the happiest results.

In New York also women devoted to music have greatly contributed toward its development, but occasionally the result of their efforts has not been so beneficial. Not so long ago a handsome but incompetent foreign musician (I will not disclose any name or dates in this story) came to New York and enlisted the sympathies of a few enthusiastic women. As many women need some personality on which to centre their devotion to art, they decided that New York should have this particular gentleman to direct its symphonic future. The American business man is proverbially good-natured to his womenkind and ready to pour out money for music provided he is not compelled to listen to it, and so these ladies gathered a huge fund with which to give a series of orchestral concerts. The amount was large enough to maintain a good symphony orchestra in proper hands for an entire winter, but in this instance was to be expended on six concerts only. The handsome young foreigner gave his first concert, which was a failure so complete and dismal—he being not only without any reputation but with hardly any experience in work of this kind—that even his little group of adorers became appalled and proposed to cancel the rest of the concerts. One lady, however, who had her own special favorite conductor, suggested that a complete disgrace might be averted if her protégé were invited to conduct the remaining concerts. As he was an excellent artist and thoroughly routined in the handling of orchestral players the results were so good and, above all, such a contrast to the dire tragedy of the first concert that the enthusiastic lady devotee saw her opportunity and suggested that a new orchestra should be formed for the following winter, the concerts of which should be conducted by the man who had saved the situation for them. New York had already an average during the winter of a hundred and fifty symphonic concerts by the New York Philharmonic, the New York Symphony, the Boston Symphony, and the Philadelphia Orchestra, and it would seem from this that the symphonic needs of our public were already more than amply supplied; but an enthusiastic woman, especially when driven by devotion for some pet artist, refuses to recognize practical conditions, and so this little group proceeded to gather more funds, amounting to hundreds of thousands of dollars, in order to put the new orchestra properly on its feet.

Their first difficulty was to find good players. There are never very many first-class symphonic players to be found. Not only do the two old-established New York orchestras employ about a hundred players each, but the orchestras of other cities come to New York to fill their vacancies. For years the Philharmonic, the New York Symphony, and other out-of-town orchestras had a gentleman's agreement that they would not steal each other's players, but this new organization immediately proceeded to take thirty-seven from the Philharmonic by offering them immensely higher salaries. They did not take a single player from the New York Symphony Orchestra because, as they vowed, of their great personal respect for me, but I think it was partly because we happened to have a two-year contract with all our men which bound them to us very effectively for another season. They filled their ranks further from members of the Boston Orchestra and from other out-of-town organizations, and then proceeded on their first regular season as a New York Orchestra with loud protestations that New York at last had an organization worthy of the metropolis. This orchestra carried on its existence for two years, at the end of which it came to a dismal close with an expenditure for the three seasons over and above the receipts of the box-office of nearly a million dollars, which their surprised and chagrined men guarantors had to pay. This is but one of several such irregular ventures, each one of which has swallowed hundreds of thousands. One would think that the inevitable failure of these efforts would deter others from undertaking them, but such is not the case. Hope springs eternal in the breast of the musical woman devotee and I have just heard of a new orchestra now being formed in order to enable still another foreigner, whose interpretations will of course be a revelation to our public, to wield his stick in this country as his own has refused to accept him at his own valuation.

In recent years chamber-music in New York has received great encouragement and intelligent support from women. Mrs. Frederick S. Coolidge has proved a veritable godmother to this lovely branch of musical art, and every fall the festivals of chamber-music which she gives in Pittsfield in the Berkshire Hills bring together notable gatherings of musicians and music-lovers as her guests. For several years she has offered generous prizes in competition for various forms of chamber-music. But to me the most encouraging thing that she has done is the commissioning of certain composers to write compositions for these festivals. Neither string quartets nor violin sonatas can ever become profitable to the composer in the ordinary way of commerce, as the number of copies which can be sold of such works is necessarily limited. Even young American composers must live, and if they are to devote their time to the creation of serious forms of art they should be assured of at least some financial recompense for the time they must give to it.

Mrs. Ralph Pulitzer has entirely maintained an excellent string quartet for the past three years, and I should like to see such excellent examples followed by others among our well-to-do, as chamber-music is essentially written for performance in the home and loses much of its charm and intimacy if given in a larger hall and before hundreds of people.

For some time to come the initiative for a more general musical education of our people will have to come from the women. If American mothers will demand and obtain for their sons the same musical privileges and opportunities which their daughters now enjoy America will speedily become the most musical country in the world.

So much has already been done, but much remains, and I should like to live a hundred years longer just to watch this development and to rejoice in its results.

XVIII

BOSTON

In 1887 I visited Boston for the first time professionally. I had begun my Wagnerian lecture recitals in New York a year or two before, and they had spread like wildfire in all directions. The enthusiasm for Wagner, which had been kindled into a bright flame by my father's founding of German opera at the Metropolitan Opera House, had produced a wide-spread desire for better acquaintance with Wagner's music and his theories regarding the music-drama.

I received an invitation from a group of Boston women, including Mrs. John L. Gardner, Mrs. O. B. Frothingham, Mrs. George Tyson, and Mrs. Henry Whitman, to give my lecture recitals on the "Nibelungen Trilogy."

Boston at that time occupied a unique position as the only city in America which possessed a permanent orchestra, maintained by Major Henry Lee Higginson, for the cultivation of symphonic music. A small group of highly educated and socially prominent Bostonians, belonging to the oldest New England families, made this orchestra almost the focus of their social life. The weekly concerts were the great events, the programmes eagerly discussed, and its conductor, Wilhelm Gericke, was alternately cursed or blessed according to their attitude toward some novelty which he had just produced.

Among this group I was made heartily welcome. The atmosphere was intensely local, if not provincial, and as against the searching, feverish life of a great metropolis

333

like New York, with its many conflicting interests and
racial currents, the tranquillity and purely American
quality of Boston life, as it presented itself to me, was a
complete contrast. I am speaking of Boston of thirty-five
years ago and of conditions that have to a certain extent
disappeared, for to-day even the young descendants of the
New Englanders of that era seem to find their pleasures
in different and more restless fashion.

In the group of which I have spoken, Mrs. Gardner was
among the most original and fascinating. She was certainly the leaven in the Boston lump and sometimes
shocked the more staid element by her innovations and
interest in more modern currents in art and literature
than had hitherto rippled its calm Emersonian surface.
Boston was at that time perhaps the best example of that
typically American musical culture of which I have spoken
elsewhere, which instead of growing upward from the
masses was carefully introduced and nurtured by an aristocratic and cultivated community through symphony
concerts and lectures on music. Its original impulse
sprang perhaps more from the head than the heart, but
it would not be fair therefore to say that New Englanders
approached music only from the intellectual standpoint.
I have seen very emotional outbursts among Boston
audiences, both at my Wagner recitals and years after
when I returned with the Damrosch Opera Company
to give the Wagner music-dramas. While it is possible
that they felt heartily ashamed of these enthusiasms afterward, and exclaimed, "Is this Boston?" the fact remains that even a Bostonian is human, like other Americans, and needs only to be encouraged to prove that he
too has a heart which can beat warmly and respond to the
emotions kindled by art.

Their capacity for friendship in the finest sense of the word is wonderful, and I achieved many of my dearest friends at that time. We have all grown much older since then, with the exception of Mrs. Gardner, on whom the years leave no imprint and whose enthusiasms for life and art flame just as brightly to-day as then.

I was certainly very young in those days, and remember, after one of my lectures, which had gone off with great enthusiasm, walking along Boylston Street toward my hotel, thinking in my young conceit that I was evidently a good deal of a personage, when I saw that the street was filled with crowds of people and the police were making a passage with difficulty so as to allow an open carriage, drawn by two horses, to pass through. In it sat a rather stout, smooth-shaven gentleman with a very shiny high silk hat, and the people were cheering him like mad. "Who is this?" I asked a bystander. He gave me a contemptuous look and stopped cheering just long enough to say: "Don't you know John L. Sullivan when you see him?" I accepted the rebuke meekly and entered my hotel a much more modest man than I had left it a few hours before. John L. Sullivan, "Boston's greatest citizen," had just come home from a fight in London, but I do not know to this day whether he had won or lost.

The Boston orchestra was at that time conducted by Wilhelm Gericke, who had brought it to a remarkable state of proficiency. I found him to be a very likable man, a thorough musician, and always gentle and friendly in his attitude. I used to envy him because, while I had to maintain my orchestra at that time by my own exertions, he had a great philanthropist behind him. His orchestra was engaged by the year, played under no other conductor, and assembled every morning at 9.30, like clockwork, for rehearsal. Gericke brought the orchestra up to a high standard of virtuosity. His sense of values was absolute, and under his training and greatly assisted by Franz Kneisel, his concert master, the strings soon acquired great unanimity and a ravishing quality of tone. His readings were always musicianly, although I felt occasionally that they were too reserved. He had a horror of the exaggeration of the brass instruments, and perhaps erred on the other side in subduing them too much; but when he returned, years after, for another five years in Boston his readings had gained in freedom and elasticity, and the balance of the different choirs seemed perfectly adjusted. Boston, and indeed the country, owes him much. He was fortunate in his opportunities, but he proved himself worthy of them.

Rightly or wrongly, Major Higginson had made it his rule to engage none but German conductors for his orchestra. He had gained his first enthusiasm for symphonic music as a young man in Vienna, and had got the idea firmly in his mind that only Germany could give his orchestra the leaders which it required. Among the long line of conductors who came and went, not all, naturally, were of equal worth. A few were distinctly second-raters, and I remember one whose blustering incompetence and conceit finally so enraged Major Higginson that, as the gentleman would not resign when requested because his contract still had another year to run, Higginson sent him a check for the entire amount and dismissed him. Curiously enough the impetus which the reputation of having been conductor of the Boston Symphony Orchestra gave was so great that it landed him in two other American orchestras, one of which he brought to the very verge of ruin and the other he ruined altogether, so that the city which had founded it and lavished hundreds of thousands upon it is now without any symphony orchestra and seems to have lost the courage to begin again.

But among the conductors of the Boston Orchestra two stand out as among the best that Europe has sent over. These are Arthur Nikisch and Doctor Karl Muck. The one died last winter, beloved and mourned by the musical public of all Europe and of North and South America; the other was sent from our country back to Germany after the war in deserved disgrace, after having been interned as prisoner of war at Fort Oglethorpe.

When I first met Arthur Nikisch in 1887 he was conductor at the Leipsic Opera House. I had gone there to attend an annual meeting and festival of the Tonkünstler-Verein, an association of which Franz Liszt had always been the president and which had originally been formed by a small group of Liszt-Wagner-Berlioz adherents, of whom my father was one. One of the features of the festival was a stage performance of Berlioz's "Benvenuto Cellini," given in honor of Liszt. The work fascinated me, and its performance under the young Nikisch delighted me beyond words. In appearance he already had the same characteristics which his enemies decried but which among his friends only aroused a delighted chuckle when he appeared on the platform, and which quickly changed to a hurricane of enthusiasm after he had demonstrated his marvellous skill as an interpreter. I refer to the long black lock which always hung low over his forehead and his still longer white cuffs which more and more enveloped his little white hands as the performance progressed.

Gericke had developed the orchestra into a perfect instrument, and when Nikisch arrived he played upon it like a virtuoso. I have always maintained that Nikisch achieved still greater mastery during his years in America, because until then he had had no such orchestra at his disposal. The much-vaunted Leipsic Gewandhaus and the Berlin Philharmonic, which he conducted, suffer from the troubles common to all co-operative organizations. Their members outstay their period of usefulness and retain permanent places in the orchestra after they should give way to younger and better men.

The readings of Nikisch were distinctly personal and therefore, because they reflected his own nature, so ingratiating that I have often enjoyed certain of his interpretations although I considered them wrong and contrary to the intentions of the composer. Nikisch made them convincing for the moment.

Doctor Muck, who became conductor of the Boston Symphony some years later, was less personal in his readings. His principal work in Germany had been the conducting of opera, and occasionally a lack of routine in symphonic work showed itself in badly combined programmes, but only in that one respect. As a conductor of the symphonies of Beethoven and Brahms he was a master, and to me his interpretations of Brahms rank among the finest that I have heard. It was a tragedy that this man, who had gained not only the confidence and respect of his patron, Major Higginson, to a greater degree than any other of the Boston conductors, who was admired not only in Boston but in every city which the orchestra visited, and to whom America had given unbounded acclaim, should at the crucial moment have proved himself a supercilious, arrogant Prussian of the worst Junker type, ungrateful toward the man to whom he owed his many successful years in America, and finally even an abject coward and renegade toward the country to which he owed national allegiance.

The story in its entirety is too unpleasant to be told, but as after Muck's return to Germany he saw fit to indulge in the most violent diatribes against America and its treatment of him, it is justifiable to tell a little of the truth in these pages.

In order to understand the story properly it is necessary to recall the excitement which swept through the country when we finally entered the Great War. Wars arouse prejudice as well as patriotism, and suspicion as well as faith. One of the curious, almost pathological, results of the psychosis of war is the spy mania, and this manifested itself in the years of 1917 and 1918 to a remarkable extent—in America as well as in Europe. One need only recall the many stories of concrete tennis-courts which were discovered and vouched for by reputable people as having been built years before by German army officers, who, disguised as "rich American financiers" (!) had constructed lavish country places along the Atlantic seaboard, all of which possessed these remarkable concrete tennis-courts. These were to support great guns which at the proper moment were to put the American navy out of existence! There were also wonderful stories of secret wires discovered in private houses, and of strange beacon-lights suddenly flaming up at regular intervals along the coast in order to signal messages to some mysterious German submarine.

It was all like a war novel of Oppenheim, and as some of our ladies joined the secret service in an unofficial capacity, they together with others—who conceived it to be the height of faithlessness to our country to enjoy a

symphony of Beethoven or an opera of Wagner while
we were at war with Germany—had a beautiful time in
the happy illusion that they were doing real war work.

Doctor Muck immediately became a centre of suspicion. He had taken a cottage at Seal Harbor, Maine,
for the summer of 1917, and of course he was immediately
accused of having a wireless outfit and signalling to a
whole fleet of German submarines which were cruising off
Mount Desert Island and whose immediate object was,
of course, to capture all the millionaires of Bar Harbor
and hold them captives for huge ransoms.

According to others he had placed a telephone receiver
in the cellar of his house in Boston which skilfully tapped
the wire of the telephone of the lady next door, and she,
to her horror, had one morning on lifting her telephone, in
order to call up her butcher, heard his "guttural" German
voice conversing with some mysterious German at the
other end about a shipment of dynamite, which was to be
used, of course, to destroy Faneuil Hall and the birthplace of Henry W. Longfellow in Maine.

There was not a story so wild that it did not gain cre-
dence, but it was not so strange that many of these pre-
posterous rumors should centre around Doctor Muck.
His attitude toward us had become more and more supercilious. That he should sympathize with his own country was perhaps natural, but that he should use some tact
and reticence in this respect was equally to be expected.
He might have taken example from Fritz Kreisler who,
as an Austrian citizen, served at the beginning of the war
in the Austrian army, but was retired and returned to
this country before we entered the conflict. From then
on he acted with such dignity and tact, giving up all
playing in public during that critical period, that he re-

tained the personal respect and affection of all right-thinking Americans.

As the war situation became more and more serious, Doctor Muck seemed to become more and more supercilious. In response to a perfectly natural impulse, the public demanded that our orchestras begin or end their concerts with the playing of the national anthem. This had become the symbol of our patriotism, and as millions of our young men began to gather in the camps and to be sent abroad in the transports, "The Star-Spangled Banner" was beginning to awaken in every heart emotions that were hardly known to our generation before the war. Doctor Muck refused to play the anthem. Not from Boston nor New York, alas, but from Providence, Baltimore, and Pittsburgh angry mutterings began to be heard. These cities insisted that an orchestra which in time of war was not willing to play our national anthem should not be permitted to play at all. Doctor Muck's answer to this, in a newspaper interview, was that he conducted an artistic institution, that "The Star-Spangled Banner" is not a work of art, and therefore "only fit to be played by ballroom orchestras and military bands."

Up till then I had upheld Doctor Muck in so far as it seemed just as bad taste for him, as a German, to conduct our national hymn in time of war with his country as it was for our public to insist that a German should do so. He could have said: "I am a German; my country is at war with yours. I am your guest because in 1915 Major Higginson insisted that I should return to America as he thought that the orchestra could not exist without me. I am now in an unfortunate position. Let me retire from conducting here during the war, or at least let your national anthem be conducted by the concert-master."

But this interview was a flippant evasion of the real point at issue, and when the reporter of the *New York Tribune* brought it to me, I exclaimed that I did not believe Doctor Muck could have said anything so outrageous, whereupon the reporter told me that his editor had expected me to say this and had therefore telegraphed to Boston and obtained a confirmation of the interview. I then expressed myself in very plain language regarding Doctor Muck's attitude, but his only answer was a new interview in which he declared that it was all a mistake, that he was not a German but a Swiss! This belated claim, which was based on technicalities and contrary to the facts, was promptly denied by the Swiss minister in Washington, and then suddenly Doctor Muck proceeded to conduct "The Star-Spangled Banner," but in listless fashion, although half a dozen cities by that time barred their doors to him and the concerts of the orchestra had to be cancelled.

In the meantime the secret-service men of the government had been patiently following every rumor and clew regarding Muck's supposed spy activities, and while they discovered that his attitude toward us was absolutely inimical and that he was therefore decidedly *persona non grata*, there was no foundation of truth in the rumors connecting him with wires, wireless, beacon-lights, dynamite, or German submarines. The secret-service men, however, discovered other disagreeable things in regard to him which had no connection with the war but which made him liable under the laws of our country. An incriminating package of letters was shown to him, and on his acknowledgment that he had written them he was given the choice of internment as a prisoner of war at Fort Oglethorpe or of being arrested on another charge and brought before the civil courts for trial. He naturally threw up his hands and accepted the former as the lesser evil. As he was released after the war on condition that he return to his own country, I cannot see that he has cause for anything but gratitude toward this country and its lenient treatment of him.

The whole affair was a terrible shock to Major Higginson. He was an old man and the discoveries regarding Doctor Muck, in whom he had placed such confidence and for whom he had vouched so absolutely, were unendurable to him. He had expected to continue his support of the orchestra, and it was generally assumed that he would leave the organization an endowment sufficient to maintain it after his death. Instead of this, he announced his determination to withdraw altogether, and left the decision whether they wished to continue the orchestra with a group of music-lovers whom he had called together. For a time its future was in great doubt. Thirty of the players were discharged because of their German nationality, but money was subscribed by various Boston citizens to rebuild the orchestra, and to-day, under the leadership of Pierre Monteux, it is fast regaining its old excellence. It will never again occupy the unique position it held twenty-five years and more ago, because since then so many other symphony orchestras have been founded in America on similar lines and with similar generous endowments. But to Major Higginson will always belong the glory of having blazed the trail. He set the standard, and America will give his memory loving reverence and gratitude.

XIX

MARGARET ANGLIN AND THE GREEK PLAYS

During the winter of 1915 I received a letter from Margaret Anglin, our distinguished American actress, asking me to compose the incidental music for two Greek plays which she intended to produce the following summer at the great open-air Greek Theatre in Berkeley, California. The plays selected were the "Iphigenia in Aulis" of Euripides and "Medea" of Sophocles. I was fascinated by the problem involved, as it necessitated not only the composing of the music but the creation of a form in which it was to be cast.

We know very little of the music of the ancient Greeks, and if we sought to imitate that, it would sound so archaic and even unnatural to our modern ears as to fail in properly supporting the emotions of the drama for us. While the Greeks had developed the technic of the drama to a remarkable extent, music as an art was at that time in its infancy, although its importance was fully recognized by Plato and the great dramatists.

The problem for me was to write music which should take full advantage of the modern development of harmony and orchestration, and form an emotional current on which the drama could float without being in any way submerged. The treatment of the Greek chorus was another problem for which I had no precedents. Mendelssohn had written incidental music to "Antigone," but this music does not represent Mendelssohn at his best, as much of it is dry and academic in character.

The Greek choruses usually begin with a recital of some old story of mythology, with which every Greek in the audience of that era had been familiar since childhood. Gradually this story is brought into connection with the situation on the stage and reaches its climax when the chorus implores the actors to draw their lesson from it. These choruses I treated in various ways, according to the needs of the dramatic situation. Some were recited to a soft but expressive undercurrent of music, others were sung, and still others were a combination of both. I would have the story of the old Greek legend recited by the first leader of the chorus. Then the second leader, as he applied it to the dramatic situation, would burst into song, until, in the third phase, the entire chorus would join in their impassioned pleadings or warnings.

In the spring of 1915 I took a little cottage in Setauket, Long Island, and there within six weeks wrote the entire music for the two plays, the orchestra parts being copied sheet by sheet as my score was finished. In June I packed them in my bag and travelled across the continent to meet Margaret Anglin and take charge of the musical part of the production.

On arriving in San Francisco I found the great World's Fair already in full operation. Its Spanish architecture and the luxuriant verdure in which it was enclosed made it a perfect dream of beauty, but I gave myself little opportunity to enjoy it, as my real mission was across the bay at the Greek Theatre in Berkeley, where Margaret Anglin and a company of players were already busily engaged from morning till evening in rehearsing. They were anxiously awaiting my music in order to make it fit in properly with the stage arrangements.

The Greek Theatre at the California University is one

of the most remarkable structures of its kind in the world. Built amphitheatrically against the side of a hill and absolutely on the lines of the old Greek theatres, its top is fringed by sombre eucalyptus-trees.

A few years before I had seen a performance of the "Bacchante" of Euripides given by a company of Roman actors at an antique amphitheatre on the side of a hill overlooking Florence. Much of this performance had been impressive, but the music was tawdry, and as the play was given according to old Greek custom in the late afternoon, the cruel sunlight made the make-up of the actors and the garish colors of their costumes doubly prosaic. The ancient Greeks had no artificial lighting and were therefore compelled to give their performances in daylight, although they sought to temper it so that night would fall at about the end of the play. Margaret Anglin, with her characteristic genius, perceived that a much greater glamour and stage illusion could be produced by giving her performances at night, leaving the audience in darkness and marking out the stage with great electric lights from above, which could be heightened or lessened according to the actual needs of the drama.

If the drama in America had been treated as seriously by its cultured citizens as music has been, Margaret Anglin would perhaps be to-day the artistic head of an endowed theatre devoted to productions of Shakespeare, Goethe, Molière, Calderon, Æschylus, Sophocles, and Euripides. These great masters of the stage would form just as important a part of her repertoire as the symphonies of Beethoven and Brahms make up an important part of the programmes of the New York Symphony Orchestra. Margaret Anglin is to-day the greatest tragedienne of the

American stage, and should be acting *Medea* and *Lady Macbeth*. But instead of that she has to tour the country, playing "Green Stockings" and similar piffle, and only indulges her artistic ambitions and ideals in occasional productions of Greek dramas at her own risk and very much at her own expense.

I was immensely interested in the rehearsals on the stage of the Greek Theatre. They began at nine-thirty in the morning and would often last—with an intermission of an hour or two for lunch—until eight o'clock at night, but as they were held outdoors in the glorious fresh air of California there was but little fatigue, and all concerned gave themselves up enthusiastically to Miss Anglin's direction and picturesque conception.

She had hired a bungalow near the theatre and a Japanese butler-cook. This little Jap would always appear at one o'clock with a basket filled with the most delicious luncheon dishes, artistically decorated in real Japanese style by his own deft fingers. He seemed to have a great penchant for the stage, asserted that he had acted *Hamlet* in Japan, and would sit for hours after luncheon watching the rehearsal, with his little inscrutable eyes fixed on the stage. I have often wondered whether on his return to Japan he gave performances of the Greek plays to his own compatriots and whether any great changes or adaptations were necessary to make them comprehensible to his audiences.

While the general plan of the action and grouping had been carefully worked out by Miss Anglin, she had an open mind and eye, and would often change the arrangement completely if an improvement could be effected thereby. This meant incessant repetitions, during which her patience and cheerful courtesy never failed her.

A grand piano had been rolled into a corner of the stage, and I was so fascinated in watching the rehearsals and the gradual evolution of the stage pictures under her skilful hands, that I insisted on always playing the incidental music myself, even though some of the scenes were repeated dozens of times.

Miss Anglin had enlisted the services of fourteen of California University's loveliest and most talented co-eds to form her Greek chorus. Beauty seems to flourish naturally on the Pacific coast, and some of these young ladies were glorious specimens of a truly Greek and statuesque charm. The recitation of one of the choruses, which was to be spoken in a kind of elastic rhythm to the music of the orchestra, was intrusted to one of these Dianas of Berkeley, and as she had no conception of this, to her, novel combination, Miss Anglin asked me to give her a separate rehearsal after lunch. I sat down at the piano and recited the chorus to her while I played the accompanying music. She stood by my side listening intently and looking like a statue of Diana of Ephesus. Then, bending her head with stately dignity, she said: "I get ya!" Alas! the illusion was gone, and her voice brought me back suddenly from my dream of 400 B. C. to California of 1915. She had not "got me," however, and I was finally compelled to give this chorus to another young lady, less statuesque in form but more clever in achieving plastic unity between speech and music.

But my real troubles began when I tried to collect an orchestra of fifty for the performances. At that time there were not many good players in San Francisco, and even those few were permanently engaged in the big World's Fair orchestra. My first rehearsal was truly pathetic—I had been so spoiled by the many years of association with my lovely New York Symphony Orchestra. But where there is a will there is a way, and by stealing a few men from the local theatres and borrowing a few more from the exposition orchestras, we were enabled to get a fairly good body of men assembled.

The success of Miss Anglin's productions was truly remarkable. There were ten thousand people at each performance, and "Iphigenia in Aulis" had to be repeated twice. In this work the camp of *Agamemnon* and its atmosphere of war were graphically illustrated, and five hundred Berkeley students, picturesquely attired and well trained, gave a very vivid picture of the soldier's camp, especially at the end of the play when the Oracle has announced that the wind has changed, and these hundreds of soldiers rushed across the stage in a tumult of joy to board their ships and sail for Troy.

The "Electra," for which William Furst had written music for Miss Anglin years before, was also performed. Eventually I also composed music for this play, and all three of the dramas were performed in New York a few years later at the request of Mr. Flagler, on the stage of Carnegie Hall, which had been skilfully converted for the occasion into a Greek theatre.

We all marvelled how vividly modern these plays, written more than two thousand years ago, seemed as given under the artistic direction of Margaret Anglin. *Electra,* waiting outside the walls of the palace for the sound that shall announce to her the death of *Ægisthus* and *Clytemnestra; Medea,* having entered the palace to kill her own and *Jason's* children in order to punish him for his marriage to the young Princess, while the chorus, shaking the iron grill of the doors, implore *Medea* not to slay her children; *Iphigenia,* youngest daughter of *Aga-memnon,* descending alone the great flight of steps to suffer death in the sacred grove of the goddess Artemis, that her wrath may be appeased and favorable winds may send the armies of *Agamemnon* to Troy—all these are unforgetable scenes, and I was overjoyed to feel that the music which I had written was not inappropriate, but formed a good background for these crucial moments.

XX

DEAD COMPOSERS

I have a large library of musical works. It was begun by my father in 1857, and contains many scores of the composers of that period, sent to him for first performance in Germany. He added to it considerably during his thirteen years in America as founder and conductor of the Symphony and Oratorio Societies, and I have still further enlarged it since I became conductor of these two organizations. My library now virtually represents the entire symphonic development up to the present time, and as I look through my catalogue I am amazed at the number of dead composers which it contains. By this I do not mean those who have passed away, but those who were once celebrated, were hailed as great, but whose works are now forgotten and only repose undisturbed on dusty shelves like mine, for no efforts or housewife's art will prevent dust from seeping into the shelves of a New York City library!

To mention a few of these "dead" composers alphabetically: Who now plays the overtures of Auber's "La Muette de Portici" and "Fra Diavolo"? Yet they figured frequently in my popular programmes thirty years ago, and both operas deserve more than a passing recognition. The first was a stroke of genius in which the commonplace Auber rose to real heights. The heroine is a dumb girl, a prima donna without a voice, but very dramatically portrayed in the orchestra, and the atmosphere of a people fighting for freedom pervades the entire story. "Fra Diavolo" is a delightful comic opera. The only trouble is that the music is too good for the abjectly dull audiences that now frequent our theatres and want to see a "musical show." Its plot is delightfully consistent, which is another reason for looking on it with disfavor to-day; but I have always regretted the Nemesis which overcomes *Fra Diavolo* in the last act. This delightful robber has by that time so endeared himself to us that he should be allowed at the end to escape, in order that the public may live in the hope of further pranks and misdeeds from him.

Thirty years ago I gave the first performance in America of a "Symphony in D Minor," by Anton Bruckner. He was a man with the brains of a peasant but the soul of a real musician, and with a marvellous gift for improvisation, although he was, intellectually, incapable of developing and balancing his themes properly. A noisy party in Vienna wished, at the time, to acclaim this disciple of Wagner as a genius, to counteract the constantly growing admiration for Brahms, and more recently such eminent conductors as Mahler have tried to popularize Bruckner's symphonies, but they have never gained a permanent hold on our public. Several years after my performance of his "Symphony in D," I was in Berlin, and Siegfried Ochs, the conductor of the famous Philharmonic Choir, brought a little bald-headed man of over seventy years of age to my table at the Kaiserhof. On my being introduced to him, he suddenly grabbed my hand, and saying, "You are the Mr. Damrosch who has given my symphony in America!" he proceeded, to my great embarrassment, to cover my hand with kisses.

Vienna is full of stories of his childlike gentleness and

modesty. Hans Richter once invited him to conduct one of his own symphonies with the famous orchestra of the Vienna Society of Friends of Music. At the rehearsal he stood on the conductor's platform, stick in his hand, with a beatific smile on his face. The orchestra were all ready to begin, but he would not lift his stick to give the signal. Finally Rosé, the concert-master, said to him: "We are quite ready. Begin, Herr Bruckner." "Oh, no," he answered. "After you, gentlemen!"

At that time he was also commanded to appear before the old Emperor Franz Joseph to receive a decoration. After he had been decorated, the Emperor turned to him and said very kindly: "Herr Bruckner, is there anything more I can do for you?" Bruckner answered in a trembling voice: "Won't you please speak to Mr. Hanslick (the famous musical critic of Vienna) that he should not write such nasty criticisms about my symphonies?"

In my father's time the overture to Cherubini's "Anacreon" had a frequent and honored place on his programmes. A modern audience would vote it too dry and old-fashioned.

The music of Niels W. Gade was quite a favorite with our grandfathers and grandmothers, but he is unendurable to-day.

A new orchestral composition of Carl Goldmark was eagerly waited for, forty years ago, and there was great rivalry between my father and Theodore Thomas as to which should have the privilege of performing it first. People used to revel in his "exotic and luxuriant orchestration," but to-day his colors have faded before the greater glories of Strauss and Debussy and Ravel, and only his "Rustic Symphony" occasionally figures on cur programmes.

During the second year of the German opera at the Metropolitan, Goldmark's "Queen of Sheba" made a success which equalled that of the Wagner operas. Solomon's temple, painted in gold, the Jewish rituals, the Oriental harmonies, and the naïve surprise of the public on seeing biblical characters upon a modern operatic stage, all combined to make the work a sensational success. To-day it has disappeared completely from the repertoire of European and American opera-houses.

The fate of Franz Liszt as a composer is still more tragic because it is partly undeserved. He created the form of the symphonic poem, but those who succeeded him have developed it so much farther as to leave his works somewhat submerged. I still have great admiration for his "Faust" Symphony, but neither I nor others of my colleagues who share this admiration have been able to make this work really popular with the general public. His "Dante" Symphony, "Festklänge," and "Orpheus" receive still fewer public performances, and his "Ce qu'on entend sur les montagnes" has never been performed here to my knowledge. But "Les Préludes" and the two Piano Concertos, on the contrary, are still played *ad nauseam*.

The symphonies of Gustav Mahler have never received genuine recognition here, although he was a very interesting apparition in the musical field. He was a profound musician and one of the best conductors of Europe, and it is possible that, in the latter capacity, he occupied himself so intensely and constantly in analyzing and interpreting the works of the great masters that he lost the power to develop himself as composer on original lines. All his life he composed, but his moments of real beauty are too rare, and the listener has to wade through pages of dreary emptiness which no artificial connection with philosophic ideas can fill with real importance. The feverish restlessness characteristic of the man reflects itself in his music, which is fragmentary in character and lacks continuity of thought and development. He could write cleverly in the style of Haydn or Berlioz or Wagner, and without forgetting Beethoven, but he was never able to write in the style of Mahler.

Of all the greater composers of the last hundred years no one has been killed oftener than Mendelssohn, yet he always seems to come back again with a new renaissance. His music for "Athalie," his "Reformation" Symphony, his overtures to "Melusine" and "Ruy Blas" are dead as a door-nail, but his Violin Concerto is still the most perfect example of its kind, his "Midsummer Night's Dream" the best incidental music ever conceived for a Shakespearean play, his "Elijah" the most dramatic oratorio ever written, and the Scotch and Italian Symphonies still possess a delightful and eternal charm.

The works of Meyerbeer, on the contrary, have deservedly disappeared even from our popular programmes. Those empty "Torchlight Dances" and the vulgar ballet music from "Le Prophète"! I confess, though, that I still have a sneaking fondness for the "Coronation March," perhaps because I had to conduct it so many times at the Metropolitan, when I first began conducting the operas there. That the same man who penned the glorious fourth act of the "Huguenots" could have been satisfied with the empty drivel which preponderates during the rest of that opera, is one of the eternal mysteries.

About thirty years ago Moritz Moszkowski was one

of the most popular composers of the day, especially for the piano, but modern ears have but little use for his delicate, though evanescent, charm, and his orchestral suites are but rarely heard to-day. He has lived in Paris for many years, and during the war he suffered greatly. Advancing years and a long illness had left him very weak, and it seemed almost as if the musical world in which he had been so popular a figure had forgotten him completely.

But last winter, Ernest Schelling, one of our best American pianists, and an old friend of Moszkowski's, conceived the happy idea of giving a testimonial concert in his honor, which should be thoroughly original in character. He, together with his distinguished colleague, Harold Bauer, accordingly enlisted the co-operation of twelve other celebrated pianists who were in America during the winter. This list, a truly remarkable one, included Elly Ney, Ignaz Friedman, Ossip Gabrilowitsch, Rudolph Ganz, Leopold Godowsky, Percy Grainger, Ernest Hutcheson, Alexander Lambert, Josef Lhevinne, Yolanda Mero, Germaine Schnitzer, and Sigismond Stojowski.

Mr. Flagler offered the services of our orchestra, but as the stage was to be completely filled with fourteen grand pianos, there was no room for an orchestra, and I had to content myself with the possibility of being taken on as a piano mover, as I longed to take part in the affair in any capacity. The morning before the concert, however, I received a hurried S. O. S. telephone call from Ernest Schelling. He said: "Please come down to Steinway's immediately and help us out. The fourteen pianists are all here for rehearsal. We have arranged for several compositions to be played by all of us, but

FRITZ KREISLER, HAROLD BAUER, PABLO CASALS, AND WALTER DAMROSCH

alas, each one has his own individual interpretation, and nothing seems to make us play together. We need a conductor!"

When I arrived at the rehearsal hall the confusion was indeed indescribable, and it took some time to bring order out of chaos. Here were fourteen of the world's greatest pianists, veritable prima donnas of the piano, but several had never learned to adapt themselves to play together for a common musical purpose, and when I rapped on my stand for silence in order to begin the "Spanish Dances" of Moszkowski, at least five or six continued their infernal improvising, playing of scales, and pianistic fireworks. By using heroic measures I gradually produced a semblance of order, and gave the signal for the beginning of the music. The effect was extraordinary! Several of these pianists had never followed a conductor's beat, and after the first ten bars, two of them rushed over to me, the one violently exclaiming that the tempo was too fast, and the other insisting with equal vehemence that it was too slow. Finally I obtained silence, and told my pianistic orchestra that they were, undoubtedly, the fourteen greatest pianists in the world, and that the interpretation of each one of them was undoubtedly equally the greatest in the world, but as they represented fourteen different grades and shades of interpretation, I intended to take the matter into my own hands and they would just have to follow my beat whether they liked my tempo or not. This was greeted with a roar of approval, and we now settled down to the work of rehearsing as solemnly as if these prima donnas of the ivories were orchestral musicians and routined members of the New York Musical Union. Order followed anarchy, and the results achieved were not without higher artistic interest, especially as I detailed such accomplished and routined musicians as Harold Bauer, Ernest Schelling, and Ossip Gabrilowitsch to use their own discretion in "orchestrating" the "Dances." Gabrilowitsch, for instance, reserved himself for the entrance of the "brasses"; Bauer invested some of the more delicate portions with agile runs of flutes and clarinets, while Schelling imitated the kettle-drums and cymbals with thrilling effect.

Carnegie Hall was jammed and the audience in a gale of happiness at the highly original proceedings. The stage was so crowded with the fourteen huge pianos that, after threading my way through them to introduce Mme. Alma Gluck, who was to auction off one of the programmes, I said that what this concert evidently needed most was not a conductor but a traffic policeman.

Perhaps the most artistic feature of the programme was the performance of Schumann's "Carnival Scenes," in which each little movement represents a separate carnival figure. The fourteen pianists drew lots as to which was to play which. The introduction was played by all, but after that, in quick kaleidoscopic succession, the different carnival figures fairly danced from the stage into the audience, as a pianist on one side of the stage would begin, followed by one from the other side, and so on. It was a most remarkable opportunity to compare the interpretative characteristics of the different pianists.

The receipts were considerably swelled by the auctioning of programmes and autographed photographs of Moszkowski, and fifteen thousand dollars was the result of an entertainment truly unique in the history of music.

The most popular modern symphonic composer in the

'70's was Joachim Raff. He was a young Swiss who, without a cent in his pocket, had walked many miles from his little village in order to hear Liszt play at a concert in Zurich. Liszt became interested in his undoubted talent, and took him with him to Weimar as musical secretary. Raff, von Bülow, and my father became great friends. But while every one expected that Raff would continue as a true disciple of Liszt's, and write in the revolutionary style of his master, he gradually turned from him and leaned more and more on classic models, although in several of his symphonies he retained the Lisztian idea of programme music. As he grew older his conservatism became more and more marked. He had great facility and produced works in every known form of music, and his vanity gradually made him believe that his string quartets were equal to Mozart's, his symphonies to Beethoven's, and his oratorios to Handel's and Mendelssohn's. His fecundity was astonishing, but his pen too fluent for real musical depth. There was hardly a winter, however, that Theodore Thomas or my father did not perform "Im Walde," or the very programmatic "Lenore" Symphony. This work, in which the last movement follows closely and dramatically Burger's famous ballad, had an enormous popularity, and is occasionally performed by us to-day, but in general the name of Raff means but little to modern concertgoers.

But perhaps the greatest tragedy of all was Anton Rubinstein, who became, after Liszt, the world's greatest piano virtuoso. The world fêted him, spoiled him, and sated him with adulation. It all brought him no satisfaction. He was consumed with the ambition to be considered a great composer, and wrote incessantly, never criticising what he wrote. His "Ocean" Symphony had a tremendous popularity in New York fifty years ago, but to-day no one would listen to it. His "D Minor Concerto" has been played, *ad nauseam*, by every pianist, but to-day it is threadbare and frayed at the edges. Only the supreme skill of a Josef Hofmann can make his "G Major Concerto" endurable and cloak its musical emptiness. He wrote opera after opera in a feverish desire to eclipse Wagner, whom he hated, and whose popularity he envied, and after "Parsifal" had been proclaimed at Bayreuth as a "Sacred Festival Play," he immediately proceeded to write an opera on the life of Christ, which is so dull and unconvincing that it has hardly had a performance anywhere.

His personal popularity was so great that Pollini, the astute manager of the Hamburg Opera, occasionally used to put on one of his operas on condition that he himself would come to Hamburg to conduct the opening performance. His presence would insure a crowded house.

At the last rehearsal of one of these operas Rubinstein was so well pleased with the work of the orchestra that he turned to them and said: "Gentlemen, if my opera is a success you must all come to my hotel after the performance for a champagne supper." Unfortunately, the opera was a decided frost and the audience so undemonstrative that Rubinstein, in absolute disgust, laid down the stick after the second act, and, bidding the local conductor finish the opera, returned dejectedly to his hotel and went to bed. At eleven o'clock there was a knock at his door. "Who is it?" he shouted in great irritation. "It is I, Herr Rubinstein, the double-bass player from the opera orchestra." "What do you want?" "I have come for the champagne supper."

"What nonsense!" raged Rubinstein. "The opera was a ghastly failure." "Well, Herr Rubinstein," answered the thirsty and undaunted double-bass player, "*I* liked it!"

The disappearance of Schumann's symphonies from concert programmes is due to the fact that he was never at ease in writing for the orchestra. His instrumentation is so thick and turgid as to be the despair of conductors. So much of the music is exquisite, but it is like a precious jewel imbedded in a foreign substance which conductors try in vain to remove by changing the dynamics of this or that instrument, or by leaving out an unnecessary doubling up of certain harmonies. All these devices, however, can do but little. More heroic measures are necessary, and I was much interested last summer when Sir Edward Elgar asked me what I would think of his deliberately reorchestrating an entire symphony of Schumann's. I heartily applauded such an idea and begged him to carry it out speedily as there is perhaps no one living to-day who better understands the colors of the orchestra and knows how to produce the most subtle shades in the intermingling of the different instruments. In the meantime Frederick Stock, the noted conductor of the Chicago Orchestra, has taken the bull by the horns and has written a new orchestration of Schumann's "Rhenish Symphony" which I hope to produce this winter.

Are Sousa's marches played nowadays? They should be. They are better than the military marches of Europe of to-day, and while one cannot put them into the category of higher musical efforts they are the only American compositions of musical worth that have triumphantly blazed their way all over the world.

Richard Strauss, who twenty-five years ago was the most interesting star in the musical firmament, has lived long enough to have outlived a part of his popularity. He never originated a musical form, but accepted the symphonic poem of Liszt and the music-drama of Wagner as models. His workmanship is infinitely greater than Liszt's, his counterpoint stupendous in its boldness, and in his treatment of the orchestra he sometimes transcends even Wagner in the originality of his orchestral combinations. But his compositions lack the ideality of either of these masters, and because of this and in spite of his marvellous paraphernalia, his works seem to carry within them the seeds of their own decay.

The gods endowed this man at his birth perhaps more richly than any other musician of our time, but something within him has made him relinquish the greatest of their gifts and has turned him to less pure ideals. In the "Sinfonia Domestica" the daily life of husband, wife, and baby are characterized by an orchestra of one hundred and ten players with such noisy fury and realistic prose as to give one an altogether distorted insight into what is supposedly a page from the composer's diary. But the music descriptive of the composer who, after these dreadful domestic squabbles, retires to his workroom, lights his lamp, and begins to communicate with his muse, is so beautiful as to fill us with a deep regret that one so winged for flight in the ether should be so content to walk on the earth.

The instrumental devices, depicting *Don Quixote's* adventure with the sheep and his fight with the windmill, which aroused such astonishment and admiration when they were first heard, have already lost their effect and are listened to to-day with hardly a smile. The final scene, however, depicting the dying of *Don Quixote*, is so beautiful and tragic in its expression as to bring tears to the listener. The "Heldenleben" is to me a work of noisy bombastic emptiness from beginning to end, and one might call it typical of certain German currents of to-day. It would, however, be manifestly unfair to call it typically German, as a race that has produced Bach, Mozart, Beethoven, and Wagner will surely find other men to continue their glorious traditions.

A composer's fame is not affirmed by professional musicians but by the general public whose judgment in the end is infallible. A great masterwork that is not destroyed will always eventually be recognized as such whether, like the "Venus de Milo," it has lain hidden for centuries beneath the earth or, like the "Matthew Passion" of Bach, equally hidden in the dusty shelves of the Royal Library of Berlin, to be rediscovered by Mendelssohn and pronounced the greatest religious choral work ever written.

The two works of Strauss which have retained their popularity with the public are undoubtedly his best, as their requirements do not enlist such qualities as he does not possess or has not sought to develop. In "Till Eulenspiegel" Strauss's talent for mordant realism finds full expression. The wild pranks of *Eulenspiegel* follow each other in mad, cynical humor, and, in the limited form of programme music, the work is flawless.

His "Salome" is as perfect a union with Oscar Wilde's marvellous play as the "Pélléas" and "Mélisande" of Maeterlinck and Debussy. In both the composers have so steeped themselves in the spirit of the poem as to enhance its beauty. But with all my admiration for "Salome" I have never been able to sit through the final scene without a feeling of disgust, which sometimes mounted even to physical nausea. When *Salome* sings her horrible love music to the head of *John the Baptist* it has always seemed to me a parody on the glorious finale of "Tristan and Isolde."

I have spoken in another chapter of Tschaikowsky's visit to America in 1891 as a guest of the Symphony Society. For twenty-five years his popularity was enormous and the mere announcement of his "Symphonie Pathétique" was sufficient to draw a crowded house. His symphonies appeared more often on our concert programmes than those of any other composer. They have a rhythmic and elemental strength which appealed even to the unmusical, but to-day a distinct lessening of this popularity is noticeable. There is a lack of real symphonic development of his themes, and certain crudities of workmanship stand out more clearly as the works have become better known. Young conductors, anxious for ready and cheap applause, still choose one of his symphonies for their début, and the melodic charm of his lighter music, if not heard too often, will retain its place in the affection of our public for some time longer.

And now we come to the greatest genius of the nineteenth century—Richard Wagner. "What!" exclaims my reader. "Do you consider him dead?" God forbid! The wings of his genius are still soaring aloft in the ether, but there is no doubt that the attitude of the world of to-day toward his music is absolutely different from that of fifty or sixty years ago when he first electrified or infuriated a public, amazed at his daring innovations. The inevitable has happened—Wagner has become a "classic."

I was a boy of fifteen when I heard the first performance of "Lohengrin" at the old Academy of Music. The opera was sung in Italian with Italo Campanini as *Lohengrin*, Valeria as *Elsa*, and our own Anne Louise Cary as

Ortrude. The conductor was old Luigi Arditi. I sat in the front row in the family circle, and was so excited by the drama and the music that at the end of the double male chorus—which accompanies the approach of *Lohengrin* in the boat drawn by the swan as the God-sent deliverer of *Elsa*—the tears rushed down my cheeks. But they were happy tears and a natural relief from the tension which the music had created in me.

Each succeeding opera of Wagner's was a similar revelation. I pored over the scores of the "Nibelungen Trilogy" during every hour left me from school work and piano practice. In fact, I often stole time from the latter and would gladly have given up my entire school if my parents had not very properly kept me where I belonged. Later on my founding of the Damrosch Opera Company for the sole purpose of producing Wagner operas seemed an inner necessity, and I was driven to it by a force stronger than myself. For years a Wagner programme, whether it was at a symphony concert in New York, or in Oklahoma on a Western tour, or at the Willow Grove summer concerts, drew the largest audiences, and the same orchestral excerpts were repeated by me and other conductors year after year and received by our public with excited enthusiasm. To-day the amazement which his music called forth is no longer apparent. He is admired and loved, but the nerves of the younger generation are not thrilled by his harmonies as ours were. His works repose upon our shelves bound in morocco and gold and occupy places of honor, but, alas, on several of them the dust is beginning to gather and many of the young people of to-day find "Lohengrin" monotonous, and vote unanimously that *Tannhäuser's* recital of his pilgrimage to Rome is too long.

Time and continued occupation with Wagner's music may have made me more critical and analytical, and I am no longer in complete and enthusiastic accord with some of his theories regarding the music-drama. But much of his music still sweeps me off my feet, and his "Meistersinger"—which is so happy and perfect a compromise between the opera and the music-drama—is to me still the greatest musical work of our times.

I have spoken above of the finality of the judgment of the public regarding the ultimate vitality of an art work. Conductors have had their personal convictions and have tried to force them upon our audiences, but unless these convictions were based on actual worth the public has in the end consciously or unconsciously rejected them. Sometimes unworthy composers have had momentary popularity, but they were born but to dance in the sun for one day and then to die.

My orchestral parts of the symphonies of Beethoven, Mozart, and Brahms are old and worn by many rehearsals and performances, and some of them have been patched up and pasted together by my librarian so many times that they have had to be replaced by new ones twice over. I have performed them for nearly forty years, and the grandchildren of my audiences of 1885 are now listening to them with equal happiness. A few years ago I discovered a lovely symphony by Mozart, which had never been played in New York, and I was as proud of this as if it had been the fourth dimension.

The works of these masters are lifted above the fashion of the moment, and their creators smile upon us serenely and eternally from the heavens in which they dwell as gods among the gods.

XXI

MUSIC AND MODERN MAGIC

Although I am not running for any public office and have no "phony" stock to sell, I have been receiving letters during the past three years from people all over the United States, and at the rate of thirty thousand a year. These letters come from old and young, rich and poor, educated and illiterate, and nearly all of them contain such friendly expressions and such gratitude for what they think I am giving to them that I often blush while reading them, knowing my own unworthiness. Here is how it all happened:

From 1885 to 1926 I officiated as regular conductor of the New York Symphony Orchestra, and I have told elsewhere of its activities during this long period of forty-one years. I was beginning to feel that the daily rehearsals and four weekly concerts during a long winter season, all of which were necessary in order to maintain such an organization at its highest level, were becoming a bit irksome. I began to long for greater freedom from such routine, and suggested to our president, Mr. Harry Harkness Flagler, that he relieve me of these responsibilities but permit me to continue my association with the beloved orchestra as a guest conductor for a short period every season. During my long term of service I had given thousands of concerts, had been the first American conductor to tour the entire country almost every spring, and had been rewarded far beyond my deserts by audiences to whom I had given the first hearing of the music dramas of Wagner and the symphonies of Brahms, Tschaikowsky, and others.

To be a pioneer is in my blood, and the fact that many of the Western and Southern cities which we visited had never, or but rarely, heard a symphony orchestra acted as a spur to my activities as a musical missionary.

But gradually symphony orchestras were founded in the cities which I visited. Philadelphia, Rochester, Detroit, St. Louis, Omaha, Los Angeles, and San Francisco no longer needed a visiting orchestra to satisfy their newly awakened desires for symphonic music. Excellent local symphonic orchestras under accomplished conductors amply supplied their artistic needs, and I began to feel that my work in that direction was over, and that at best I could not do more than repeat myself in continuing to perform to my own home audiences the works of the masters, with the beautiful orchestra which time and infinite care and affection had enabled me to develop.

Incidentally, especially since the World War, there did not seem to be any new great composer for whom I could break a lance as of yore for Wagner and Brahms. I was naturally deeply grateful for the appreciation of my concert audiences, but at sixty public applause does not excite one so much as at twenty-five. Then—literally out of the blue, which is out of the ether—something came and beckoned to me with such a lure of new possibilities, such new virgin fields, and such new attachments to my fellow citizens, that I found myself suddenly again in a turmoil of fascinating adventure and with an intense and happy conviction that there was still work for me to do.

In the spring of 1925, just before leaving for Europe, I received an invitation from A. Atwater Kent to conduct a concert with my orchestra in his radio series. I accepted, and just before the concert one of the officials of the National Broadcasting Company asked me to give a few explanatory remarks before each number, such as for many, many years I had given at my Children's and Young People's Concerts in Carnegie Hall in New York.

The effect of this concert seems to have been quite extraordinary, but beyond the assurance of the broadcasting officials that it had been successful I thought nothing further about it and sailed the following week for Europe. I had hardly been in Paris a week when I received a cable from the broadcasting company asking me to accept a contract for twenty concerts for the following winter.

It was only then that I realized at least some of the possibilities which this opened before me; audiences of millions at one concert instead of the three thousand in a concert-hall; the greater proportion of these radio listeners absolutely virgin soil instead of a more or less sophisticated metropolitan audience which had heard many orchestras, and for whom I might be either best-beloved or their most-hated interpreter.

I, therefore, acted as guest conductor of the New York Symphony Society for one month, but gave one weekly radio concert during the entire winter of 1927–28.

The response throughout the country was amazing to me. Thousands of letters began to pour in, and I was particularly astonished at the fact that most of them especially mentioned my voice as being peculiarly adapted to radio transmission. I had always been interested in diction and proper voice modulation in speaking, and had developed this through the many thousands of dramatic lecture recitals on the Wagnerian music dramas which I had given all over the country, but I could not claim any credit for the fact that my voice seemed to carry well over the radio. Nature had done that trick, and evidently successfully, as the people in Colorado or in New Mexico or Saskatchewan wrote me that my voice sounded as if I were in the same room with them and talking with them as one friend would to another.

Ever since then I continued these concerts—during the season of 1927–28 under the auspices of the Radio Corporation of America, and during 1928–30 for the General Electric Company. My audiences grew every season by the millions and the statisticians of the National Broadcasting Company, computing every Saturday-night audience at ten millions, claim that I, therefore, played and talked to an incredible total of three hundred and forty millions during the thirty-four concerts. As the majority of these people, living far away from the centres of musical culture, had never heard the kind of music which I gave them, and as even the names of Mozart, Beethoven, and Wagner were unknown to them, it was a joy to cultivate such a virgin field and to find out how easy it was to make willing converts of my listeners. My programmes were, of course, especially adapted for this purpose, but they contained nothing but music by the best of composers, by which I led this gigantic audience gently but firmly into the higher fields of symphonic art.

During the season of 1927–28 I mentioned to Mr. Aylesworth, the president of the National Broadcasting Company, that it seemed to me that the radio had enormous possibilities for educating the young people of our country musically and thereby supplying them with a very necessary and ideal outlet for their emotions.

Mr. Aylesworth was delighted, as this suggestion chimed in with his own dream of a "University of the Air," and Mr. David Sarnoff, the general manager of the Radio Corporation, with quick and sympathetic response offered to let me give three such concerts as an experiment. If this experiment was successful they would organize a regular educational series for the following winter over a network that would take in all the schools and colleges in the cities, towns, and villages as far west as the Rocky Mountains and as far south as New Mexico and Louisiana. Through the radio and the newspapers of the country the schools and parents were informed of our intended innovation.

Giving such concerts for the schools over the radio presented many new problems, and was therefore very much in the nature of an experiment. At my Carnegie Hall Young People's Concerts the children not only heard the music and my short verbal explanatory comments, but could see me and the orchestra with their musical instruments, and watch their playing and my conducting. All this is not yet possible over the radio, and I could not tell how far I would be able to interest an audience of youngsters that could see nothing but the loud speaker from which the sounds of the orchestra and of my voice emanated. Mechanical problems of sound reception also had to be solved, but soon after our first concert the reports which arrived in the form of thousands of delighted letters from all over the country proved that in the main we had achieved our aims, and Mr. Sarnoff felt that the time had come to inaugurate a gigantic and new system of music education.

In order to gauge its importance we must envisage the average musical conditions surrounding the majority of the young people in our country. A small percentage living in the great centres may have had an opportunity to hear an orchestral concert now and then, but at least ninety-eight per cent of our school population had never realized that music is a beautiful and highly developed universal language, which as a vehicle for human emotions and æsthetic perceptions goes way beyond the spoken word. In many of the schools singing had been introduced and the rudiments of music were taught. A few of them had even organized school orchestras, but some quickening impulse was necessary in order to increase the perception of the higher possibilities of music and to develop a joy in hearing and in cultivating it themselves. The children in the little red schoolhouses in the farming districts, in the small country towns, and indeed even in the larger cities, had grown up for the greater part as heathens as far as music is concerned, and what musical instincts they had, threatened to become vitiated by a monotony and monopoly of jazz, which excites the nerves without feeding either the heart or the head. Something had to be done and done quickly in order to balance the marvellous material development of our people and to teach the younger generation that all this prosperity was useless unless it not only permitted but encouraged beauty and its cultivation through art to permeate our lives.

The radio has proved itself as the great democratic leveller and uplifter. It has been so widely distributed among millions of American homes that it has become the natural medium not only for amusement but for information and education of all kinds, and its entry into our schools marks a new era in the dissemination of education.

6. *Q.* What instruments, seldom used melodically, play the opening theme of the trio, or middle part, of this movement?
   A. The violoncellos and double basses.
7. *Q.* What does the finale of the Fifth Symphony express?
   A. Triumphant joy at victory over the adverse forces of Destiny. (Illustrated by the principal theme.)
8. *Q.* What innovation of formal design does Beethoven introduce in the finale of this symphony?
   A. He interpolates, in the middle of the finale, a fragment of the third movement.
9. *Q.* Why does he do this?
   A. As a reminder, in the hour of triumph, of the pains and travail through which victory has been achieved.

Such questions and answers aroused great interest, and the letters which I received from students as well as teachers show that the radio is making them ear-minded, and that the influence of music seemed just as strong even though my performers were invisible and the imagination of the listeners was stirred only by what they perceived through the ear.

During last winter over five million school children were reported as listening in on Friday mornings. I received thousands of letters from teachers and pupils from all parts of the country, literally from every State in the Union east of the Rocky Mountains.

I was amazed at the keen interest and imaginative qualities which most of the writers displayed, and certain of our programmes aroused their special delight. Fairies in music, containing Mendelssohn's Overture to Shakespeare's "A Midsummer Night's Dream," Berlioz's "Dance of the Sylphs," and the fairy tale of "Beauty and the Beast" as depicted in music by Ravel. Animals in music, as so delightfully pictured by Saint-Saens, Rimsky-Korskaoff, and Strauss.

The children were quick to perceive the musical possibilities of the heavy-footed elephant, the buzzing bumble-bee, and the graceful dragon-fly. That the percussion instruments, with the fascination of the kettledrums, military drums, the xylophone and cymbals, especially charmed the youngsters was to be expected, but perhaps one of the principal results was the greater interest that the youngsters took in the instruments of the orchestra and their immediate desire to learn how to play them. From their letters it seems that the existing high-school orchestras were greatly stimulated and new school orchestras have been formed in many places. I hold this to be one of the most important results and, as now seems certain, if these concerts can be continued for a series of years, the result will be the formation of town bands all over the country.

These bands will supply a great need in the community. Their members will be composed of the former high-school students who will continue to practise and perform on their respective instruments as a pleasant occupation for their leisure hours and as a welcome relief from their daily work in shops, offices and farms. Such town bands will meet once or twice during each week for rehearsal, and you may be quite sure that they will practise not only jazz but some of the real music of the masters, and on holidays and ceremonial occasions they will furnish welcome music for their community. This will mean an America in which music will be cultivated not only by a small, over-fed and sometimes over-critical community, but by millions of farmers, carpenters, plumbers and factory employees all over the country, to whom the names of Mozart, Beethoven and Wagner will be household words, and all this, thanks to the greatest invention of our age—the radio.

Do you wonder that I am looking forward eagerly to Friday morning, October 10, when, under the auspices of the National Broadcasting Company, I shall inaugurate our third year of school concerts over the radio?

I consider myself fortunate, through these school concerts, to be able to contribute something toward the musical future of our country.

POSTLUDE

These reminiscences were begun in New York in April, 1922, and finished the following August in Bar Harbor, Maine.* My friends had urged me for some time to write down my experiences because they thought that the many and varied events in a long musical life would prove interesting to American musicians and readers generally.

I do not know. On re-reading the foregoing pages in the proof-sheets I feel that many happenings which seemed of great importance to me may prove but dull reading to others. But at least I have tried to tell a truthful tale and to give an honest account of my aspirations and struggles.

I have climbed a few hills, but only to see the mountains beyond rising higher and higher, the path upward often indiscernible through the mists surrounding the peaks.

I love the people among whom my father settled because he firmly believed that in America his children would have a greater opportunity for development than in old Europe.

The musical field in America is certainly wonderful in its possibilities, and all my life I have reached out with both hands and have worked incessantly and enthusiastically in my calling. In part at least I have tried to repay what I owe to my compatriots for their confidence and help. But the power of the individual is compara-

---

* The last chapter, XXI, called, "Music and Modern Magic," was added in 1930 for the new popular edition of the book then published.

tively small, and while our musicians have already accomplished miracles within the short period that music has played a part in our civilization, so much yet remains to be done that I long for at least one hundred more years of life, partly to continue my work but still more to satisfy my eager curiosity as to the musical future of our people.

If this book serves to encourage my younger colleagues in their efforts to increase the love and appreciation of music in our country, it has not been written in vain.

INDEX

Abbey, Henry, 104, 106 *ff*., 113, 116, 121 *ff*., 129 *ff*., *et passim*
Abbey, Schoeffel, and Grau, 51 *ff*., 72, 113, 116, 121, 130, 133, 182
Abbott, Lawrence, 31
Abt, Franz, 75
Academy of Music, 52, 116, 118, 120
Accademia Santa Cecilia, 295 *ff*.
Achenbach, Andreas, 142
"Acis and Galatea" (Handel), 178
Adamowski, Tim and Joe, 149
Æolian Hall, 219
Æschylus, 346
Allan, Mr., 295
Allen, General, 41
Allen, Sir Hugh, 319
Alvary, Frau, 137
Alvary, Max, 63, 109 *ff*., 112, 130, 142 *ff*., 172, 211
Amato, 152
American Academy in Rome, 302 *ff*.
"American Friends of Musicians in France," 221 *ff*., 239, 244
American women and music, 323 *ff*.
Andersen, "Fairy Tales," 5
Anderson, Mary, 51
Anglin, Margaret, 19, 344 *ff*.
"Arabian Nights," 5
Architecture, 285
Arditi, Luigi, 365
Arion Society, 9, 12, 25, 27
Arnold, Matthew, 90
Arnold, Richard, 208 *ff*.
Auber, 351
Auer, 2
Augustus Cæsar, 296
Austro-Prussian War, 1866, 1

B——, Madame, 87 *ff*.
Bach, 23, 57, 75, 152, 169, 171, 181, 262, 363
Backhaus, Wilhelm, 217
Baermann, 47

Ballay, Captain, 235
Banda Communale di Roma, 297 *ff*.
Bandmaster's School, 251 *ff*., 311 *ff*.
Bandsmen in American army, 233 *ff*., 247 *ff*.
Barrère, George, 46, 194 *ff*.
Baton, Rhene, 228
Bauer, Harold, 356 *ff*.
Bayreuth, 143, *et passim*
Beale, Walker Blaine, 18 *ff*.
Beethoven, 9, 33, 40, 75 *ff*., 81, 83 *ff*., 86, 88, 97, 99, 120, 148, 153, 155, 157, 164, 190, 196, 216 *ff*., 259 *ff*., 262, 278 *ff*., 282, 292, 298, 324 *ff*., 338, 340, 346, 366, *et passim*
Belcher, Zach, 35
Benedetti, 7, 41
Berlioz, Hector, 23, 27, 31 *ff*., 34, 43, 164, 180, 278, 292, 337
Berthold, Barron, 115
Bible, 5
Bigelow, Doctor Sturgis, 120
Bismarck, 2, 41, 140
Bispham, David, 19, 115, 129, 132, 159 *ff*.
Blaine, Emmons, 20 *ff*., 101
Blaine, Harriet, 91
Blaine, James G., 90 *ff*., 95 *ff*., 100 *ff*.
Blaine, Mrs. James G., 90 *ff*., 95 *ff*., 101
Blaine, Margaret (later Mrs. Walter Damrosch), 90 *ff*., 97, 100 *ff*., 103, 118, 121, 129, 291 *ff*.
Blaine, Walker, 103
Blanc, M., 293 *ff*.
Bliss, Mr. and Mrs. Robert, 241.
Boccaccio, 304 *ff*.
Boeckelman, 11
Boieldieu, 60
Boito, 144
Bonnet, M., 311
Bonsal, Stephen, 96
Bordeaux concert, 1920, 284 *ff*.
Boston musical affairs, 333 *ff*.
Boston Symphony Orchestra, 22, 123,

128, 150, 186, 207, 210 *ff*., 236, 268, 330, 333 *ff*., *et passim*
Boulanger, Mlle. Lili, 258
Boulanger, Mlle. Nadia, 156, 238, 258 *ff*., 279
Bowing, 320
Boyd, Colonel, 264
Brahms, 23, 25 *ff*., 47, 79 *ff*., 86 *ff*., 183, 184, 217, 259, 319, 324 *ff*., 338, 346, 352, 366
Brandt, Marianne, 53, 60, 65, 73, 140 *ff*., 172
Brema, Marie, 109, 111 *ff*.
Brisbane, Arthur, 96
British music, 319 *ff*.
Bronsart, Hans von, 7
Brown (coachman), 119
Bruch, 144
Bruckner, Anton, 352 *ff*.
Bruneau, Albert, 311 *ff*.
Brussels concert, 1920, 314 *ff*.
Bryce, Viscount, 321
Bülow, Hans von, 2 *ff*., 6 *ff*., 39, 54, 74 *ff*., 157, 216, 300, 359, *et passim*
Bundy, General Omar, 246 *ff*., 249
Burger, 359
Burns, Robert, 94

Calderon, 37, 346
"Caligula Seidenschwanz," 84 *ff*.
Callender, Miss Mary R., 106, 215
Callender, May, 85
Calvé, Madame, 122, 162
Cambridge University, 144 *ff*.
Campanari, 306 *ff*.
Campanini, Italo, 121, 364
Caplet, André, 255
Carnegie, Andrew, 90 *ff*., 113, 143
Carnegie Hall, 94 *ff*., 143, 179, 183, 219, 349, 358
Carnegie, Louise, 90
Carreno, Madame Teresa, 28, 167
Carter, Ernest, 240, 242
Cary, Anne Louise, 364
Casadesus, Francis, 250, 254 *ff*., 264, 310 *ff*.
Casadesus, Henri, 156, 221 *ff*., 238, 240, 311
Casella, 301
Chamber-music in New York, 331 *ff*.
Château-Thierry, 231

Chaumont, Band school at, 251 *ff*., 311 *ff*.
Chausson, 260
Cherubini, 353
Chicago Orchestra, 204, 211
Chicago, "Tannhäuser" in, 57 *ff*.
Chickering Piano Company, 74
Children and music, 326 *ff*.
Chopin, 166
Christmas celebrations, 17 *ff*.
"Christus" (Liszt), 49 *ff*.
Clemenceau, M., 147, 224
Coates, Albert, 319
Collins, Lieutenant-Colonel, 245, 249, 264
Cologne Music Festival, 86 *ff*.
Columbia Theatre, Chicago, 58 *ff*.
Coman, Miss Wynne, 198 *ff*.
Conductors and conducting, 45 *ff*., 64 *ff*., *et passim*
Conried, Heinrich, 173 *ff*.
Conservatoire Orchestra, party, 282
Converse College for Women, 192
Cook (Thomas) and Sons, 276 *ff*., 315
Cooke, 19
Coolidge, Mrs. Frederick S., 331
Coppinger, Mrs., 100, 103
Cornelius, Peter, 43, 66, 184
Cortada, 32
Cortot, Alfred, 155, 222, 231, 235, 238, 311
Cowdin, Mr. and Mrs. John E., 147
Cowen, 23
Cravath, Paul, 238 *ff*.
Croix Rouge Française, 234
"Cyrano" (Damrosch opera), 150 *ff*.

d'Agoult, Countess, 164
d'Albert, Eugene, 40, 187
Damrosch, Alice (later Mrs. Pennington), 19, 238, 265, 267 *ff*., 270 *ff*.
Damrosch, Anita, 270
Damrosch, Clara (Mrs. Mannes), 214
Damrosch-Ellis Opera Company, 123
Damrosch, Frank, 1 *ff*., 10, 58, 102, 179, 182 *ff*., 217, 254, 327 *ff*.
Damrosch, Gretchen, (later Mrs. Thomas Finletter) 154, 285
Damrosch, Hans, 1
Damrosch, Doctor Leopold (father of author), 2, 5 *ff*., 10 *ff*., 22 *ff*., 36, 52

ff., 74, 79, 86, 90, 97, 140 *ff.*, 149, 169 *ff.*, 351, *et passim*

Damrosch, Mrs. Leopold (mother of author), 1

Damrosch Opera Company, 16, 67, 69, 104 *ff.*, 129, 134, 205, 276, 334, 365, *et passim*

Damrosch, Mrs. Walter (Margaret Blaine), 90 *ff.*, 97, 100 *ff.*, 103, 118, 121, 129, 291 *ff.*

Dana, Charles A., 14

David Mannes Music School, 214

Davis, Ambassador, 321

Dawes, General Charles, 243, 262

Debussy, 238, 260, 353, 363

Defoe, "Robinson Crusoe," 10

de Forest, Miss Caroline, 85, 106, 215

Deis, Karl, 191

de Reszke, Edouard, 129 *ff.*, 149

de Reszke, Jean, 129 *ff.*, 149, 159, 292 *ff.*

de Reszke, Madame Jean, 292 *ff.*

de Vere, Madame, 178

Dewey, Admiral, 179 *ff.*

di Lasso, Orlando, 184

d'Indy, Vincent, 278 *ff.*

di Sabata, Victor, 301

Dodge, Miss (Gail Hamilton), 95, 99

Doll's theatre, 14 *ff.*

Draesecke, Felix, 6

Drew, John, 199

Dubois, Theodore, 279

Duff-Gordon, Lady, 304

Du Maurier, 319

Dumesnil, M., 311 *ff.*

Dvořák, Anton, 155, 183

Eaton, Doctor Charles, 95

Elgar, Sir Edward, 183, 319, 361

Ellacott, Captain, 255

Eller, Joseph, 110

Ellis, Charles, 123 *ff.*, 128 *ff.*

Emma, Queen Mother of Holland, 317

Endicott, Governor, 115

Engelhardt, Frau, 69 *ff.*

Engles, George, 200, 273, 276, 282, 284, 287 *ff.*

Euripides, 344, 346

European tour, 1920, 272 *ff.*

Fairchild, Blair, 244

Fauré, Gabriel, 260, 279, 282

Faversham, Julie, 19

Ferrero, 304

Festival of 1881, 30 *ff.*

Finci, Signor, 306

Finletter, Judge, 154

Fischer, Emil, 63, 66, 105, 109, 134 *ff.*, 172, 178

Fischer, Mrs. Emil, 135 *ff.*

Flagler, Harry Harkness, 136, 186, 210, 218, 222, 239, 272 *ff.*, 322, 349, 356

Flagler, Mrs. Harry Harkness, 218

Flagler, Mary, 285

Florence concert, 1920, 304

Foch, General, 246 *ff.*

Folk-music, 323

Fontainebleau concert, 1920, 312

Fontainebleau summer music-school, 311

Fourth of July, Paris, 231 *ff.*, 248

Fragnaud, M., 311 *ff.*

Franck, César, 43, 74, 155, 238, 257, 281, 316

Franko, Sam, 149

Franz Joseph, Emperor, 353

Franz, Robert, 177

Frederick, Crown Prince, 2

Friedman, Ignaz, 356 *ff.*

Frohman, Daniel, 211

Frothingham, Mr. O. B., 333

Furniss, Sophie and Tina, 118 *ff.*

Furst, William, 349

Gabrilowitsch, Ossip, 356 *ff.*

Gade, Niels W., 353

Gadski, Johanna, 109, 115, 118, 122, 129 *ff.*

Ganz, Rudolph, 356 *ff.*

Garde Républicaine, 235

Gardner, Mrs. John L., 115, 333 *ff.*

Gartlan, Mr., 327

Genoa concert, 1920, 294 *ff.*

George II, King, 176

George V, King, 273

Gericke, Wilhelm, 333, 335 *ff.*

German music during the war, 260 *ff.*

German Opera at the Metropolitan, 51 *ff.*, *et passim.*

Giucciardi, Countess, 164

Gladstone, 92

Gluck, 60
Gluck, Mme. Alma, 358
Godowsky, Leopold, 356 *ff.*
Goethe, 37, 49, 262, 346
Goettich, Hans, 71, 200
Goldmark, Carl, 353 *ff.*
Goldmark, Leo, 88
Goosens, Eugene, 319
Gounod, 54, 286
Grainger, Percy, 356 *ff.*
Grau, Maurice, 104 *ff.*, 113, 116, 120, 121, *ff.*, 124, 129, 148, 160, 206, 300, 316
Grau Opera Company, 162, *et passim*
Greek plays, 344 *ff.*
Greek Theatre, Berkeley, Calif., 344 *ff.*
Grell, Edward, 180 *ff.*
Grew, Mr., 283
Grieg, 144
Grimm, "Fairy Tales," 5
Guegnier, Captain, 259

Haenselt, 2
Halévy, 65
Hamilton, Gail (Miss Dodge), 95, 99
Handel, 23, 33 *ff.*, 169 *ff.*, 175 *ff.*, 181, 183
Hanslick, Mr., 353
Hanson, Howard, 302
Harris, Doctor and Mrs. George, 19
Harrison, Benjamin, 98, 100
Harvard University, 161
Haven, George, 123
Hawthorne, "The Scarlet Letter," 114 *ff.*, 121, 160
Haydn, 23, 181, 183
Healy, 48
Hegemann, Mme. de, 29
Heimburg, Marie von (Tante), 4, 10, 175
Henderson, William J., 109
Henschel, George, 150
Herbert, Victor, 237
Herty, 152
Hesse, Landgravine, and Prince of, 79 *ff.*
Hewitt, 236
Higginson, Major Henry Lee, 22, 150, 186, 205, 207, 333, 336, 338, 341, 343
Hock, Wilhelm, 54
Hofmann, Josef, 360
Hohenlohe, Cardinal Prince, 48
Holland concerts, 1920, 317 *ff.*

Homer, "Iliad" and "Odyssey," 4
House, Colonel, 147
Hulsen, Baron von, 85
Hutcheson, Ernest, 356 *ff.*
Hyde, E. Francis, 208

Institute of Musical Art, 183
Italy, new musical development in, 299 *ff.*

Jackson, Schuyler Brinkerhoff, 35
Jazz music, 268
Jeanne (pianist), 166
Jeanne d'Arc, 263
Joachim, 2 *ff.*
Johnson, Reber, 236
Johnson, Robert Underwood, 275 *ff.*, 301
Joseffy, 187
Joukowski, Baron von, 39, 47 *ff.*
Jurgenson, 145

Kalisch, Paul, 66 *ff.*
Kant, 262
Kautsky and Briosky, 109
Kelley, Lieutenant, 262
Kerensky, 283
Klafsky, Madame Katherine, 111, 114, 117, 120 *ff.*
Knabe Piano Company, 23
Kneisel, Franz, 336
Kochanski, Paul, 149
Kossman, 74
Kraemer, 172
Krauss, Ernst, 138
Kreisler, Fritz, 152, 340
Kubelik, 187

Lafere, M., 272
La Fontaine, 157
Lambert, Alexander, 149, 356 *ff.*
Lamond, Major Felix, 303
Lamperti, 142, 160
Lassen, 14, 37 *ff.*, 48
Lathrop, George Parsons, 115
Laub, 7
Lorenziti, 238
Lehmann, Lilli, 63 *ff.*, 85 *ff.*, 111, 122, 130, 132
Lehmann, Marie, 67
Lekeu (the elder), 316

Lekeu, Guillaume, 316
Leon, Paul, 282, 311, 313
Lettelier, 47
Levi, Herman, 42
Lhevinne, Josef, 356 *ff.*
Liebling, Max, 28
Lindemann, 47
Liszt, Franz, 2 *ff.*, 6, 14, 23, 36 *ff.*, 66, 74, 97, 146, 148 *ff.*, 154, 156 *ff.*, 164, 181, 337, 354, 359, 362
Littleton, Augustus, 273, 321
Loeb, James, 183
Loeffler, Charles Martin, 149 *ff.*
London concerts, 1920, 318 *ff.*
London Telegraph, 97
London Times, 97
Longfellow, Ernest, 49
Longfellow, Henry Wadsworth, 48, 340
Longy, 236
Louise (pianist), 166
Louisville, Southern Exposition, 190 *ff.*
Lund, John, 58, 61

MacKenzie, Sir Alexander, 319
Maeterlinck, 151, 363
Mahler, Gustav, 138, 352, 354 *ff.*
Malipiero, 301
Mancinelli, Signor, 300
Mangeot, M., 311
"Manila Te Deum," 179 *ff.*
Mannes, David, 214
Mannes, Mrs. David (Clara Damrosch), 214
Mannes (David) Music School, 214
Mantel, M., 154, 228
Mapleson, Colonel, 51 *ff.*
Marburg, University of, 81 *ff.*
Marseilles concerts, 1920, 287 *ff.*
Mary Queen of Scots, 98
Materna, Madame, 53, 55, 59 *ff.*, 105, 140
Mathieu, 46
McCormick, Anita, 101
McKim, Miss Letty, 265, 267
McLane, Thomas, 223, 239
Meiningen, Orchestra of Grand Duke of, 77
Melba, Madame Nellie, 123, 129, 155
Mendelssohn, 23, 28, 34, 181, 344, 355, 363
Mendelssohn Choir, Toronto, 171

Meredith, George, 304
Mero, Yolanda, 356 *ff.*
Messager, André, 261, 279, 282
"Messiah" (Handel), 175 *ff.*
Metropolitan Opera House, New York, 51 *ff.*, 55 *ff.*, 61 *ff.*, 69, 72, 80, 88, 104 *ff.*, 116, 122, 123 *ff.*, 129, 134, 136, 142, 148, 160, 170, 172 *ff.*, 183, 206, 292, 300, 316, 355
Metz concert, 1920, 309 *ff.*
Meyerbeer, 55, 64 *ff.*, 85, 355
Milan concert, 1920, 306 *ff.*
Minna (Swedish nurse), 18
Molière, 346
Molinari, Maestro, 296 *ff.*
Moltke, 2
Monte Carlo concert, 1920, 291 *ff.*
Monteux, Pierre, 343
Morley, John, 92, 95, 100
Moszkowski, Moritz, 355 *ff.*
Mozart, 23, 155, 177, 190, 257, 259, 281, 300, 315 *ff.*, 325, 366
Muck, Doctor Karl, 225 *ff.*, 337 *ff.*
Music Festival Association, 30 *ff.*
Musical Union, 212
Musin, Ovide, 97, 319

Napoleon III, 8, 29
National Federation of Musicians, 213
Neilson, Mrs. James, 25
Neuendorf, 55
New York Festival Chorus, 32
New York Oratorio Society, 22 *ff.*, 30, 32, 35, 43, 57, 80, 92, 143, 169 *ff.*, 217, 255, 327
New York Philharmonic Society, 186 *ff.*, 206 *ff.*, 330, *et passim*
New York Symphony Orchestra, 27, 46, 80, 143, 186 *ff.*, 236, 260, 330, 346, 349, *et passim*. See also Symphony Society of New York
Newark Harmonic Society, 32, 34 *ff.*, 171
Ney, Elly, 356 *ff.*
Niemann, Albert, 42
Nikisch, Arthur, 337 *ff.*
Nilsson, 52
Nordica, Madame Lillian, 72 *ff.*, 132 *ff.*, 158 *ff.*
Notman, John, 208
Novello & Co., 273

Ochs, Siegfried, 352
Oratorio Society of New York, 22 *ff*.,
    30, 32, 35, 43, 57, 80, 92, 143, 169 *ff*.,
    217, 255, 327
Orchestral Conditions, 26
Outlook, 31

Paderewski, Ignace, 146 *ff*., 187
Pappenheim, Madame, 55
Paris concerts, 1920, 278 *ff*., 313
Paris Conservatoire, 46 *ff*.
Paris in war time, 229 *ff*.
Parker, Horatio, 181
Parma concert, 1920, 305 *ff*.
"Parsifal," 44 *ff*., 171 *ff*., *et passim*
Pasdeloup Orchestra, 223, 228
Patti, 52
Peary, 19
Pendennis Club, 190
Pennington, Mrs. (Alice Damrosch),
    19, 238, 265, 267 *ff*., 270 *ff*.
People's Choral Union, 183
Pershing, General, 185, 234, 243, 245 *ff*.,
    251 *ff*., 265
Philadelphia Academy of Music, 121 *ff*.
Philadelphia Orchestra, 204, 330, *et
    passim*
Philharmonic Society of New York,
    186 *ff*., 206 *ff*., 330, *et passim*
Phillips, William, 317 *ff*.
Phipps, Mr. and Mrs. Henry, 95
Piano ensemble for Moszkowski, 356 *ff*.
Pichon, M., 224
Pierné, Gabriel, 183, 279, 327
Pinner, Max, 11
Pizzetti, 301
Plato, 326, 344
Pohl, Richard, 7
Polignac, Marquis de, 222
Polish artists, 146 *ff*., 149
Pollain, Captain, 236
Pollini, 360
Popovici, Dimitri, 121
Porges, 14
Powell, John, 275, 281, 285, 301
Preller, Friedrich, 4
Programmes of Paris Concerts, 1920,
    278, 281
Pruckner, 11
Pulitzer, Mrs. Ralph, 332
Punch, 319

Raff, Joachim, 7, 14, 77, 81, 193, 359
Ravel, 278, 280, 353
Renz, Herr, 85
Respighi, 301
Richter, Hans, 319, 353
Rieger, William, 178
Rieman, Doctor, 47
Rissland, Rudolf, 196, 200
Roberts, Field-Marshal Lord, 145
Robinson, Adolf, 55
Rodgers, Admiral William, 270 *ff*.
Roebbelin, August, 208 *ff*.
Rome concert, 1920, 295 *ff*.
Roosevelt, Hilborn, 52
Roosevelt, James, 52
Roosevelt, Theodore, 179 *ff*., 223, 269
Ropartz, M., 309
Rosé, 353
Rosebery, Lord, 95
Ross, Mrs. Janet, 304 *ff*.
Rubinstein, Anton, 2, 22 *ff*., 33 *ff*., 79,
    359 *ff*.
Rummel, Mrs. Franz, 88
Russell (librarian), 88 *ff*.

Saint-Saëns, Camille, 43, 144, 153 *ff*.,
    180, 237, 258
San Martino, Count, 296
Sanford, Samuel, 211 *ff*.
Sarasate, 187
Sauveur, Doctor, 31 *ff*.
Sayn-Wittgenstein, Princess Carolyn, 6
Scaria, 45
"Scarlet Letter, The" (Damrosch
    opera), 114 *ff*., 121, 160
"Scarlet Letter, The" (Hawthorne),
    114 *ff*., 121, 160
Scharn, Fräulein von, 39, 47 *ff*.
Scharwenka, Xaver, 138 *ff*.
Schelling, Ernest, 356, 358
Schieffelin, Mary, 154
Schiller, Friedrich, 164
Schiller, Lorchen, 165 *ff*.
Schirmer, Gustav, Jr., 14 *ff*., 25 *ff*.
Schirmer, Gustav, Sr., 13
Schirmer, Rudolph, 14
Schloetzer, Baron von, 29
Schnitzer, Germaine, 356 *ff*.
Schoeffel, John, 104
Schools, music in, 326 *ff*.
Schott, Anton, 53 *ff*., 105

Schroeder-Hanfstangel, Madame, 54
Schubert, Edward, 9, 22
Schubert, Franz, 10, 11, 75, 260
Schumann, Robert, 10, 43, 75, 358, 361
Schumann, Clara, 2
Schumann-Heink, Madame, 132, 159
Scott, Walter, 98
Sealey, Frank, 35
"Seidenschwanz, Caligula," 84 ff.
Seidl, Anton, 54, 63 ff., 66, 77, 102, 107, 116, 121, 142, 206
Seidl-Kraus, Madame, 54 ff.
Seligman, Isaac N., 215
Sembrich, Madame, 52, 149
Shakespeare, 36, 94, 217, 346
Shinkle, 35
Shirk, Lieutenant, 227
Singer, 7
Sinigalgia, 301
Sloane, William, 223, 239
Smith, John Cotton, 32
Smithson, Miss, 164
Society of Musical Art, 184
Sophocles, 344, 346
Sousa, 361
Sowerby, Leo, 302
Spalding, Albert, 155, 275, 281, 284, 286, 304
Spring-Rice, Sir Cecil, 196
Stanford, Sir Charles Villiers, 144, 319
Stanton, Edmund C., 62 ff., 66, 102, 134
Staudigl, 55, 61
Steers and Coman, 198 ff.
Steers, Miss Lois, 198 ff.
Stehmann, Gerhardt, 137 ff.
Steinmetz, General, 2
Steinway, William, 107 ff., 138
Steinway & Sons, 22, 146
Stevens, Director, 303
Steyl, 81
Stock, Frederick, 204, 361
Stoessel, Albert, 185, 255
Stojowski, Sigismond, 356 ff.
Stokowski, Leopold, 204
Stone, Melville, 225
Strakosch, Maurice, 28, 75
Strakosh, Max, 53
Strassbourg concert, 1920, 309 ff.
Strauss, Johann, 190
Strauss, Richard, 33, 353, 361 ff.

Subscribers to New York Symphony Orchestra Fund, 215 ff.
Sucher, Rosa, 109 ff.
"Sulamith" (cantata of L. Damrosch), 47
Sullivan, John L., 335
Sulzer, M., 225 ff.
Sun, New York, 14, 96, 109
Symphony Society of New York, 22 ff., 30, 43, 52, 55, 57, 92, 121, 187, 272 ff. See also New York Symphony Orchestra.

Tafanel, 46
Tagliapietra, 167
Talbot, Mrs., 327
Tardieu, Mr., 222
Taussig, 2 ff., 7
Tennyson, 20
Ternina, 111, 114, 120, 129, 132
Thomas, Theodore, 22 ff., 34, 53, 186, 201, 204, 206, 353, 359
Thursby, Emma, 75
Tivin, Morris, 290 ff.
Tommasini, Signor Vincenzo, 295, 297 ff., 301
Ton-künstler Verein, 47
Toscanini, 300, 308
Townsend, Roger, 282
Trebelli, 52
Tribune, New York, 342
Tschaikowsky, Peter Iljitsch, 143 ff., 364
Tyler, Bandmaster, 248 ff.
Tyson, Mrs. George, 333

Untermyer, Samuel, 208

Valeria, 364
Van Dyk, 316 ff.
Vecella, Maestro, 298
Verdi, 34, 64, 188, 300
Versailles Conference, 147, 263
Vidal, Paul, 279
Vitali, 153
Vogt, Jean, 11, 171
Volstead Law, 35
von Bülow, see Bülow, von
von Inten, 11
Voss, translation of Homer, 4

Wagner, Cosima, 42, 75, 132, 143, 173 *ff.*
Wagner, Richard, 1 *ff.*, 11, 13 *ff.*, 34, 36 *ff.*, 52, 64, 68, 74, 77, 86, 92, 99, 102, 104 *ff.*, 116 *ff.*, 127 *ff.*, 140, 143 *ff.*, 156, 164, 171 *ff.*, 188, 190, 192, 196, 205 *ff.*, 252, 259 *ff.*, 281, 292, 297 *ff.*, 300, 316, 333 *ff.*, 337, 340, 360, 362, 364 *ff.*, *et passim.* Music dramas, *passim*
Wagner Society, 106
Walter, Bruno, 178
War, the Great, 221 *ff.*, 339 *ff.*
Ward, Major Cabot, 241
Warren, Mrs. John Hobart, 152
Webber, Amhurst, 292
Weber, Joseph N., 213
Weill, Lieutenant Michel, 252 *ff.*, 255, 260, 262, 264 *ff.*
Welling, Richard, 121, 215
Wendell, Evart, 245
Wendell, Lieutenant, 245
Wesendonck, Madame, 164
Wharton, Edith, 244 *ff.*

Whitlock, Mr. and Mrs. Brand, 314
Whitman, Mrs. Henry, 333
Widor, Charles Marie, 157 *ff.*, 238, 257 *ff.*
Wieniawski, 22
Wilde, Oscar, 363
Wilhelmj, August, 28 *ff.*
Willeke, Willem, 284
William I, Emperor, 2, 7, 41, 79, 86
Wilson, Admiral, 265, 268
Wilson, President, 295
Wolf-Ferrari, 183
Women in musical affairs, 323 *ff.*
Wood, Sir Henry, 319
World, New York, 96

Y. M. C. A., 222 *ff.*, 239 *ff.*, 265
Yale University, 212
Young People's Symphony Concerts, 183, 328
Ysaye, Eugene, 150, 152 *ff.*, 187

Zimbalist, Efrem, 193 *ff.*, 217
Zimmerman, Mrs., 118